"Professor Susan Long opens a portal for a new ⌐⌐
scholars to appreciate an old idea that was ove⌐ ·
stood at worst. Her capacity to underst⌐
such a complex idea and its evolution
scholarly gifts. She invites the reader to
in new ways.

From Schelling to Freud and out into th   ⌐ok is a
tour de force. The unconscious and its evolut⌐   as the world
collapses under its own weight of greed and t⌐   ⌐on, this text offers
those with a curiosity about the human conditic   ⌐ndow on where we have
been and where we could go next. The reconnection of the unconscious with
the spirit is a bold and radical act – and timely! It is a courageous exposition
that resituates the unconscious and our current world in profound entangle-
ment that has quantum opportunities for the human species and its relationship
to life. This is a creative and scholarly contribution to a field that is struggling
to find its way in the emerging age of artificial intelligence."

Dr Leslie Brissett, *formerly of the Tavistock Institute,*
St Leonards-on-Sea, Sussex, UK and Dumas, Arkansas, USA

"Susan Long lives in the spaces between us, uncovering the hidden connections that link our unconscious minds, each other and the world around us. In
this moving exploration, she guides us through the ideas of various clinical and
social theorists, offering an engaging and accessible journey towards a moving
and thought-provoking synthesis. For anyone seeking to better understand the
complexities of the human experience, I highly recommend joining her on this
illuminating journey."

Edward R. Shapiro, MD, *author,* Finding a Place to Stand:
Developing Self-Reflective Institutions,
Leaders, and Citizens *(Phoenix, 2020)*

"This landmark book on the unconscious will help you in navigating the endless seas of human reality, with all its mysteries and challenges. The unconscious as a source, an ally and compass, for making sense and better choices."

Erik van de Loo, *psychoanalyst, affiliate professor*
of organizational behavior, at business school INSEAD

The Evolution of the Unconscious

Drawing on over four decades of professional and academic experience, Susan Long explores how the concept of the unconscious has evolved from the nineteenth to the twenty-first century, showing that it is not only an individual phenomenon, but it is also a group, organisational and institutional phenomena.

Each chapter examines theories that use the idea of the unconscious, first covering the work of Schelling, Freud, Bion and Lacan. After examining traditional psychoanalytic ethos, the author takes a look at the mid-twentieth-century extension of the meaning of the unconscious in the social field. Here, she explores three main traditional categories of approaches: the Neo-Freudians, the Frankfurt School and social scientists, historians and anthropologists. The book also covers the idea of approaching the unconscious from the perspective of the neurosciences, as well as its connections with nature, showing a broader, more cosmic view of the unconscious in nature and the universe. Lastly, Long looks at how we might understand today's organisations and society through the lens of the changing ideas presented throughout the book.

Broad sweeping and accessible, this book is a valuable resource for organisational psychologists, consultants and managers exploring psychoanalytic and socioanalytic approaches, as well as those in academic settings wanting to pursue an interest in the unconscious.

Susan Long is Emerita Professor and PhD Co-Lead at the National Institute of Organisation Dynamics Australia (NIODA). She has more than four decades' experience teaching psychoanalytic and socioanalytic approaches to managers, organisational consultants, organisational psychologists and other professionals.

The Evolution of the Unconscious

Exploring Persons, Groups, Nature and Spirit

Susan Long

Routledge
Taylor & Francis Group

LONDON AND NEW YORK

Designed cover image: Art image of a vast dark cavern deep underground illuminated by a bright fiery orange light from a tunnel leading to a magma river. art inspired by the "Dwarf fortress" video game; Shutterstock

First published 2025
by Routledge
4 Park Square, Milton Park, Abingdon, Oxon OX14 4RN

and by Routledge
605 Third Avenue, New York, NY 10158

Routledge is an imprint of the Taylor & Francis Group, an informa business

British Library Cataloguing-in-Publication Data
A catalogue record for this book is available from the British Library

ISBN: 9781032907925 (hbk)
ISBN: 9781032907918 (pbk)
ISBN: 9781003559818 (ebk)

DOI: 10.4324/9781003559818

Typeset in Galliard
by Deanta Global Publishing Services, Chennai, India

Contents

Acknowledgements

I acknowledge the help and guidance of many people, too numerous to name, who have helped me throughout my career. Special thanks go to those who have read sections of the manuscript and given me their comments and support: Sean McGrath, Phillip Boxer, Janet Duke, Mark Solms, Margo Lockhart, Maurita Harney, Carolyn Cooper and Leslie Brissett. Their comments have been informative and have helped me to hone my ideas. Any misconceptions or errors in the book are, of course, mine alone. I acknowledge also the support of my husband Michael Long who always stands by me in my work.

I also acknowledge the traditional custodians of the lands upon which I write this book – the Wurundjeri people. I gain inspiration when looking out of my window, near my computer and see beautiful bushland with its birds and the occasional wombat, wallaby or echidna.

1   An Introduction

This book is a result of my lifelong interest in the idea of the unconscious. It is, perhaps, a book near the end of my career. I recognise that the literature and thinking about the unconscious are vast and far beyond what I can hope to navigate. Moreover, the more I now read, the more trepidation I feel about putting forward my ideas. I am in a sea without a horizon, a landscape stretching in infinite directions. But the unconscious has been an idea that has informed my work and life and continues to drive my curiosity. With this book, I hope to bring forward my interpretation of its evolution, unapologetically drawing out those strands of thought that have influenced me over the years. I recognise that many have written about this subject, and many have been more comprehensive than I, and most likely more accurate in their renditions of its theorisation, if accuracy is the right perspective from which to view one's own incorporation of the ideas of others. Attempting to be true to their meaning while expanding one's own understanding is a better way of expressing this, and it is what I attempt to do.

This work contains many autobiographic hints in the sense of how one person, me, has grown in understanding from experience, practice, study and interest. Perhaps it will help the reader to appreciate their own growth in knowledge and understanding from their experience, recognising its limitations and that truth comes in many guises. Indeed, it is the idea of reaching unconscious truth that drives many of the theories I examine.

I do not attempt to evaluate the theories in the sense of arguing for their veracity or misguidedness. My interest lies in seeing how an idea that has been central to my work and life evolves over time. The history of an idea is important because meaning is embodied and retained, unconsciously one might claim, within the idea as it develops over time. Writing about the history of a concept presents the difficulties of accessing and studying a vast literature, the failings of memory and the many varied interpretations of its expression. In a recent volume written as an introduction to the unconscious (Newirth 2023), the author remarks that the development of the idea should not be seen as an evolution because its development is not linear. He places Freud at the centre of the ever-growing spokes of a wheel. My perspective, though looks outside the psychoanalytic wheel, sees that a journey, while not strictly

DOI: 10.4324/9781003559818-1

linear, has progress. Moreover, to take out one concept from the theories that surround it renders it necessarily incomplete and struggles to give it justice. Nonetheless, I will try to capture some of the main streams of development as they have captured me.

An idea is a social construction built through a process of interacting thinkers. While each thinker may hold a similar meaning, there will be as much diversity within even the same theoretical school for the idea to evolve and change in its usage. Indeed, an idea will grow and change within the lifetime of any one theorist and writer. I do not intend to thoroughly trace it through each biography, looking intensively, for instance, at how the early Lacan differs from the late Lacan or how the middle period of Bion differs from his later theorising, or how Freud or Schelling's late work grew or challenged their early work. Although, of course, all this occurs, and I do mention some developments internal to each theory. I stay with what seems most central and pivotal in my own thinking. Nor do I want to be caught deep in the web of how the biography of each theorist interacts with the ideas produced, important and interwoven as this may be. I leave that to others, except where such interweaving substantially shifts my meeting the idea of the unconscious. The personal life of each thinker is a minefield of interesting distractions, and takes great care in its negotiation.

As I noted in Long (2016, p. 32f.f.), we tend to say such things as "ideas or thoughts come to us".[1] We "entertain" them. We "develop and nurture" them. Sometimes they "strike us". Other times they creep up on us surreptitiously and hide "at the back of our minds". We have good ideas and bad ideas. Some thoughts are unbearable; some are wicked and some are creative. Embedded in this language is the sense that ideas and thoughts have a life somewhat independent of us. We relate to them, and they to us. In our groups and societies, they are born, come of age, are popular or hated and they fade out and die. Our ideas for explaining the world are no more static than the processes and phenomena that they attempt to explain. So, we may expect the idea of the unconscious to be in constant evolution.

The idea of the unconscious is a thought about thoughts, an idea about ideas. It is an idea about how thoughts, perceptions and memories influence us even though we may not be aware of them. It is an idea about what we do with unwanted thoughts or thoughts that we are not ready to entertain. It is an idea about how thoughts shape and are shaped by our experience. It is an idea that responds to the question: what lies beneath consciousness? Or put another way: what prevents our consciously thinking thoughts? But it is also an idea about the hidden "not yet thought" embedded in the nature of our universe.

We tend to think and speak of *the* unconscious as a mysterious, unknown terrain that influences us from inside. But it is not so much a hypothetical place as it is a function or a state of mind: unconsciousness. I prefer to think in terms of unconscious processes and unconsciousness rather than *the* unconscious as a static container or object, and the reason for this becomes evident as I trace the history of the idea. Nonetheless, I may simply say "the unconscious" because that is how usage has prevailed, and I want to explore the usage of the idea in the various theories that reference it. And, at times, it seems as if it is a container as well as a process, just as in physics light may behave both as waves and particles.

The book contains an introduction to many theorists and practitioners who have approached the idea of the unconscious. I can only hope to introduce a few of the ideas in a fairly simple way. Each writer I approach has a complex, lifelong body of work, and I hope to discuss some of their central approaches to the topic. As I have been writing, I realise that my own conception of the unconscious has grown through the years as a kind of amalgam of the ideas of different thinkers and from my own perspective of a systems psychodynamic or socioanalytic lens. I have always thought and felt that I am part of something much greater than myself as a person. Moreover, when reading commentaries on the work of the different theorists, I see that each can be, and is, read in many ways, some of which may be close to the original, others seen through extended perspectives. I am now attempting to tease out my strands, knowing that such an endeavour is limited and that the threads I choose will reflect as much about me as about the various authors I approach. That is the fate of all readers gaining their own interpretations of what is written or said and will be yours, my reader, as much as mine.

Each of the theorists/practitioners I discuss has taken the idea of the unconscious in new directions from the early beginnings of the idea – since humans first started considering their own actions, thoughts and feelings – to the most recent formulations. Each has explored unconscious processes and their links to emotion and action. One major thread that I pursue is the link between unconscious processes and the idea of free will. There is a question of how far our thoughts, feelings and actions are determined by unconscious, systemic, physical and contextual forces and how much we are free to make decisions and act. This is a complex conundrum that has puzzled philosophers and scientists for aeons. How we look at the issue of free will enters all institutions and their practices: from the family, through health and the law, economics, politics and education. It underlies how we see authority, responsibility and accountability, personally and organisationally; it infuses our feelings of guilt, shame, blame, anger, remorse, love and empathy. And it is no simple either/ or issue but a weaving together of many factors: one being the nature of our subjectivity – who is the I that decides or is driven or compelled? The idea of the unconscious is integrally implicated in this, and each iteration of the idea has something to say.

My studies have also led me to the ideas of emergence, transcendence and spirit. The unconscious is somewhat the opposite of, or at least understood as in relation to, consciousness, itself a phenomenon barely understood. Questions are raised about the "hard problem of consciousness" (Chalmers 1995), referring to how phenomenal consciousness arises. Much is understood about the functional connections of the brain and behaviour, and about the dynamics and structure even of conscious thinking. But how and why phenomenal consciousness occurs; explaining "why there is 'something it is like' for a subject in conscious experience" (Internet Encyclopedia of Philosophy 2023) continues to be elusive. I currently understand the mind as an emergent and yet transcendent property of our corporeality, broadly incorporating conscious and unconscious aspects, with both having many forms, qualities and expressions. I hope to show how this view has grown through the many theories and explorations that I discuss. The nature of spirit is caught up in this and is also elusive; perhaps not to be understood as much as to be experienced both consciously and unconsciously.

Why is this important today in the twenty-first century? The history of an idea is of interest in itself – there is always something about beginnings and developments that grasp the human imagination, probably because our own beginnings are lost in the mists of the unreachable unconscious. However, the effects of ideas are often long-reaching and affect us in the here and now of living. The world is made up of nation states and multinational corporations whose leaders make critical decisions about policies and actions on global issues such as economies, wars, climate change, carbon emissions, environmental health, species survival, immigration and human rights. Large international conglomerate organisations have great power and influence. Decisions made on a weekly, daily, even hourly basis by governments and corporations have long-lasting effects. Even small group, community and family decisions can reverberate throughout a society. I explore how the unconscious is not just an individual phenomenon – not even mainly. It is present as group, organisational and institutional phenomena. In what ways and how it is present are critical for our futures.

An idea has a birth, it grows and develops, and eventually, perhaps, dies through irrelevance. Some ideas have shorter lives than others. We have yet to see how long the idea of the unconscious will last and be useful to humanity. I have chosen to look at it as an evolution, believing that some transformation of the idea will continue indefinitely because what it alludes to is central to the nature of humans and perhaps of all living things. So long as we have subjectivity, self-consciousness, curiosity, creativity and a thirst for truth, we will wish to explore that realm that lies within us and around us, influences and eludes us, yet gives us enough glimpses of its possibilities both dangerous and exciting that we know we must approach it.

> In the corner of my eye
> I glimpse a 'me', another I.
> I fear its tread, its soft pursuit.
> I turn away, I tell a lie -
> I didn't see it, I insist,
> The tale it wants to tell can't be!
> And yet an echo in my mind
> Calls out .....
> It is essential me.

(Long: poem written in 2023)

Although I started my career as a psychoanalytically informed clinical psychologist, I am now an organisational researcher and consultant, so my interest will most often turn to organisational dynamics, the people in roles within organisations and the social contexts within which they exist. As Wilfred Bion was acutely aware – we are primarily social animals. I extensively use the Transforming Experience into Authentic Action in Role Framework (TEF) as a basis to explore organisational and social contexts (Long 2016). The choice of theorists and practitioners I present here is idiosyncratic to my own biography and to my perspectives, and each has had a substantial impact on the evolution of the idea of the unconscious.

I start with the philosopher Friedrich Schelling, said to be the first to use the idea in a systematic way, although its origins can be found much earlier (Whyte 1962; Long 2016; Weinberger and Stoycheva 2020), and outside of Western thinking (Mathur 2016). Many of the ideas put forward by Schelling seem to anticipate psychoanalytic thinking, or maybe it is better said that later psychoanalytic thinking elaborates and extends Schelling. It must be kept in mind, though, that the times and cultures later psychoanalysts and social theorists live in have influenced them and are different. I came to Schelling late in my career, having previously been steeped in psychoanalytic thinking. I am grateful for reaching his ideas because they link the unconscious to spirit, and in what ways we might conceive this, and bring me closer to some understanding of how the spiritual side of nature might link to the physical and corporeal.

I then move to consider Freud and the psychoanalysis that he delivered. The unconscious is central to Freudian theory and practice. It incorporates the repressed dynamic unconscious that heralds those ideas familiar in the twentieth century and beyond. Such an idea has permeated popular thought. My own practice as a psychotherapist, and later as an organisational researcher and consultant, has been deeply influenced by tuning myself to recognise the effects of the repressed.

From here, I move to Wilfred Bion and Jacques Lacan. Both have influenced my thinking and practice. There are, of course, a myriad of psychoanalysts whose ideas have entered into the mix of my thinking, and I cannot name them all here. I have chosen Bion and Lacan to discuss because I have found their work, more than that of others, helps me in understanding psychosis, or what we might call madness, whether of individuals or of society. I could have moved from here to Bergson and from his work to Deleuze, as they formulate different ideas of madness and the unconscious – perhaps their emphasis on the creative potential of the unconscious being more in line with Carl Jung. But I am not as familiar with their work despite having read *Anti-Oedipus* (Deleuze and Guattari 1984) and am unable to devote a whole chapter to them. Similarly with Jung, although his influence has come to me through the social dreaming methodology developed by Gordon Lawrence, and my early days of working with dreams in psychotherapy. But I have had to put limits on what I can do here.

I have sadness that, although all these theories, both psychoanalytic and others, and the theories and practices of those who later incorporate them, while explaining the madness in the world, have not yet provided enough influence to stop its overall large-scale destructiveness, especially the traumas of war and the attendant grief, hatred and revenge, notwithstanding the many efforts that have been successful in small ways (see, for example, descriptions and interventions described in Volkan et al. 2023). The hope is that such interventions that are successful can expand.

Whereas Bion and Lacan could be said to stay within the traditional psychoanalytic ethos, albeit with quite radical extensions and interpretations of the Freudian unconscious, many theories from the broader social sciences of the mid-twentieth century begin to extend the meaning of unconscious processes away from the individual towards the social field. I am dealing here with this period of history. What is central is that there is a consideration of unconscious processes at societal and cultural levels. While this has become acceptable in the twenty-first century, it was in the twentieth century that some radical thinking emerged. Some of the theorists examined here take the psychoanalytic meaning of "unconscious" as their basis; others take on different perspectives. Having permeated the social sciences, the idea of the unconscious is linked to societal repression and intergroup relations. Of interest are the ideas coming from the Frankfurt School with its attempts to integrate Freud and Marx, and later sociologists who examine social conditions in light of unconscious dynamics. I explore three main traditional categories of approaches, although grouping these into categories does not do justice to the very rich differences within the categories. Each of the theorists I approach uses the idea of the unconscious but often in quite different ways.

The idea of a social unconscious and some of its implications are then explored. In doing this, the perplexing question of the nature of the "mind" is necessarily confronted, more so when the idea of a social mind is invoked than when an individual mind is discussed because we tend to think of the mind as an individual possession. This chapter questions such a colloquially held belief. The idea of a social unconscious with a social "mind" appears at first as counterintuitive, mainly because our way of thinking puts individual persons as central and individual minds as a given. But the perspective of the individual mind as the centre of thinking has to change just as the Copernican Revolution changed thinking about the universe. While Freud showed how unconscious thoughts could overthrow the conscious so-called rational ego, so Bion, Foulkes and those who follow argue for the centrality of an unconscious field of associative and connective thinking. This social and associative unconscious becomes embedded in the very fabric of our institutions (family, the law, education, industry) and is thus passed from generation to generation. Our freedom as a species is integrally linked to our understanding and experience of this unconscious.

In the next chapter, I approach the unconscious in our everyday work organisations, bringing my understanding of the unconscious to the task. Rather than being devoted to a particular theorist, this chapter presents, through a series of vignettes, the way I work as a socioanalytically informed organisational consultant.

But perhaps the greatest changes in the idea of the unconscious come from neuroscience. I investigate how these ideas, especially those of Mark Solms, not only follow earlier psychoanalytic ideas but also challenge them. The early work of Julian Jaynes is examined, followed by more recent theories with a focus on the work of Mark Solms and his neuropsychoanalysis. Attempts are made to understand psychoanalytic concepts through the lens of neuroscience; nonetheless, the idea of the unconscious here is quite different. This is explored in a chapter raising the question of how we define consciousness as well as unconsciousness.

I then turn to the idea of the unconscious in nature, which raises many questions about the definitions of life, the mind and consciousness. I am committed to seeing how ideas of the unconscious help us to understand the deep connections throughout nature. Notwithstanding the important contributions of psychoanalysis, we need to extend our ideas about the nature of the "mind" and how its various forms emanate from all living things and from the planet as a whole. This at least requires exploration, not simply for the future of the human race through the interconnectedness that sustains us, not only for our place as the means by which the universe can understand itself, but also for the deep meaning of our choice for life and our ethical responsibilities in pursuing this choice. This chapter explores the idea of the unconscious as presented in nature other than the human mind.

I then turn to a broader, more cosmic perspective of the unconscious in nature and the universe – some ideas returning to Schelling and the philosophers, but clothed also in the psychoanalytic embracement of the unconscious. My own questioning is in the place of spirit and how the experience of spirit fits with the body and mind. My hypothesis is that spirit resides in the collectivity of each species and in their interconnectivity.

The final chapter of this book revisits each of the theories that have been examined in light of the questions of free will and the emergence of ethical choice. This opens up many questions about our humanity, its spirit and our position in nature. These questions, many of which I cannot even formulate, I hope will be considered by my readers.

I have one regret: I have been unable to chronicle the work of the many women who have contributed to the idea of the unconscious and have influenced my thinking: Anna Freud, Melanie Klein, Jessica Benjamin, Margaret Mahler, Dorothy Dinnerstein, Marion Milner, Maud Mannoni, Margaret Rioch, Luce Irigaray, Juliet Mitchell, Carol Gilligan, Isobel Menzies-Lyth and many others, past and current, especially my many female colleagues. Maybe that's another book.

Note

1 Some of what I write here contains words from my previous publication in S. Long (2016) *Transforming Experience in Organisations* published by Routledge. The work there, however, is extended here.

References

Chalmers, D.J. (1995) 'Facing up to the Problem of Consciousness', *Journal of Consciousness Studies,* vol. 2, pp. 200–219.

Deleuze, G. and Guattari, F. (1984). *Anti-Oedipus: Capitalism and Schizophrenia.* London: The Athlone Press Ltd.

Internet Encyclopedia of Philosophy (2023). https://iep.utm.edu/hard-problem-of -conciousness/ [accessed 2 October 2023].

Long, S.D. (ed.) (2016). *Transforming Experience in Organisations.* London: Karnac.

Mathur, A.N. (2016) 'Spirituality in Management and Management of Spirituality: Connecting inner and outer worlds', paper presented at the International Conference on Spirituality and Management: Bangalore, 4–6 January 2016.

Newirth, J. (2023). *The Unconscious: A Contemporary Introduction.* London: Routledge.

Volkan, V. Scholtz, R. and Fromm, G. (eds.) (2023). *We Don't Speak of Fear: Large Group Identity, Societal Conflict and Collective Trauma.* Oxfordshire: Phoenix Publishing.

Weinberger, J. and Stoycheva, V. (2020). *The Unconscious: Theory Research and Clinical Implications.* New York: The Guilford Press.

Whyte, L. (1962). *The Unconscious Before Freud.* New York: Basic Books.

2 Schelling[1]
The Beginnings

In this chapter, I explore some of the origins of the idea of the unconscious crystallised in the work of Friedrich Schelling. Although the idea was certainly in discourse and thought well before the nineteenth century, he provides its first systematic theorising, at least in Western thought. His thinking is infused with spirit (seen as God) as the infinite basis of the mind. Some interpreters find it easy to understand his tracing the history of the world from a religious perspective as a metaphor for the development of the human mind and we can read Schelling from the vantage point post Darwin and Freud. And certainly, Schelling seems to predate in startling ways much of what comes later. But the age he lived in should also remind us to read his work as a product of that age without twisting it into a narrative that we, in our age, would prefer.

From where does the idea of the unconscious come?[2] Prior to any thinking about psychology, philosophers, religious thinkers and scholars tended to refer primarily to the soul or spirit as the one immaterial essence of human beings. For Aristotle, the soul was the essential form of life. The soul was immortal yet embodied. Moreover, religious mystics such as Ignatius of Loyola engaged in long-term and deep exploration of processes within themselves, initially hidden from awareness, in what might be seen as self-analysis long before Freud developed the method of psychoanalysis and the theory of repression. Colleague Ajeet Mathur has reminded me that ideas of the unconscious have long been a part of thinking in the Indian sub-continent (see, for example Mathur 2018). Such thinking, although of great interest but relatively recent to me, is not included here. Here, I briefly introduce the idea of the unconscious prior to its uptake by psychoanalysis, in Western thinking.

Other scholars have done this (Ellenberger 1957, 1970; Whyte 1962; Ffytche 2011; Rabstejnek 2015) and I only briefly trace some lines of development leading up to Friedrich Schelling, whose work I will draw upon more fully. Whyte (1962) examines the history of thinking about the unconscious, focusing on European thinking from the seventeenth to nineteenth centuries. The unconscious, he claims, was an inference needed once humans became "intensely aware of his (sic) own faculty of consciousness, and then balanced this by becoming aware, by inference, of much in his own mental processes of which he is not directly conscious" (p. viii). The seventeenth-century

DOI: 10.4324/9781003559818-2

Enlightenment, following the foundations of scientific thinking, formally established the idea of a mind that was different from the body.[3] Descartes placed an emphasis on the mind and our capacity to think rationally. His thinking founded what is known as Cartesian dualism: in very rough terms this considers the body as a kind of machine animated by the mind. The thinking mind is the essence while perception and experience in the body can fail: "Cogito, ergo sum; I think therefore I am".[4] This dualism has been influential in Western philosophy where the soul/mind and body distinction has become part of general parlance. It is at the basis of much of psychology and popular thinking into the twenty-first century. The mind and rational thought have become regarded as the centre of consciousness apart from the illogical processes of the body and its emotions, albeit sometimes influenced by that irrationality. The subject, that is, the thinker is regarded as different from the object, i.e. that which can be thought about – even the object that is one's own body. However, even Descartes argued that the body could influence the mind and rationality through the passions. His own thinking could not make this separation a total split (see Whyte 1962, pp. 26–28).

Many philosophers have challenged the dualist position: especially Heidegger and the existentialists who argue that existence in the world precedes any essential nature of consciousness. The challenge is also from the movement of Idealism and many of the nature philosophers, an allied tradition that has held the mind and body as a unity with consciousness arising from an unconscious unity. What then of unconsciousness? The influential philosopher Immanuel Kant (1724–1804) implicitly wrote of unconscious processes when introducing the idea of a "noumenal self" "that fits the theory of the system unconscious; an inner self that was unknown to the conscious self, but profoundly influenced the sense of self experienced" (Chessick 1992 cited in Rabstejnek 2015, p. 4). Kant believed that ideas, the raw matter of knowledge, must somehow be due to realities existing independently of human minds; but he held that such things in themselves must remain forever unknown. Human knowledge cannot reach them because knowledge can only arise in the course of synthesising the ideas of sense (German idealism | philosophy | www.Britannica.com). This was his position on transcendental idealism. The ideas of the unconscious and unconsciousness had so permeated thinking in the eighteenth century that by 1869, Von Hartmann wrote a widely read book, *The Philosophy of the Unconscious*, a topic he continued to explore throughout his life (Rand 2004). However, philosophy in the nineteenth century was not so interested in finding the unconscious as in trying to understand how consciousness arose – an interest taken up more recently by neuroscientists (see Chapter 9 in this book).

The term unconscious or unconsciousness was first used in a systematic way by the late eighteenth-century, early nineteenth-century German Romantic Idealism philosopher Friedrich Schelling and was understood as a source of creative power (McGrath 2012; Ffytche 2011). Despite a wane in Schelling's popularity as a significant philosopher during the late nineteenth and the twentieth centuries at a time when psychoanalysis was being formulated and extended, his influence is apparent. Perhaps this is due more to his ideas infiltrating the discourse about the unconscious through his lectures rather than any direct reading of him by Freud and his followers, although Jung's library contained his works and it is arguable that Jung's archetypes and collective unconscious are more heir to Schelling than has been recognised (Barentsen 2015). As we move through his ideas, you, like me, may find many as implicit within later psychoanalytic thinking.

Let me first say that I am neither a philosopher nor an expert on or scholar of Schelling. I can only speak from the little I currently know and what has stimulated me in looking at the idea of the unconscious. I have read some Schelling directly and some commentaries and studies written by others – finding Sean McGrath, Joseph Carew and Teresa Fenichel perhaps most accessible at this stage. But the debates among philosophers are long and complex and, as a socioanalytic thinker, wandering into them is like entering an almost impenetrable forest.

Friedrich Schelling was a post-Kantian philosopher named as one of three influential German Romantic Idealist philosophers: Hegel, Fitche and Schelling. To give you an idea of what Idealism is: "idealism, in philosophy, is any view that stresses the central role of the ideal or the spiritual in the interpretation of experience" (from Brittanica). It may hold that the world or reality exists essentially as spirit or consciousness, that abstractions and laws are more fundamental to reality than sensory things or, at least, that whatever exists is known in dimensions that are chiefly mental – through and as ideas. Schelling's work, which was perhaps neglected for some time, is now undergoing somewhat of a revival (Segall 2014). He was the first to systematically use the term the unconscious and have a philosophy that held this idea centrally. Schelling's concern with the rise of self-consciousness led him to argue that consciousness itself could not be aware of its own origins. He postulated the existence of an unconscious as a substrate prior to consciousness. This unconsciousness underpins self-consciousness; (called "ungrund" or unground to emphasise its primacy, its indifference in his early thinking); not as a known and experienced grounding but an unknown and mostly unknowable substrate (Carew 2014, 2015; Fenichel 2019). Unconsciousness, he argued, was to be found in nature before any split into a subject that knows and an object that is known – a split, as I have indicated, that was conceptualised by Descartes but not accepted as fundamental by Schelling.

That which is not constituted by consciousness is Schelling's "barbarian principle": the unruly, destructive, unpredictable ceaseless productivity of nature, which he first described in the *Naturphilosophie* and further developed its implications in the *Freedom* essay and *The Ages of the World*. It is the most compelling description of the problem phenomenology must confront: how to think the world of nature in which we find ourselves.

(Snow 2014, p. 1.)

Schelling's central concern is about human freedom.

> Schelling was the first thinker to make freedom the basis of his philosophy. His other interests, about nature, cosmos, time, moral law, culture, death, evil, etc, were secondary to his interest in human freedom. In a letter to his one-time friend Hegel he said, that the alpha and omega of all philosophy is freedom. In fact, as far as Schelling was concerned, freedom was the central premise behind German Idealism.....What mattered to Schelling, and to Kant before him, is that one lives a virtuous life. This alone is Godly, because one's *morality* is the outward expression of freedom, which is in turn the means by we are directly connected to God, a connection that exists in this world, here and now.
>
> (Tsarion; 2020, pp. 1-2)

I return to this idea of freedom later in the chapter.

Scholars have noted three main phases in Schelling's work: (i) his early work on nature philosophy; (ii) his mid-career work on identity and the emergence of consciousness; (iii) his late career work on what he termed negative and positive philosophy and the importance of myth. Although these phases seem to mark quite different thinking, McGrath argues that Schelling never completely left his ideas from the early nature philosophy. "The early Schelling and the romantics constructed the unconscious in order to overcome the modern split between subjectivity and nature, mind and body, a split legislated by Cartesian representationalism" (McGrath 2010, p. 72). Schelling argues that nature (the body and all in nature – plants, animals and all that is physical) is the physical presence of spirit. Nature is in itself unconscious – consciousness has evolved and through this – through self-consciousness, spirit comes to know itself.

In more psychological parlance, we each go through this evolution – unconscious of our own birth, our spirit or subjectivity grows and grows to know itself through interactions with others: subjectivity here being equated not only to consciousness but also unconsciousness. "For the early Schelling, nature is a dynamic evolving system, internally directed to self-manifestation, which it achieves when self-consciousness emerges" (McGrath 2010, p. 75). "Schelling regarded nature as *both* organizing itself in a rational way *and* embodying a pure upsurge of creative energy" (Stone 2023). Barentsen (2019) argues that Schelling's nature is "a 'speculative physics' (something Schelling himself says) which aims to discover the fundamental dynamic forces and drives – the ground of nature's infinite productivity" (p. 94) not a static system to be exploited by neo-liberalism: such a conception being necessary, if somewhat paradoxical for an ecological civilisation to counter the degradation afforded by our anthroprocentric cultures. Wirth (2013) reminds us of Schelling's *Barbarian Principle*, stating that there is within us *natura naturans*, an irreducible remainder that cannot be thought. It just is. We cannot think about nature as positivistic science attempts, divisible into deterministic components, but as "with, of and from nature" (Wirth 2013, p. 32). For Schelling, we can know nature because we are of nature. "Schelling was concerned not only to show the cognitive conditions for objective knowledge, but the nature of the world that enables it to be known objectively, and to produce beings which could achieve objective knowledge of it and of themselves" (Gare 2011, p. 44).

The idea of nature philosophy permeates the thinking of James Lovelock and Lynn Margulis in their GAIA hypothesis of the earth as a living, self-regulating, complex system (Lovelock 1979), and other ideas of a whole earth consciousness and unconsciousness, ideas that I will return to in Chapter 10. The early Schelling attempts to find intuitive forms of thought in nature and links nature to spirit through this unconscious ground (McGrath 2012, kindle edition). "Schelling proposed nature as unconscious spirit, and spirit as nature become conscious of itself" (Matthews 2012). This was an idea of God/Spirit as revealed through nature: "The universe or totality is the self-revelation of the absolute" (Schelling 1942, p. 17).

The idea of nature as unconscious was linked to the development of consciousness and self-consciousness in a way that anticipates some aspects of the psychoanalytic focus on biography, denial and repression. Schelling says,

> Certainly, one who could write completely the history of their own life would also have, in a small epitome, concurrently grasped the history of the cosmos. Most people turn away from what is concealed within themselves just as they turn away from the depths of the great life and shy away from the glance into the abysses of that past which are still in one just as much as the present.
>
> (Schelling 1815a, pp. 93–94).

Moreover, for Schelling, nature is impelled by a drive for infinite development; a dynamic within that is later elaborated by him in his *The Ages of the World* referred to as *Weltalter*.[5]

Later, in the period termed his identity philosophy period, he explored ideas that led, I think, to a more developed idea of unconscious processes – about how the particular is related to the whole – the many to the one; explaining how the one of God/Spirit is present in the many of the world and yet how free will can also be present. In this, Schelling is revealed as a complex self-organising systems thinker.

> In the circle out of which everything becomes, it is no contradiction that that through which the One is generated may itself be in turn begotten by it. Here there is no first and last because all things mutually

presuppose each other, no thing is another thing and yet no thing is not without another thing.

(Schelling transl. 2006, p. 28)

If we are to say the world *is* spirit revealed, what do we mean? Let's diverge to understand identity in Schelling's terms. To say something *is* something, although seeming to be identity between the two is also not identity but an explication of what is implicit in the first something. Schelling gives an example that McGrath explains:

"The perfect is the imperfect". If identity is sameness, this statement amounts to a denial of difference between the perfect and the imperfect; such that: "The perfect and the imperfect are the same [einerlei], all is the same [geich] in itself, the worst and the best, foolishness and wisdom" (Schelling 1809, p. 13). However, if identity is identification of difference the claim means something else entirely, namely, that imperfection is consequent upon perfection, presupposes it, unfolds something implicit in it, or more helpfully, imperfection does not ground itself but presupposes something opposed to it yet intimately related to it, which makes it possible. As Schelling puts it, "The imperfect is not due to that through which it is imperfect but rather through the perfect that is in it (op. cit. p. 13)".

(McGrath 2015, p. 7)

Through this argument, Schelling considers how evil and good each exists through the other: they explicate the implicate in each other and are interdependent; and how freedom involves a choice. David Bohm, a quantum physicist, describes the nature of the universe in terms of such an unfolding. All that comes in space-time is an explicate unfolding of what is an implicate (Bohm 1980). Schelling read widely about the science of his day.

In his treatise on freedom, choice rather than compulsion or determinism sits at the basis of being. And being reflects action taken as true to unconscious choice – the basis of character/personality.

Following his early ideas on nature as the unconscious spirit, and yet in moving away from his early idealism and criticisms that his writing was pantheist, Schelling developed an historical view about the rise of consciousness from unconscious unground (ungrund). In describing this, Das (2014) says,

It now appears that the condition of possibility of consciousness as such remains irreducible to consciousness itself. This is the problem that has become decisive, not only for Schelling's subsequent philosophical career, but for the fate of Idealism as such. It now appears as if our self-consciousness is driven or constituted by an unconscious ground, forever inaccessible to consciousness, which can never be grounded in consciousness itself.

(Das 2014)

In this construction, for Schelling the infinite spirit – God – gave rise to consciousness as "other". This was the process by which God could emerge from infinite into existence (Love and Schmidt 2006): the deep nature of will being the will to exist. The emergence of creation is a paradox because, he asks, what is needed by an infinite being other than infinity? Yet, without other (finity) the one cannot know itself; apart from its own infinity it cannot be revealed. With other there is the possibility of actuality, communion and of love. Schelling addresses this paradox through reference to the notion that the infinite can find in itself that which is finite but must make this finite part "other". "God is what is in itself and is understood only from itself; what is finite, however, is necessarily in another and can only be understood from this other" (Schelling 1815a, p. 12).

The roots of this thinking can be traced to Boehme, a seventeenth-century theosopher. (Theosophy is a combination of theology and philosophy: McGrath 2012.)

> Boehme's unground is the ineffable, non-dual, and incomprehensible darkness of the Godhead out of which the light of self-consciousness emerges through a dialectic interplay of opposites. The unground in itself "lacks" the duality necessary to revelation; Boheme repeats, like a mantra, that without distinction and duality there can be no manifestation... Duality emerges out of the non-duality of the unground in the form of hunger... nothingness as a lack and a hunger for something, ultimately for a revelation of itself.
>
> (McGrath 2012, Kindle e-version)

For Boehme, the ungrund of the Godhead cannot be reduced, but it contains a drive to reveal itself. (Chapter 4 discusses the work of Wilfred Bion, a psychoanalyst who talks of the fundamental need for discovering one's truth for psychic growth, and the need to communicate such truth. This might be understood as the will to reveal one's truth.) This need to reveal is not a perfect actualisation nor a need; not driven but an act of free will. An "other" is freely created in order that the one can know itself. (We can read this as pertaining to both spirit and the development of human psychology.) The unground creates a ground for itself. Nonetheless, Boehme argues, the desire for revelation creates a "dark fire" of "pain, unappeased desire and anxiety... the corporeality of God turned in on itself that hungers only for itself" (McGrath 2012). Its opposite is a "light hot fire" turned towards the other with love and the potential of revelation. The difference is crucial; that they are always together is part of their essence, just as self or ego and other are always in opposition but together.

Schelling takes Boehme's descriptions and creates a philosophical argument for the paradoxical presence of dual and opposing drives within the unity of the primordial infinite (God or Spirit). Yet, paradoxically, this unity contains in God what is not God and is separated out in the creation of the other – of nature (Barensten 2019). The history of the world is predicated upon this, and it is played out in the development of the human personality – a necessary reflection of the creator. The opposing drives are an inward-turning potency towards "self" and an outward-turning potency towards "other". The inward turning is a negation of the totality and in this negation is an actualisation of the ego – the ego that wants to be without other, just desirous of self (similar to Freud's primary narcissism). But it is this very turning into the darkness of self through negation (what Schelling calls the first potency) that allows for the second potency of turning out and the encounter of other, with the possibility of love. "An essence cannot negate itself as actual without positing itself at the same time as the actualizing, generating potency of itself" (Schelling 1815a, p. 112). This view predates Freud's (1925) idea that cognisance of a thought, although negated, is nonetheless evidence of the vitality of that thought. The negation cannot occur unless the "essence" is at first posited. The third potency unites these opposing drives and all three exist together in the one. Important in this argument is Schelling's view that the initial state of God is unconsciousness in a circular, rotary turmoil of drives, and that consciousness could only arise once "other" was actualised and in that process difference, otherness, narcissism and free will are revealed. All were there in potential, but the initial negation was the actualising force. Hence, the unconscious is ground to and prior to consciousness. As such, its anarchy continues to lie beneath the seeming order of the world.

Schelling's philosophy naturally developed and changed several times throughout his life. But rather than criticise his changes of direction, we can appreciate that his thinking was always a struggle in following his belief that philosophy should consist of the pursuit of knowledge. Moreover, his epistemological development can be read as containing many of the different threads emanating from his insistence on linking philosophy to the real world (White 1983; McGrath 2012). Despite the differences from Schelling developed in psychoanalysis, in particular its rejection of his theological teleology, there is much in Schelling that anticipates later psychoanalytic formulations (although Schelling should not be read entirely from the psychoanalytic perspective: see Woodard 2013). Indeed, in my reading of Schelling, I have started to discern many ideas that predate psychoanalysis. This makes his work exciting for psychoanalytic and socioanalytic researchers. For example, the place of mythology in Jung (who explores myths and archetypes as a basis of personality) and Freud (who uses myths as more than a simple metaphor for such phenomena as the Oedipus complex); the idea that intuition is not merely a gut feeling but a form of "embodied cognition versus the more detached forms of thinking (reflection and reason)" (Segall 2014) brings forward Bion's ideas of intuition as a reaching towards "O" through close embodied observation; the concept of "the indivisible remainder" being the dark side of God/Spirit – "leaving its trace in the impenetrable and inexplicable reality of things" (Segall 2014). The inextinguishable nature of desire for being that is central to spirit can be found in Freud's instinctual id and the importance of negation to create otherness; the realisation of ego and desire as founded on a lack – integral to finiteness and established within difference anticipates Lacan's (1977) reading of Freud.

Bion is heir to the notion of the unconscious as infinite. For instance, take his idea of "O" described by Grotstein (1977):

> "O" is perhaps Bion's most far-reaching conception. It designates an ineffable, inscrutable, and constantly evolving domain that intimates an aesthetic completeness and coherence. He refers to it by different terms, "Absolute Truth", "Ultimate Reality", or "reverence and awe". When preternaturally personified, it is called "God". The "Keter-Ayn-Sof" of the Zohar Kabbalah translated it as "Nothing" (Scholem, 1960; Bloom, 1983), a designation Bion (1962, 1963, 1965) focused on as the "no-thing".
>
> (Grotstein 1977)

"O" echoes Schelling's ideas of the unconscious as infinite and ground to an aesthetic completeness (see Pistiner de Cortinas 2009; Glover 2009; Aurelio 2012). Both Bion and Schelling acknowledge the influence of the Kabbalah.

There are many interpretations of Schelling – one of the most influential being that of the philosopher Zizek (2006), who looks at Schelling through the lens of the psychoanalyst Jacques Lacan. The invisible that can never be conceptualised or put into a logical system underlies Zizek's reading of Schelling. On Schelling's writing about the beginnings of consciousness and unconsciousness in *The Ages of the World*, he says,

> The true Beginning is the passage from the closed "rotary" motion to "open" progress, from drive to desire – or, in Lacanian terms, from the Real to the Symbolic.
>
> (Zizek 1996 Kindle edition)

The following passage from Schelling indicates the roots of such a reading:

> After the eternal act of self-revelation, everything in the world is, as we see it now, rule, order, and form; but anarchy still lies in the ground, as if it could break through once again, and nowhere does it appear as if order and form were what is original but rather as if initial anarchy had been brought to order. This is the incomprehensible base of reality in things, the indivisible remainder, that with which the greatest exertion cannot be resolved in understanding but rather remains eternally in the ground. The understanding is born in the genuine sense from that which is without understanding. Without this preceding darkness creatures have no reality: darkness is their necessary inheritance.
>
> (Love and Schmidt 2006, p. 29)

This, Zizek reads, as the Symbolic (rule, order and form) in the world as we see it with the Lacanian Real[6] being the anarchy that lies in the ground – the indivisible remainder; that which defies being brought to order (Carew 2015).

> In this regard, German Idealism presents us with an unconscious Grundlogik that we can only now, with the aid of Freud and especially Lacan, reconstruct, thus giving us a profoundly new and controversial view of its internal development and theoretical preoccupations.
>
> (Carew 2014, p. 37)

An overall Lacanian reading has been critiqued (McGrath 2012; Segall 2014; Boxer 2024); insofar as it appears to read Schelling from a psychoanalytic perspective post Schelling (and perhaps provides even a misreading especially of Lacan – Boxer 2024), and as such places upon his work ideas, they argue, not within it, although possibly anticipated at some level. Woodard says, "because aspects of Schelling's mid to later work is suggestive of psychoanalysis does not mean that all the stages of his work should be rewritten to make that assertion more palatable". Nonetheless, Zizek's reading of Schelling is seductive, if not completely satisfying.

Schelling's later work on myth is a forerunner to Jung. The last theme that came to preoccupy Schelling in the more religious period of his later years was that of mythology and revelation. Schelling saw mythological themes as the empirical verification of his metaphysical theory of the absolute and its genesis in the unconscious. For him, myths were an early, still unconscious historical manifestation of the absolute, while Christian revelation represented the free, intentional expression of a later stage. In his *On the Deities of Samothrace* (1815b), Schelling interprets the function of ancient Greek deities as that of precursors to the full manifestation of God. Schelling's notion that myths are not the product of a rational mind but that of a much earlier unconscious activity can be seen as a precursor to Carl Gustav Jung's archetypes.

> There is truth in mythology, but not in mythology as such. The mythological is: 1) either a mere form, disguise of a) a historic truth, b) of a physical truth; or 2) misunderstanding, distortion, a) of a purely scientific (essentially irreligious) truth, b) of a religious truth.
>
> (Schelling trans. 2007, p. 49 in Rivas 2020)

Schelling's ideas about the unconscious process may be discerned repeatedly in the two centuries following his work. Even where there is no direct reference to him, it seems that his formulations permeate the concept as it has been developed. This, perhaps, indicates its strength as an idea and its complexity insofar as its implications are constantly being realised in new ways.

As I write about these ideas, I recognise that I am simplifying. And I apologise for this, if not to you, to Schelling himself and his scholars. Schelling's work is too vast and complex for me to attempt to cover, even what I have come to understand. Perhaps most relevant to me is Schelling's stance towards freedom and his understanding of how it emerges from our willingness for self-appropriation. This is the basis of the movement towards truth so valued in psychoanalysis. McGrath (2010) says, "To appropriate myself means taking over the ground of my being as mine and taking up the burden of my willing" (p. 90). McGrath: My willing means roughly my unconscious desire but perhaps more than that – my very nature; what Schelling refers to as "ungrund" will, before even the infinite unconscious. To quote McGrath (2012) again:

> "Influenced by Boehme and Kabbalah, the later Schelling modified his notion of the unconscious to include the decision to be oneself, which must sink beneath consciousness so that it might serve as the ground of one's creative and personal acts". And "the early notion of 'visible spirit' becomes, in the later Schelling, 'ground,' the dark side of God, which leaves its trace in the impenetrable and inexplicable reality of things; 'the indivisible remainder' (der nie aufgenhende Rest), which is never subsumed into a concept and frustrates every attempt to build a rational system".

As described earlier, Schelling talks of the emergence of self-consciousness through *The Ages of the World* – his *Weltalter* – in which he attempts to see how the pre-world infinite led to the finite universe. As such, he uses God and Spirit interchangeably. (Note that Schelling, as philosopher was also acquainted with the science of his day including physics and biology. Moreover, for Schelling, God is the ultimate spirit and spirit is in all nature, including humanity.)

You can read Schelling without having to translate this to the Christian God, in whatever way you might understand this to be. Modern scholars see spirit as psyche or subjectivity, and we can read Schelling through that lens just as we can only see through the lenses of our own history (Carew 2015; Sharvit 2015). But we do this remembering that Schelling lived in a different age and terms are not easily translatable. In my understanding, the will to be, to exist, to self-manifest is eternally strong. Spirit as an infinite and unitary wished (or perhaps continues to wish) existence which implies differentiation. This is the nature of spirit – to will to be. To do this, Spirit had to create the universe as other because it is only through other that self can exist.

Schelling's ideas predate and remind one of Jessica Benjamin's work on assertion and recognition. I quote Benjamin:

> Assertion and recognition constitute the poles of a delicate balance. This balance is integral to what is called "differentiation": the individual's development as a self that is aware of its distinctness from others. Yet this balance, and with it the differentiation of self and other, is difficult to sustain. In particular, the need for recognition gives rise to a paradox. Recognition is that response from the other which makes meaningful the feelings, intentions, and actions of the self. It allows the self to realize its

agency and authorship in a tangible way. But such recognition can only come from an "other" whom we, in turn, recognize as a person in his or her own right. This struggle to be recognized by an "other", and thus confirm our selves, was shown by Hegel to form the core of relationships of domination.

(Benjamin 1988, p. 12)

It is interesting to note that Hegel and Schelling were friends and roommates before their later differences.

The late Schelling incorporated these ideas into what he called positive philosophy. This should not be confused with what is nowadays known as positive psychology – a psychology that wishes only to stress the positives in life and dismiss negativity. Schelling in no way turned from the darker side of existence. For him, spirit held all dichotomies in one: good and bad, ill and health, yes and no. These are eternals and only by a process of differentiation and self-creation can one freely choose between them. Pre-Freud, Schelling does not talk of repression in a personal unconscious. I want to quote McGrath (2010) at length here:

Nowhere does Schelling say that the unconscious is constituted by acts, contents, experiences, which are unconscious because subjectivity could not bear them. The Schellingian unconscious is not reactive but productive, not repressive but dissociative. Here we refer to a distinction between two broad classes of theories of the unconscious: the reactive unconscious, which is an effect of the loss and disowning of the individual's past (of which Lacan's is the most philosophically sophisticated account), and the productive unconscious, which is widely associated with Jung, and increasingly with Deleuze and Guattari, but whose historical inception is Schelling's Naturphilosophie. The productive unconscious is the future-oriented, creative ground of the polymorphous self, a collective layer of potencies and possibilities that are for the most part unrecognized by the ego but that make possible the development and transformations the psyche undergoes in its progressive individuation. Where the theoreticians of the reactive unconscious have broken with the theosophico romantic lineage of dynamic psychology, the advocates of the productive unconscious have actively elaborated and developed it... Something of the Schellingian unconscious survives in Bergson, Janet, Jung, and Deleuze/Guattari.

(McGrath 2010, pp. 85–86)

This idea of the unconscious is linked to Schelling's argument for freedom (Schelling 1809). Despite Freud's project to have a scientific somewhat determinist psychoanalysis, the ghost of Schelling's freedom idea persists. Necessity and freedom philosophy has long been interested in the polarity of determinism and free will – sometimes expressed as fate vs. freedom. The idea of freedom was central to Schelling's work. Schelling asserts that freedom is essentially the capacity for good or for evil (*ein Vermögen zum Guten und Bösen*) (McGrath 2015).

What Schelling called the ungrund was before Spirit; unconscious to Spirit and neutral to all. When nature or the other was created through individuation – when personality evolved, so free will was realised in this (Barensten 2019).

In Freud, freedom is a result of accepting and taking responsibility for one's unconscious, rather than getting caught in the death of repetition compulsions. For Schelling, our actions and thoughts come from our being that is self-authored, even though authored in the unconscious. A maxim comes from our being, not being from a maxim. That is, the rules by which we live our personal lives come from our central being; our character/personality which is unconsciously chosen. At the core it is the "will" that counts.

> The will acts out of the necessity of its nature. This necessity is not mechanical: it is the being of the will, the core of freedom out of which its individual acts unfold. "But precisely this inner necessity is itself freedom; the essence of man is fundamentally his own act; necessity and freedom are in one another as one being that appears as one or the other only when considered from different sides, in itself freedom, formally necessity."
>
> (McGrath 2010, p. 77)

In Schelling, the opposites of necessity and freedom, of nature philosophy and moral philosophy, are life-giving oppositions, or productive dissociations (McGrath 2010); these are the opposites of fate/determinism and freedom/ morality. Productive dissociation – a dissociation for growth – is taken up by Deleuze. Continuing identity is seen as falsely clinging to an image that doesn't reflect experience that is fragmented. Dissociation may reflect a deeper reality. The fear of dissociation is fear of being multiple, the many rather than the one that continues. For Deleuze, following Schelling, consciousness is not a synthesis but a displacement, not a resolution of unconscious conflict, but a symptom.

Importance of Schelling for the Twenty-First Century

What then can we take from Schelling about the role of the unconscious in our lives, our groups and organisations? As described earlier, Schelling's ideas, even where there is no direct reference to him in later theories, show that his formulations permeate the concept as it has been developed, indicating its strength as an idea and its complexity insofar as its implications are constantly being realised in new ways.

The unfolding of this complexity through a variety of philosophical theories each with different emphases has been concentrated around the major dimensions of joy/pain, creativity and destructivity: dimensions that Freud later came to designate within his ideas of the pleasure and reality principles. Throughout the history of the idea of the unconscious, the two qualities of the unconscious process – both its creativity and its angst – have been emphasised, sometimes in tandem and at other times independently.

Segall (2014 p. 1) argues:

> I believe his (Schelling's) philosophy provides many of the anthropo-logical, theological, and cosmological resources necessary for bringing forth alternative forms of modernity no longer bent on the destruction of earth and the disintegration of human communities.

This is because Schelling sees nature, including the physical and biological sciences, as a complex process rather than as an entity; and its study as being not from a distanced outside perspective, but from the human within nature (Stone 2023). He says, "the knower and that which is known are the same" (Schelling 1804, 1994). That is, humanity is nature and nature can know itself through itself. Our deepest exploration of the natural world is the way to understanding ourselves and understanding ourselves leads us to nature.

"Schelling posits that the only way to know the world is to know it *person-ally* – that is, in the way we become familiar with our own or another person" (Fenichel 2019, p. 196). I might add that this is in the way we know ourselves and others as interacting beings in roles in human and natural systems. How we make choices is a reflection not only of the necessities of reality – which necessities indeed we have ourselves created or co-created – but also of our unconscious will.

The importance of choice rather than determinism or compulsion is critical because our lives are comprised of decisions both small and large. Our organi-sations and institutions are dependent on the decisions of many role holders and their interactions. Daily ethics and the decisions of governments and large multinational organisations are critical to our lives. Schelling confronts us with the idea that our decisions are subject to unconscious choices and impulses that create our basic character and ethical stance in the world.

On studying Schelling, Fenichel says,

> Freedom is a confrontation with the depth of our responsibility and the limitations of our knowledge – a disturbing recognition of our inability to either escape from or to fully inhabit our subjectivity... freedom and life are inextricably joined for Schelling; objective truth is a contradic-tion in terms... the truth of creation is not *something* revealed... it is the infinite capacity to orient ourselves to otherness... to the unknowable, to the unconscious, to the liminal. In fact, to be free is to acknowledge our dependency – to claim responsibility for, to identify with the deepest foundation of our being that is expressed and developed through our choices.
>
> (Fenichel, p. 92)

The current cultures of narcissism (Lasch 1991) and perversity (Long 2008) that permeate the consumerism of the twenty-first century that we are subject to and co-create – the seeming intractable problems of anthropomorphic climate change, poverty, species loss and racism – confront us with what Erich Fromm, last century in face of the then "big questions", called an escape from freedom into totalitarianism.

> It is modernity's repressed fear of chaos and meaninglessness, in other words, that leads it to turn away from "the big questions" in favor of the instrumental solutions and small pleasures of technoscientific consumerism. Inquiring into the essence of human freedom is especially terrifying for the narcissistic ego used to the pampering of consumer capitalism. The willing soul must learn, according to Schelling.
>
> (Segall 2014, p. 26)

Throughout this book, the idea of freedom in many forms surfaces. What does it mean to be; to be free, to have free choice in a group, an organisation, a society, an institution? Equally astonishing but linked to the unconscious is the idea of something that is transcendent, beyond human comprehension but deeply part of us, just somehow to be experienced. The Quakers refer to the "light within" or the "inward teacher" (Duke 2023) ideas congruent with this. For Bion it is the infinite unconscious.

> The essence of human spirituality, according to Schelling, is freedom, the decision between good and evil. Humanity's fall into hubris is caused by the elevation of our animal nature over all other living creatures. The fall is not a fall into animality, but an inversion of the spiritual principle of freedom leading to the elevation of the periphery (our creatureliness) above the Center (our divine likeness).
>
> (Segall 2014, p. 10)

> Freedom is the very ground of subjectivity, the abyss from which subjectivity first emerges. As a human spirit, I just am the freedom to decide for good or evil, and nothing besides. This decision is the essence of my freedom – which in fact is not mine at all, since it is more correct to say that I belong to freedom. There is no me behind or before the spiritual crisis of this originally free deed.
>
> (Segall 2012, p. 2)

Notes

1 Let me say to begin with that although I have studied psychoanalysis since my early university days, what I put forward is my understanding alone – drawn from my reading and my experience. If there are rights and wrongs in reading and scholarship, then I may sometimes seem wrong in my interpretations – or at least I may

differ from the interpretations of others. I endeavour, however, to give evidence for
my thinking and welcome the thoughts of others.
2 This chapter includes but extends material from my chapter "The Transforming
Experience Framework and Unconscious Processes" in S. Long, *Transforming
Experience in Organisations: A Framework for Organisational Research and
Consultancy*. London: Karnac, 2016.
3 Whyte points out that "many religious and early philosophers, Plato for example, assumed a similar separation of soul or mind from the material universe. But
Descartes was the first thinker to assert a sharp division of mind from matter as the
basis of a systematic philosophy claiming scientific clarity and certainty" (p. 26).
However, he argues that it is following the Cartesian splitting of mind from body
that an idea of the unconscious became necessary.
4 https://philosophybreak.com/articles/i-think-therefore-i-am-descartes-cogito
-ergo-sum-explained/.
5 This work was never quite completed by Schelling and there are three versions with
several attached notes.
6 More recently, Phillip Boxer has named this the radical unconscious to draw a
distinction in light of Freud's discoveries of a repressed unconscious that may be
brought to light through psychoanalytic treatment.

References

Aurelio, M.S.G. (2012). 'Schelling's Aesthetic Turn in the System of Transcendental
Idealism', www.kritike.org/journal/issue_11/aurelio_june2012.pdf.
Barentsen, G. (2015). 'Silent Partnerships: Schelling Jung and the Romantic
Metasubject', *Symposium*, vol. 19, no.1, pp. 67–79.
Barentsen, G. (2019) 'Schelling's Dark Nature and the Prospects for Ecological
Civilisation', *Journal of Natural and Social Philosophy*, vol. 15, no.1, pp. 91–127.
Benjamin, J. (1988). *The Bonds of Love: Psychoanalysis, Feminism and the Problem of
Domination*. New York: Pantheon books.
Bohm, D. (1980). *Wholeness and the Implicate Order*. London: Routledge.
Boxer, P. (2024). 'Why Should Zizek's Misreading of Lacan Matter?', https://asy
mmetricleadership.com/2024/02/24/why-should-zizeks-misreading-of-lacan
-matter/ [accessed February 2024].
Carew, J. (2014). *Ontological Catastrophe: Zizek and the Paradoxical Metaphysics of
German Idealism*. London: Open Humanities Press.
Carew, J. (2015). 'Reading Schelling Psychoanalytically: Zizek on the Fantasy of
the Ground of Consciousness and Language', *Canadian Journal of Continental
Philosophy: Symposium*, vol. 19, no. 1, pp. 39–51.
Chessick, R.D. (1992). *What Constitutes the Patient in Psychotherapy: Alternative
Approaches to Understanding Humans*. New York: Jason Aronson.
Das, S.B. (2011). 'F.W.J. Schelling' in James Fieser and Bradley Dowden (eds.)
Internet Encyclopedia of Philosophy. London: Routledge. https://iep.utm.edu/
schellin/ [accessed 12 September 2023].
Das, S.B. (2014). 'Friedrich Wilhelm Joseph Von Schelling (1775–1854)', *Internet
Encyclopedia of Philosophy*, www.iep.utm.edu/schellin [accessed 11 September 2013].
Duke, J. (2023). *Where Do Words Come From?* Unpublished PhD thesis. Melbourne:
University of Divinity.
Ellenberger, H. (1957). 'The Unconscious Before Freud', *Bulletin of the Menninger
Clinic*, vol. 21, pp. 3–15.

Ellenberger, H. (1970). *The Discovery of the Unconscious: The History and Evolution of Dynamic Psychology*. New York: Basic Books.

Fenichel, T. (2019). *Uncanny Belonging: Schelling, Freud and the Philosophical Foundations of Psychoanalysis*. London: Routledge.

Ffytche, M. (2011). *The Foundation of the Unconscious: Schelling, Freud and the Birth of the Modern Psyche*. Cambridge: Cambridge University Press.

Freud, S. (1925). *Negation*. S.E. 19 233–240. London: Hogarth Press.

Gare, A. (2011). 'From Kant to Schelling to Process Metaphysics: On the Way to Ecological Civilization', *Cosmos & History: The Journal of Natural and Social Philosophy*, pp. 26–69.

Glover, N. (2009). *Psychoanalytic Aesthetics – Introduction to the British School*. London: Karnac.

Grotstein, J. (1977). 'Bion's Transformation in "O" and the Concept of the Transcendent Position', www.sicap.it/merciai/bion/papers/grots.htm [accessed 13 November 2014].

Lacan, J. (1977). *Ecrits*. London: Tavistock.

Lasch, C. (1991, first published 1979). *The Culture of Narcissism: American Life in an Age of Diminishing Expectations*. USA: W. W. Norton and Co.

Long, S.D. (2008). *The Perverse Organisation and Its Deadly Sins*. London: Karnac.

Love, J. and Schmidt, J. (2006). 'Introduction', in J. Love and J. Schmidt (trans.) *FWJ Schelling: Philosophical Investigations into the Essence of Human Freedom*. Albany, NY: SUNY.

Lovelock, J. (1979). *Gaia: A New Look at Life on Earth*. Oxford: Oxford University Press.

Mathur, A.N. (2018). 'Two Cultures? Frontiers of Faith in Yoga and Psychoanalysis', in A.N. Mathur (ed.). *Psychoanalysis from the Indian Terroir*, pp. 145–164. London: Rowman & Littlefield.

Matthews, B. (2012). 'Schelling: Heretic of Modernity. An Intellectual Biography of Freidrich Wilhelm Joseph von Schelling (1770–1854)', http://philosophyproject.org/schelling/ [accessed 11 September 2014].

McGrath, S.J. (2010). 'Schelling on the Unconscious', *Research in Phenomenology*, vol. 40, pp. 72–91.

McGrath, S.J. (2012). *The Dark Ground of Spirit: Schelling and the Unconscious*. London: Routledge e-version.

McGrath, S.J. (2015). 'The Logic of Schelling's Freedom Essay', https://www.metaphysicalsociety.org/2015/papers/McGrath.pdf [recovered 18 October 2023].

Pistiner de Cortinas, L. (2009). *The Aesthetic Dimension of the Mind: Variations on a Theme by Bion*. London: Karnac.

Rabstejnek, C.V. (2015). 'History and Evolution of the Unconscious Before and After Sigmund Freud', https://www.researchgate.net/publication/277871439_History_and_Evolution_of_the_Unconscious_Before_and_After_Sigmund_Freud.

Rand, N. (2004). 'The Hidden Soul: The Growth of the Unconscious in Philosophy, Psychology, Medicine, and Literature, 1750–1900', *American Imago*, vol. 61, no. 3, pp. 257–289.

Rivas, V. (2020). 'The Anthropogenic Takeover of a Dual External World', *Cosmos and History: The Journal of Natural and Social Philosophy*, vol. 16, no. 1, pp. 317–348.

Sharvit, G. (2015). 'Schelling and Freud on Historicity and Freedom', *Idealistic Studies,* vol. 42, no. 2, pp. 149–167.

Schelling, F.W.J. (1804). 'System of Philosophy in General and of the Philosophy of Nature in Particular', in D. Snow (ed.). *Idealism and the Endgame of Theory.* Albany, NY: Suny Press.

Schelling F.W.J. (1809/2006). *Philosophical Investigations into the Essence of Human Freedom.* Jeff Love and Johannes Schmidt (trans.). Albany, NY: SUNY.

Schelling, F.W.J. (1815a; 1942). *The Ages of the World.* F.D. Wolfe Bowman Jr. (trans.). New York: Columbia University Press.

Schelling, F.W.J. (1815b; 2024). *On the Deities of Samothrace.* A Bilder, J. Wirth and D. Farrell Krell (trans.). Bloomington: Indiana University Press.

Schelling, F.W.J. (2006, first published 1809). *Philosophical Investigations into the Essence of Human Freedom,* Jeff Love and Johannes Schmidt (trans.). Albany: SUNY.

Schelling, F.W.J. (2007). *Historical-Critical Introduction to the Philosophy of Mythology.* Mason Richey and Markus Zisselsberger (trans.). Albany, NY: State University of New York Press. pp. 149.

Segall, M.D. (2012). 'Schelling's Philosophy of Freedom', https://footnotes2plato .com/2018/10/26/schellings-philosophy-of-freedom/ [accessed 18 January 2024].

Segall, M.D. (2014). The Re-Emergence of Schelling: Philosophy in a Time of Emergency. Germany: Lambert Academic Publishing.

Snow, D.E. (2014). 'The Barbarian Principle: Merleau-Ponty, Schelling, and the Question of Nature', in Jason Wirth and Patrick Burke (eds.), *Review: University of Notre Dame Philosophical Reviews.* Albany, NY: SUNY Press. https://ndpr.nd .edu/reviews/the-barbarian-principle-merleau-ponty-schelling-and-the-question -of-nature/.

Stone, A. (2023). 'Philosophy of Nature' in M. Forster and K. Gjesdal (eds.) *Oxford Handbook of Nineteenth-Century German Philosophy.* Oxford: Oxford University Press.

Tsarion, M. (2020). *The Freedom of Man* – By Michael Tsarion. https://www .schellingzone.com/chapter-3.html [accessed November 2015 & 14 July 2023].

White, A. (1983) *Schelling.* New Haven: Yale University Press.

Whyte, L. (1962). *The Unconscious Before Freud.* New York: Basic Books.

Wirth, J. (2013). 'The Reawakening of the Barbarian Principle', in J. Wirth and P. Burke (eds.) *The Barbarian Principle: Merleau-Ponty, Schelling and the Question of Nature,* pp. 1–24. Albany, NY: SUNY Press.

Woodard, B. (2013). 'Schellingian Thought for Ecological Politics', *Anarchist Developments in Cultural Studies ISSN: 1923-5615 2013.2: Ontological Anarché: Beyond Materialism and Idealism.*

Zizek, S. (1996, reprint 2007). *The Indivisible Remainder: On Schelling and Related Matters.* New York: Verso.

3 Freud
The Repressed Unconscious

This chapter is focused on the work of Sigmund Freud, father of psychoanalysis, his clinical method and substantial theory. Extensive though his work is, I focus on the basics of how he conceptualised the unconscious, recognising that to take this idea out of the context of the whole of Freudian theory renders what I say necessarily incomplete.

The chapter is, in many ways, my own rendition of his work on the unconscious, although I do attempt to be faithful to his meaning. I first heard of Freud during my last year of high school and was drawn to what seemed to me a set of ideas that might support my own thoughts about hidden secrets, the sort of skeletons in the cupboard, and anxieties that all families have, mine included. I had wanted to study biology at university but was precluded as I did not have the level of mathematics that the University of Melbourne needed for entry to science. I thought psychology might be a substitute. At least that could be taken as part of an arts degree. Disappointed by the focus on behaviourism, I spent my holiday time in the library reading Freud's collected works. Although I did not understand all at that time, much sank in, at least through my own lens of discovering the hidden, especially marvelling at the case studies.[1] They fitted with my own enjoyment of mystery and detective novels. Freud shares much in common with the fictional Holmes, with his focus on small, often overlooked details, yet such detail holding a critical meaning for the patient, unfolded in the analysis. Later, I came to see his method as abductive (Ginsberg and Davin 1980; Long and Harney 2013).

My own analysis was with a Freudian analyst. This and my own clinical training in Freudian approaches led me to wait for the signs of the unconscious to reveal themselves. I worked first with individual patients and also with families and later with organisations. While training, I read Klein, a follower of Freud, and utilised her method of play therapy with my child patients, where I learned much about the unconscious as evidenced through play and non-verbal interactions. My patients' drawings and play taught me much about their unspoken anxieties and attempted defences against these. This, the systems work with families, and my infant observation studies were foundational to my later work in organisations: always attempting to understand both conscious and unconscious dynamics. While Freud, the father of psychoanalysis, must

DOI: 10.4324/9781003559818-3

stand as fundamental to my ideas of the unconscious, I must acknowledge that many other psychoanalytic thinkers and practitioners have influenced me – too numerous to list here, but important in the further development of the idea of the psychoanalytic unconscious.

Freud and Psychoanalysis

In his new *Introductory Lectures* (Lecture 35 1933), Freud names psychoanalysis as "a depth psychology or psychology of the unconscious".[2] As with any person seriously engaged with continually learning and developing ideas, Freud's work on the unconscious evolved throughout his life. We may never come to a definitive idea of the Freudian unconscious; it has many implications, intuited but not pursued by Freud, and yet to be followed.

Contrary to some popular views, Freud's major contribution was not to discover "the unconscious" but to discover the use of free association – a method for exploring unconscious processes; although, as Rand (2004) points out, Francis Galton had been working with associative methods since 1879. There is a history to everything.

> The poets and philosophers before me discovered the unconscious. What I discovered was the scientific method by which the unconscious can be studied.
>
> (Freud 1928)[3]

Wollheim (2003, p. 23) argues that indeed, Freud discovered the unconscious "for science", and examines how Freud came to understand hidden desire as at the core of the unconscious, such understanding gained through the new psychoanalytic method. Freud's work is most often traced back through a historical link to the work of Mesmer and Charcot through the application of magnetism and hypnosis (Rabstejnik 2011), methods that he rejected in favour of his method of free association (Newirth 2023; Wollheim 2003; Rand 2004). But the influence of philosophy, given Freud's wide reading, cannot be dismissed.

In his 1900 book *The Interpretation of Dreams* – a book said to herald the birth of psychoanalysis proper – Freud says,

> It is not without intention that I speak of "our" unconscious. For what I thus describe is not the same as the unconscious of the philosophers.
>
> (Freud 1900, p. 775)

He goes on to note that their concern was with the rise of consciousness, saying about the unconscious that "the term is used merely to indicate a contrast to consciousness". Despite some evidence that Freud had met with the ideas of Schelling, and even though he does mention the followers of Schelling in *The Interpretation of Dreams*, and again in his paper on the uncanny, I think this statement indicates that his understanding of Schelling was influenced by his views on religion, dismissing much of Schelling's unconscious as unscientific and linked to idealism's teleological emphases. But, Schelling had been involved with thinking about the unconscious, and not simply as a contrast to consciousness, as is discussed in Chapter 2. And many of Schelling's ideas, as I have said, predated psychoanalysis. Nonetheless, Freud does come to conceptualise the unconscious in new ways. Throughout his publications, the unconscious is described in many different and complex versions as his thinking about this idea progressed. However, the basics of repression remained.

He developed the idea of the repressed dynamic unconscious and discovered the process of free association to access unconscious processes. He did this predominantly, although not exclusively, within the context of the clinic in order to free patients from the toxic grip of symptoms arising from what he came to see as repressed thoughts, impulses and associated psychological defences. To Freud, repression has a central place in creating the dynamic unconscious: an unconscious found through its many effects. His 1917 *Introductory Lectures*, aimed at presenting his work to a broad audience, examine these effects in detail, ranging from parapraxes (slips of the tongue and pen) to dreams and neurotic symptoms, and they discuss his methods of interpretation and the several dynamics of working with patients. The focus is on discovering unconscious processes and attempting to bring them to consciousness. Such a focus on an active, dynamic unconscious differs from the central place of the non-repressed unconscious, such as is found in the archetypal collective unconscious of Jung, regarded as having a permanent presence whether or not brought to consciousness. The non-repressed aspects of the unconscious, while still present in Freud's work, have less centrality to his theories of psychopathology.

With what seemed audacious and somewhat shocking in his own time, and still to some extent nowadays, Freud saw that the sexual desires of humans, beginning with childhood, were the basis for much that becomes repressed (Freud 1905, 1920). He demonstrates this through his case studies, where time and again his analysands, with pain and difficulty, are shown to discover childhood unconscious phantasies and their interrelatedness with facts and memories that remained unconscious yet fundamental to psychological symptoms during their development. Famously, he took the ancient Greek myth of Oedipus as a metaphor for the development of sexuality in the child, noting the boy child's desire to marry his mother and replace his father with murderous intent – all either repressed or abandoned through a resolution that brings him to so-called normal adult sexual identity and activity. That is, if all goes well. The link between sexuality and the unconscious is a strong theme throughout Freud's theorising and practice. Much is taken for granted in modern psychoanalytic psychotherapy – at least the practice of discovering traumas from the past: skeletons in the cupboard.

The influence of psychoanalytic ways of describing the unconscious has been dominant in the twentieth and early twenty-first centuries. Who now can read the Romantic poets of the eighteenth and early nineteenth centuries without the lens of psychoanalysis? Take the *Songs of Innocence and of Experience* by William Blake, or Samuel Coleridge, who described Sophocles' "Oedipus Rex" as a work with a perfect plot and whose *Rime of the Ancient Mariner* is often read as a psychological tale of internal turmoil, guilt and final reparation. Or indeed, many of the works of Shakespeare.

As background to discussing Freud's unconscious, I make the following comments:

• Freud was a man of his time: ideas on homosexuality, women and so-called primitives are generally not acceptable nowadays. They register the nomenclature and culture of his time. This should not detract from the basic arguments put forward about unconscious processes.
• There is an emphasis on observation, particularly clinical observation. He insists this is primary to theory.
• The 1915 paper on the unconscious introduces its systemic nature; the evidence for its existence; the ideation of instincts; the purpose of censorship and repression; and its special characteristics.
• His arguments sit within his general theory of the economics of psychic energy (cathexis to ideation being one part: cathexis being an energetic attraction).
• These are some foundational ideas in psychoanalysis that appear in different forms in later psychoanalytic thinking.

In *The Interpretation of Dreams* (1900), Freud argues for unconsciousness having two forms, and he names these as two systems: the system unconscious (ucs), which is not easily accessible to consciousness (often referred to as the dynamic unconscious), and the system preconscious (pcs) (often referred to as the descriptive unconscious), the contents and processes of which can be brought to consciousness through attention. He then speaks of processes of censorship that form a barrier between the pcs and the ucs, and of a barrier of censorship between the conscious (cs) and pcs. He illustrates these with clinical examples. Later (*Introductory Lectures*: Freud 1915–1916), he gives the analogy of a doorman standing between two large rooms, only letting past those ideas that please him – the censor. Such processes of barriers and censorship are at the basis of his theory of repression.

However, as his thinking develops, Freud argues more fully that the preconscious is part of the system consciousness, not part of the unconscious. The unconscious proper, he argues, includes a repressed and a non-repressed aspect.

> Everything that is repressed must remain unconscious; but let us state at the very outset that the repressed does not cover everything that is unconscious. The unconscious has the wider compass: the repressed is a part of the unconscious.
>
> (Freud 1915a, p. 166)[4]

What then is the unconscious that Freud examined? Too often the unconscious is seen as a "location" or storehouse, and Freud sometimes writes, most likely for convenience of expression, as if it were.[5] But his main emphasis is that it is a system of the mind within which certain processes take place. In his paper *The Unconscious* (1915a), Freud talks of the system unconscious as one of three systems of the mind – conscious (Cs) preconscious (Pcs) and unconscious (Ucs). Such "systems" do not indicate a static storehouse view.

From early on, he emphasises that although he uses topographical analogies about these systems, they are not to be understood as "places" and suggests that the term cathexis is better employed – seeing that ideas may be cathected (held by energetic forces) in conscious, preconscious or unconscious states (Freud 1900, pp. 770–771). And, although some of Freud's descriptions give the idea of the unconscious as a kind of place or thought repository, at other times he insists on it as a set of processes within an energetic field. Initially, Freud was a neurologist, and his ideas continued to hold much of his early perspectives in the form of what is described as his economic theory of the nervous system and somatic links to the psychic systems. It seems evident that he struggles throughout to find the right language for the unconscious, as have all those who wish to understand it.

Freud's 1915 paper on the unconscious stresses:

(i)   That it is a system in the mind. Freud had a systemic view, and this is important for thinking not simply about individual psychic systems, but also larger social systems as he enters his work on groups and societies carried out at a later time.
(ii) That repression involves ideas – emotions are suppressed, not repressed; it is in the nature of emotion that it is felt/consciously experienced.
(iii) That this unconscious produces effects, and it is by these effects that we can hypothesise its existence. The effects are often termed the "return of the repressed".
(iv) The evidence of the effects is largely in parapraxes, jokes, dreams and neurotic symptoms.
(v)   Unconscious ideation is linked to consciousness (it is latent, preconscious or repressed).
(vi) It is an idea "lacking in consciousness".

As a system, the unconscious has special characteristics. It has archaic inherited aspects (which may become energetically linked to ideation, but may not), that different impulses can coexist without contradiction, that it substitutes external reality with psychic reality and it is timeless. These ideas become foundational and persist throughout the Freudian project. They strongly influenced my reading of his case studies and my own clinical work. The thinking associated with these characteristics is called "primary process thinking".

A particularly interesting characteristic that he notes is that the unconscious of one person can connect with (talk to) the unconscious of another person without the intermediary of consciousness. This phenomenon is of interest to later psychoanalytic ideas of, for example, projective identification and transference/countertransference phenomena as elaborated by the object relations school. It should be of great interest to those interested in unconscious processes in groups and organisations because it suggests that communication in groups and organisations can occur without participants' overt awareness, and such communication can only be accessed by paying special attention to its effects. Only then can we hypothesise the message and possibly its intent. Such is the work of the systems psychodynamic or socioanalytic consultant.

In many ways, it seems as if Freud has taken the concept of the unconscious from the philosophers and turned it on its head. For instance, whereas we see in Schelling and the German Romantics an ambition to understand how an intelligent and self-conscious world arose from an infinity that was unconscious, in Freud we see an unconscious built through a process of repression occurring through personal and social history. Ideas that are repressed were once conscious, even if fleetingly. However, this difference may be more apparent than substantial because, despite the contribution of his theories of repression, Freud, as described earlier, also recognises a primordial unconscious of inherited instincts that push for expression in thought, much as the infinite spirit of Schelling wills its own realisation. Freud's primary interest becomes centred on the dynamics of this push for consciousness through the drives[6] and in the opposing forces of repression that resist this, themselves unconscious. This lies at the basis of the clinical method of psychoanalysis.

Freud's ideas have formed a foundation for our understanding of unconscious processes, and his specific theory of repression – sometimes referred to as motivated forgetting – adds a new perspective to that found in pre-psychoanalytic ideas. The term repression has many meanings in the general English language, one being a social dynamic of domination, as we shall see in Chapter 6. However, Maddox tells us that it was Freud's own insistence that his German term *Verdrangung* be translated as "repression" (Maddox 2006, p. 62).

> We have learned from psychoanalysis that the essence of the process of repression lies, not in putting an end to, in annihilating, the idea which represents an instinct, but in preventing it from becoming conscious. When this happens, we say of the idea that it is a state of being "unconscious", and we can produce good evidence to show that even when it is unconscious it can produce effects, even including some which finally reach consciousness.
>
> (Freud 1915a, p. 159)

A greater difference between the earlier views of the unconscious and the Freudian perspective is Freud's rejection of a teleological emphasis, such as may seemingly be found in Schelling's work. In Schelling, it is through the subordination of the unconscious to consciousness that its participation in love is enabled.

> Freud's dark principle (the id) is held down by consciousness. According to Schelling, the dark ground, when it acts in accordance with love, *holds itself back*; it defers to the light not because its desires are out of proportion to the modicum of pleasure reality can afford, but only by subordinating itself to consciousness can it participate in love.
>
> (McGrath 2012; 73% into Kindle version)

We might at first argue with McGrath here because the repressing action of the ego is itself part of the unconscious in Freud, according to his later work on the ego and the id (Freud 1923). The holding down is not strictly by consciousness but by those unconscious egoistic forces pressing for individual survival. But then again, repression is from an ego most probably once conscious, and a super-ego shaped by social forces.

Schelling's description is somewhat present in Freud's idea of sublimation, where erotic love in a way holds itself back and is transformed into tender love; and in Ernst Kris' notion of regression in the service of the ego (Kris 1952), where regression is not regarded as pathological but as a means by which the unconscious might express itself creatively and thus actualise itself. Nonetheless, the implication in Schelling is that the willing of the unconscious is *in order for* spirit to achieve self-recognition and a connection with the other through love (and – as it was actualised in the fall – hate), hence the seeming teleological underpinning of the idea. There is a fulfilment or greater purpose stretching back, as it were, to pull the spirit forward. Freud's scientific deterministic disposition, on the contrary, looked to the conscious psyche as largely determined through personal history and repressive forces. (Later in the book, we see that ideas of anticipation may act "as if" the future pulls us forward without this being mystical or teleological.)

In Freud's work, as I have indicated, some instincts that are wholly unconscious become represented in thoughts (1915a, 1915b, 1915c). It is in this sense that they become "drives". Whereas the person can flee anxiety-provoking stimuli that arise in the external world, the anxieties arising in relation to instinctual representations require different methods of escape, hence the use of repression. By this mechanism, the instinctual representations are forced back into unconsciousness. However, because thoughts have many associations in consciousness, more distant associations with repressed thoughts may escape repression and stay in consciousness. It is through these associations that the psychoanalytic method approaches the unconscious material.

> In carrying out the technique of psychoanalysis, we continually require the patient to produce such derivatives of the repressed, as in consequence either of their remoteness or of their distortion, can pass the

censorship of the conscious. Indeed, the associations which we require him to give without being influenced by any conscious purposive idea and without any criticism, and from which we reconstitute a conscious translation of the repressed representative – these associations are nothing else than remote and distorted derivatives of this kind. During this process we observe that the patient can go on spinning a thread of such associations, till he is brought up against some thought, the relation of which to what is repressed becomes so obvious that he is compelled to repeat his attempt at repression.

(Freud 1915b, pp. 148–149)

In *A Note on the Unconscious in Psycho-Analysis* (1912), Freud says, "I wish to expound in a few words and as plainly as possible what the term 'unconscious' has come to mean in Psychoanalysis and in Psychoanalysis alone" (p. 255). He describes an unconscious conception as one of which we are unaware but willing to admit exists due to other indications or signs – and here he talks of post-hypnotic suggestion indicating an idea that was in the mind but not consciously present.

We call a process unconscious if we are obliged to assume that it is being activated *at the moment* though *at the moment* we know nothing about it.

(Freud, 1912 p. 258)

It is interesting, though, that in this brief paper, although talking of repressive forces, he regards all conscious thought as rising through unconsciousness to consciousness. He says, "Every psychical act begins as an unconscious one, and it may either remain so or go on developing into consciousness, according as it meets with resistance or not" (p. 261). Does this not echo some of the earlier Schelling ideas?

In his 1915 paper on the unconscious, as I indicated earlier, he distinguishes between the preconscious that contains thoughts able to be accessed through memory and the unconscious that contains thoughts unable to reach consciousness without great effort (i.e. the dynamic unconscious). Although initially looking at an unconscious censorship occurring between the pcs and cs (an issue of some censorship and memory), he later elaborates, reserving the notion of unconscious censorship to that dynamic between the systems unconscious and conscious (now including the pcs) in the following way:

We are led to look for the more important distinction, not between the conscious and the preconscious, but between the preconscious and the unconscious.

(Freud 1915a, p. 192)

Here, he is pointing to the idea of repression not as a simple failure of memory or consciously setting aside an idea into the preconscious but as an active energetic force.

> For the present let it suffice us to bear in mind that the system Pcs. shares the characteristics of the system Cs. and that the rigorous censorship exercises its office at the point of transition from the Ucs. to the Pcs. (Or Cs.).
>
> (Freud 1915a, p. 172)

This is energetically described as

> an anticathexis, by means of which the system Pcs. protects itself from the pressure upon it of the unconscious idea. We shall see from clinical examples how such an anticathexis, operating in the system Pcs., manifests itself. It is this which represents the permanent expenditure [of energy] of a primal repression, and which also guarantees the permanence of that repression. Anticathexis is the sole mechanism of primal repression; in the case of repression proper ("after-pressure") there is in addition withdrawal of the Pcs. cathexis.
>
> (Freud 1915a, p. 180)

In this, he is outlining a theory of energies and uses the term after-repression to indicate the fate of thoughts once experienced but now intolerable – the dynamic unconscious. The term primary repression is given to repression that occurs in relation to unconscious instinctual forces. He distinguishes between instinctual forces and their ideational representations. Instincts, he claims, and I continue to express, can never be conscious in themselves.

> I am in fact of the opinion that the antithesis of conscious and unconscious is not applicable to instincts. An instinct can never become an object of consciousness—only the idea that represents the instinct can. Even in the unconscious, moreover, an instinct cannot be represented otherwise than by an idea. If the instinct did not attach itself to an idea or manifest itself as an affective state, we could know nothing about it. When we nevertheless speak of an unconscious instinctual impulse or of a repressed instinctual impulse, the looseness of phraseology is a harmless one. We can only mean an instinctual impulse the ideational representative of which is unconscious, for nothing else comes into consideration.
>
> (Freud 1915a, pp. 176–177)[7]

Unpleasant memories and thoughts being repressed (termed after-repression) are derived through experience, particularly in childhood although he had changed his original ideas that infantile thoughts were derived from actual events and changed to the belief that they came from infantile phantasies.

> What is unconscious in mental life is also that which is infantile. The strange impression of there being so much evil in people begins to diminish. This frightful evil is simply the initial, primitive, infantile part of mental life which we can find in actual operation in children.
>
> (Freud 1916, p. 247)

Freud's early theories are based on the idea of the mind as being formed and altered through psychic energy that is either bound to particular thoughts (cathected) or unbound and experienced as anxiety.[8] His later theories became increasingly more focused on the symbolic processes of meaning-making. Anxiety became not simply unbound energy but a signal or sign that a repressed idea or wish may become conscious and thus a threat to the ego and the person's narcissistic investments. In this later thinking (Freud 1923), he moved to a model of the mind based on id, ego and super-ego: three systems of mind roughly representing (i) instinctual forces; (ii) the part of the mind in touch with perception, conscious reasoning and reality; and (iii) the conscience and ego ideal. This model lies over his older model of the systems unconscious, preconscious and conscious. It regards the id as totally and always unconscious and sections of each of the other two systems as being either conscious or unconscious.

By 1933 in the new *Introductory Lectures*, he is attributing to the id much of what he earlier said about the unconscious.

> We perceive that we have no right to name the mental region that is foreign to the ego "the system ucs" since the characteristic of being unconscious is not restricted to it. Very well, we will no longer use the term "unconscious" in the systemic sense and we will give what we have hitherto described a better name and one no longer open to misunderstanding... we will in future call it "the id"... It is the dark inaccessible part of the personality... the logical forms of thought do not apply in the id... contrary impulses sit side by side... they may converge to form compromises... there is nothing in the id that corresponds to the passage of time... the Id makes no judgements of value: no good and evil: no morality.
>
> (Freud 1933, p. 71)

This may be of interest to us when we consider modern ideas of the unconscious, such as unconscious bias in perception.

But now, with the systems id, ego and super-ego, Freud can attribute aspects of the ego and super-ego to the unconscious – they are not simply conscious systems of the mind, and the unconscious aspects of the censorship processes can be understood.

Many later psychoanalysts tend to avoid the idea of psychic energies as described by the early Freud, and the theory of id, ego and super-ego has become dominant in the popular mind. Nonetheless, repression *is* an energetic term – pushing ideas out of the mind – and the idea of the unconscious has always been formed with the implication of energetic forces.

> The nucleus of the ucs consists of instinctual representatives which seek to discharge their cathexsis; that is to say, it consists of wishful impulses.
>
> (Freud 1915a, p. 190)

Moreover, the very ideas of psychological defence and psychic conflict imply forces that act on one another: the theory of the defences being a foundational theory for psychoanalytic psychotherapy (for example, Malan 1999) and later for ideas of social defences (Jaques 1955; Menzies 1970; Armstrong and Rustin 2014). The idea of energetic forces in relation to the unconscious is an important stream of thought that has echoes both at a bodily somatic level and at an intergroup relational level. A move away from a systemic topographical emphasis to a structural emphasis of id, ego and superego could be regarded as a retrograde step because of its leading to simplified views by some of the psyche as a set of structures rather than ongoing systems.

Nonetheless, the earlier energetic dynamics persist in Freud's thinking and although a powerful psychic force, repression is never whole or complete. Freudian psychoanalysis is concerned with the return of the repressed: how repressed thoughts influence current thinking, feelings and actions. The method of Freudian psychoanalysis attempts to retrieve repressed thoughts and free the person from their domination.

So, we have in Freud's idea of the unconscious a dynamic system of the mind where threatening thoughts (instinctual representatives) are kept from consciousness, but not from having an impact on other thoughts, feelings and behaviours. As Freud says, "a repression is something very different from a rejection" (Freud 1914, p. 317). Freud's analysis of dreams, parapraxes, jokes and symptoms gives a picture of repressed ideas seeking to express themselves, to return to consciousness, at times cleverly evading the censorship of the conscious ego by mechanisms such as displacement and condensation – the primary mechanisms of dream work; processes that Freud describes as primary process thinking – or by rationalisations, denial, reaction formations or other such defensive mechanisms. Perhaps the most ingenious mechanism, if we are to anthropomorphise these processes as Freud does for descriptive clarity (even as late as 1938 describing a defensive process as "artful"; Freud 1938, p. 277), is where the defence mechanism is "won over" so that the defence itself expresses the repressed thought: the hand-washing rituals of the obsessive neurotic being a prime example. The washing represents both the thought *and* the dismissal of the thought. Similarly, both loving and hating attitudes can be expressed in the same symptom. Freud calls these compromise products and describes such a defensive solution in his case study of the Wolfman, whose obsessive thoughts linked God to faeces "in which a part was played no less by an affectionate current of devotion than by a hostile current of abuse" via the patient's anal eroticism (Freud 1918, p. 321). Clever! Such mechanisms illustrate how the ego itself is partly unconscious; striking deals, as it were, between combating forces. These ideas expressed by Freud through metaphors of attack and defence – censors and evaders – bring images of an internal world of conflictual systems that require neutralisation and provide a vision taken up more fully by later object relations theorists such as Melanie Klein, who describe an inner world of objects and partial objects striving among each other for expression in the experience of the person (subject).

The inner world as a place of conflict and turmoil is not new. The Ancient Greeks wrote this into their plays – where the conflicts between the gods paralleled and interacted with the internal conflicts of the human protagonists – as did Shakespeare where the forces were often as much between natural forces as within human political intrigue. Inner conflict and turmoil are also at the centre of the tussle between temptation and piety as portrayed in the great religions. But for Freud, the turmoil has its developmental roots specifically in childhood sexuality and its conflict with the repressive forces of social mores and authority. For psychoanalysis, the nursery is the crucible of conflicts rather than the heights of Mount Olympus.

Within this picture of an active, influential unconscious, insofar as unconscious ideas seek expression and other forces seek to prevent this, there is also the view of a somewhat unchanging scene. The system unconscious is regarded by Freud as entertaining no doubts or uncertainties, is free from internal contradictions, not altered over time and pays "little regard to reality" (1914, p. 191). Repressed material, it appears, is held in the grip of an extremely conservative and illogical system of the mind, out of touch with reality and subject to phantastic satisfactions. More recent authors have taken up this view and regard this conservative and illogical system as an internal, somewhat dictatorial "establishment" (Bion 1970; Hoggett 1998). We come to this later when considering groups and organisations.

Freud's whole oeuvre is large and, of course, contains contrasting and conflicting ideas developed throughout his lifetime. This is natural insofar as an idea – such as the unconscious – is worked through and developed in the light of practice and experience. The determinist stance that drove him to create psychoanalysis as scientific by the standards of his time is matched by the influences of a more hermeneutic tradition or beyond this, as a psychoanalytic method *sui generis* (Long 2001). Freud follows Descartes insofar as "Lacan argued that the true significance of the *Cogito* was not perceived until Freud, who identified the true subject as the subject of the unconscious, the existence and nature of which is only detectable via the mediation of symptoms" (Restivo 2013, p. 54). Yet, Freud's unconscious, while emphasising the dynamic forces of instincts, drives and repressions, also owes much to the influence of the Romantic philosophers. And it should not be forgotten that Freud acknowledged that there was more to the unconscious than repression and repressed material. "Not all that is unconscious is repressed". This aspect of the unconscious, including the instincts that are totally unconscious and their representations that sometimes reach consciousness, is a whole different yet connected area.

Drawing from ideas on pleasure/unpleasure as driving the ego, in arguing that unpleasant stimuli come from both without and within, he points out that protection against strong stimuli from the outside may occur through the use of a shielding process in the brain as well as from psychological defences. Not so simple is protection from within. Heightened disturbances from within, coming either from repressed ideas or even ideas that represent unconscious instincts, may, claims Freud (1920), be treated as if they were external stimuli and hence shielding defences are used. This, he believes, lies at the basis of projection as a defence.

> Internal perceptions yield sensations from processes arising in the most diverse and certainly also in the deepest strata of the mental apparatus.
>
> They are more primordial, more elementary than perceptions arising externally and they can come about even when consciousness is shrouded.
>
> (Freud 1923, pp. 14–15)

The Unconscious and Freedom

So far in this book, I have put forward the position that Schelling sees freedom as a result of self-authorisation. The will to be, to exist, to self-manifest – the unground – is eternally strong. To appropriate myself means taking over the ground of my being (i.e. the unconscious) as mine and taking up the burden of my willing. This is to be free.

In Freud, freedom is a result of accepting and taking responsibility for one's unconscious, rather than getting caught in the death of repetition compulsions. These ideas place Freud in a tradition that was present in the nineteenth century.

> For Kierkegaard and Heidegger, repetition is the act that allows a human being to embrace the fact that his actions are not determined, whether by an essential nature or by the past. We finally confront the emptiness of the future and our responsibility for our actions only by confirming our past as radically contingent. Whatever happened to me in the past I accept as my responsibility. I can do otherwise now; therefore, I could have done otherwise then.
>
> (Kerslake 2007, p. 25)

The concept of the unconscious, so far, is inextricably intertwined with the idea of freedom; not the freedom of a narcissistic pursuit of entitled desires, but the freedom of knowing the truth about oneself, of knowing the constraints placed upon one and knowing when and where to challenge those.

Notes

1 Meltzer (2018) describes the development in Freud's thinking through the case studies, each of which demonstrates new ideas that often overturned Freud's past thinking.
2 I have taken some of this chapter directly from my chapter on "The Transforming Experience Framework and Unconscious Processes" in *Transforming Experience in Organisations* (Long 2016). However, my research and thinking are continuing to develop; therefore, much new material has been added. I am indebted to Philip Boxer for drawing my attention to some differences in the interpretation of Freud's work.
3 Credit for tracking down this one goes to Jeffrey Berman. He believes that the remark was made in 1928 to Professor Becker in Berlin. http://www.freud.org.uk /about/faq/ recovered 8/10/14.
4 Boxer's (2022) reading of Freud on this point emphasises the economic or energetic neurological principle of cathexis that is part of Freud's theory of instinctual excitations. Boxer points to Freud's often overlooked distinction between an instinct and its psychical representation, the former always being unconscious. Only the instinctual representation can become conscious through thought or via an emotional expression. This leads him (Boxer) to distinguish the general idea of the repressed unconscious from what he calls the "radically unconscious" (Boxer 2022). This conceptualisation will be pursued in Chapter 5 on Jacques Lacan.
5 As this paper progresses, it is evident that the complexity of the idea of the unconscious for Freud leads to many struggles to articulate its essence and its many aspects, especially the way that the different systems – conscious, preconscious and unconscious – are distinguished, related and interact.
6 Drives are the psychical representation of instincts represented in thought.
7 Some of the later developments in the idea of the unconscious, as expressed in neuropsychoanalysis (described in Chapter 9), seem implicit here. For example, there are instinctual forces located deep in the brain that are unconsciously and automatically enacted.
8 The idea of energetic forces in relation to the unconscious is an important stream of thought that has echoes of energetic forces both at a bodily somatic level and at an intergroup relational level, as explored later in this book.

References

Armstrong, D. and Rustin, M. (2014). *Social Defences Against Anxiety: Explorations in a Paradigm*. Tavistock Clinic Series. London: Karnac.

Bion, W. R. (1970). *Attention and Interpretation*. London: Tavistock.

Boxer, P. (2022). 'How Are We to Distinguish a "Repressed Unconscious" from a "Radically Unconscious?"', *Lacanticles*. https://lacanticles.com/how-are-we-to-distinguish-a-repressed-unconscious-from-a-radically-unconscious/ [accessed November 2022].

Freud, S. (1900). *The Interpretation of Dreams*. James Strachey (trans.). Revised by Angela Richards 1976. Pelican Freud Library Vol 4. Harmondsworth: Penguin Books.

Freud, S. (1905). *Three Essays on the Theory of Sexuality*. J. Strachey (trans. and ed.), S.E. Vol. VII, pp. 130–243. London: Hogarth Press.

Freud, S. (1912). *A Note on the Unconscious in Psycho-Analysis*. J. Strachey (trans. and ed.), S.E. Vol. XI, pp. 255–266. London: Hogarth Press.

Freud, S. (1914). *On Narcissism: An introduction*. J. Strachey (trans. and ed.), S.E. Vol. 14, pp. 73–102. London: Hogarth Press.

Freud, S. (1915a). *The Unconscious*. J. Strachey (trans. and ed.), S.E. Vol. XIV (1914–1916), pp. 159–215. London: Hogarth Press (1957).

Freud, S. (1915b). *Repression*. J. Strachey (trans. and ed.), S.E. Vol. XIV, pp. 141–158. London: Hogarth Press (1957).

Freud, S. (1915c). *Instincts and their Vicissitudes*. J. Strachey (trans. and ed.), S.E. Vol. XIV, pp. 117–140. London: Hogarth Press (1957).

Freud, S. (1915–1916) *Introductory Lectures on Psycho-Analysis*. J. Strachey (trans. and ed.), S.E. Vol. XV (Parts I and II). London: Hogarth Press.

Freud, S. (1916). 'The Archaic Features and Infantilism of Dreams', Lecture 13 in J. Strachey (trans. and ed.). *Introductory Lectures on Psycho-Analysis*, S.E. Vol. XV (Parts I and II). London: Hogarth Press.

Freud, S. (1918). *From the History of an Infantile Neurosis*. J. Strachey (trans. and ed.), S.E. Vol. XVII, pp.7–122. London: Hogarth Press.

Freud, S. (1920). *The Sexual Life of Human Beings: A General Introduction to Psychoanalysis*, S.E. Vol. XX London: Hogarth Press. https://pages.uoregon.edu /eherman/teaching/texts/Freud%20The%20Sexual%20Life%20of%20Human %20Beings.pdf.

Freud, S. (1923). *The Ego and the Id*. J. Strachey (trans. and ed.), S.E. Vol. XIX, pp. 1–66. London: Hogarth Press.

Freud, S. (1928). 'Remark made to Professor Becker in Berlin', http://www.freud.org .uk/about/faq/ [accessed 8 October 2014].

Freud, S. (1933). *New Introductory Lectures on Psycho-Analysis*. J. Strachey (trans. and ed.), S.E. Vol. XXII (1932–1936), pp. 1–182. London: The Institute of Psychoanalysis and the Hogarth Press.

Freud, S. (1938). *Splitting of the Ego in the Process of Defence*. J. Strachey (trans. and ed.), S.E. Vol. XXIII, pp. 271–278. London: The Institute of Psychoanalysis and the Hogarth Press.

Ginzberg, C. and Davin, A. (1980). 'Morelli, Freud and Sherlock Holmes: Clues and Scientific Method', *History Workshop*, vol. 9, pp. 5–36.

Hoggett, P. (1998). 'The Internal Establishment', in P.T. Bion, F. Borgogno and S. Merciai (eds.) *Bion's Legacy to Groups*. London: Karnac.

Jaques, E. (1955). 'Social Systems as a Defence against Persecutory and Depressive Anxiety', in M. Klein, P. Heineman and R. Money-Kryle (eds.) *New Directions in Psychoanalysis*. London: Tavistock.

Kerslake, C. (2007). *Deleuze and the Unconscious*. New York: Continuum.

Kris, E. (1952). *Psychoanalytic Explorations in Art*. New York: International Universities Press.

Long, S.D. (2001). 'Working with Organizations: The Contribution of the Psychoanalytic Discourse', *Organisational and Social Dynamics*, vol. 2, pp. 174–198.

Long, S.D. (ed.) (2016). *Transforming Experience in Organisations: A Framework for Organisational Research and Consultancy*. London: Routledge.

Long, S.D. and Harney, M. (2013). 'The Associative Unconscious', in S. D. Long (ed.). *Socioanalytic Methods*, pp. 3–22. London: Karnac.

Maddox, B. (2006). *Freud's Wizard: Ernest Jones and the Transformation of Psychoanalysis*. Cambridge, MA: Da Capo Press.

Malan, D. (1999). *Individual Psychotherapy and the Science of Psychodynamics*, 2nd ed. Oxford: Butterworth Heinemann.

McGrath, S.J. (2012). *The Dark Ground of Spirit: Schelling and the Unconscious.* London: Routledge e-version.

Meltzer, D. (2018). *The Kleinian Development Part 1: Freud's Clinical Development – Method-Data-Theory.* London: Karnac.

Menzies, I.P.M. (1970). 'The Functioning of Social Systems as a Defence Against Anxiety: A Report on the Study of a Nursing Service of a General Hospital', in *Tavistock Pamphlet 3.* London: Tavistock Institute.

Newirth, J. (2023). *The Unconscious: A Contemporary Introduction.* London: Routledge.

Rabstejnek, C.V. (2011). 'History and Evolution of the Unconscious before and after Sigmund Freud.' http:www.houd.info./unconscious.pdf.

Rand, N. (2004). 'The Hidden Soul: The Growth of the Unconscious in Philosophy, Psychology, Medicine, and Literature, 1750–1900', *American Imago*, vol. 61, no. 3, pp. 257–289.

Restivo, G. (2013). 'Jouissance and the Sexual Reality of the (Two) Unconscious', PhD Thesis: Aukland University of Technology. https://openrepository.aut.ac.nz/server/api/core/bitstreams/86d5b839-19cf-4c50-abd4-592e0a81dc6b/content.

Wollheim, R. (2003). 'On the Freudian Unconscious', *Proceedings and Addresses of the American Philosophical Association*, vol. 77, no. 2 (November), pp. 23–35. American Philosophical Association.

4 Bion and the Infinite Unconscious

It could be said that the psychoanalyst Wilfred Bion was more of an heir to Schelling and the Romantics than was Freud. Bion is well known for his exemplar in psychoanalytic practice to eschew memory and desire. Schelling (1811/1942) says, "those who look for true philosophy must be bereft of all hope, all desire, all longing" (Kindle version).

Bion's work is a mixture of the scientific close observational stance of Freud and yet a dive into the mystical and poetic: a way towards conceptualising an "inner space", echoing the vastness of "outer space"; an inner space where much is unconscious and infinite. This is not to lodge Bion in the "mystical" as such, but to support his rejection of positivism when dealing with psychic reality, and link him to Bergson, Poincare, Husserl and Whitehead (Rugi 2016). In any case, John Rickman, a Quaker, was his initial analyst and influenced him before the influence of his second analyst Melanie Klein. One of my PhD supervisees and now colleague, who is also a Quaker, believes that Rickman's Quaker influence shows up more strongly than usually acknowledged; or at least this aspect of his work deserves more attention. The Quaker ideas of the "inner teacher" and "emergence" are certainly echoed in Bion's thought about the inner life and its emergent transformations (Duke 2023). Moreover, in his practice and writing, Bion shows an ability to step aside from himself in ways that invite a stance of "not knowing" and curiosity rather than certainty, showing a "systematic doubt" (Civitarese 2013a, p. 630) not resolved but leaving open a passage for the truth to emerge.

In this chapter, I outline the major ideas of Bion that have most influenced me. His early work on group dynamics is well known and foundational to the Group Relations movement, which I discuss more briefly. Here, I am primarily interested in how he broadly conceptualised the mind and the unconscious.

Bion's work is extensive across psychotic functioning, the development of the mind, and group and social dynamics. Here, I touch upon a few of his ideas in relation to the unconscious, and my scoping may move backwards and forwards across his varied interests because they are interconnected. In many ways, he took the idea of the unconscious process and transformed it. While Freud and Klein formulated their theories predominantly around sexuality, life and death instincts, and the Oedipal family configuration (all of which Bion

DOI: 10.4324/9781003559818-4

also took into account), Bion developed a meta-psychoanalysis around episte-mology: how we come to know about the world and ourselves, including our own inner lives (Grotstein 1997). His focus was on how emotional experience is transformed into thoughts and how the mind develops or fails to develop in order to think those thoughts.

While Freud talked of an "unrepressed unconscious" (Freud 1915; Bergstein 2019) and further developed the thinking in this regard through his study of the instincts, Bion describes this unconscious as a mental area that is infinite, accessed by an intuitive process and distinguished from the finite mental area of sensuous experience that is derived from perceptions from the external world. It may be said by some that Bion renamed the unconscious, "the infinite". But in this, he is pointing to a realm of mental experience dif-ferent from the repressed unconscious of Freud, not replacing it.

Bion's ideas are expansive, digging deep into emotional experience in terms not only of an individual mind but also conceptualising the mind as a collec-tive phenomenon; regarding truth in experience as essential for the growth of the individual and the group; his inquiries into epistemology – how we come to know, as much as what we know – were perhaps influenced by his early studies of Kant (Mancia and Longhin 2000). The ideas of container/ contained infuse his theorising and his clinical approach (Bion 1970). They allow a theory that can examine boundaries and differentiation; minds that contain or do not contain thoughts; cultures and establishments that can be "exploded" due to their inability to contain new ideas; language that can or cannot contain words and experiences, as in his description of a man who stammered, his words unable to contain his thoughts (Bion 1970, p. 94). Containers can be flexible or porous or brittle. Containment provides a well-used metaphor. Yet, it is beyond metaphor insofar as it describes a function of psychic experience: the processes that enable raw experience to form a mind that can think, communicate and grow humanity.

I argue that the unconscious for Bion is, in terms of his own ideas on the container and the contained (Bion 1970), beyond containment. It is not something simply contained in a mind – neither individual nor social; and it is not itself predominantly a container of taboo ideas, as in the repressed unconscious, although he does not eschew the repressed. The unconscious is an infinite pre-experience that can come into being through the emotional experiences of people as they grow within their groups and societies.

Bion (1977) quotes Martin Buber's *I and Thou*:

Every developing human child rests, like all developing beings, in the womb of the great mother – the undifferentiated, not yet formed primal world. From this it detaches itself to enter a personal life, and it is only in dark hours when we slip out of this again (as happens even to the healthy night after night) that we are close to her again.

(Bion 1977, p. 59)

In this, he and Buber show their Schellingian inheritance: the conceiving of an infinity that comes into being through the emotional experience of living; a primitive experience that is somewhat transformed into consciousness as an emergent process, yet still ever present as a dream-like uncontained force.

For now, I will spend some time examining Bion's psychoanalytic theories as they relate to the unconscious because they inform how he understands the human mind and how humans learn and develop emotionally. What follows is an all-too-brief description of his view about how thinking develops largely unconsciously in the person (for a fuller description, see Grotstein 2007; Bion 1963, 1965, 1967a). But these ideas strongly influence an understanding also of the unconscious psychodynamics of social systems, to which Bion contributed and to which I turn later in the chapter.

Bion was deeply interested in emotional truth. By this, he meant the truths that lie behind or beneath conscious knowledge; those truths that are painful and hard to face and yet are central to us. Such truths, whether or not we consciously know them, show themselves through means other than direct ones. Bion explored ways in which we turn away from and discard the pain given by the truth. For him, psychoanalysis is about discovering those truths, albeit through toleration of the pain involved in that discovery. "Progress in psycho-analysis is inseparable from a need to tolerate the painful concomitants of mental growth" (Bion 1967b, p. 137). Grotstein (2007) says that Bion goes beyond many Freudian ideas in his search for the ultimate reality and absolute truth – a transcendent position that yet paradoxically "is within us as our unconscious" (Grotstein 2007, p. 122); hidden behind the illusions that disguise what is real. In reading Bion, there is a strong sense of his own growth through facing painful realities, many of which must have come to him through his command role in World War I.

However, I should emphasise that the truth in everyday life for Bion is neither absolute nor a definitive opposite to lying. The transcendent position is infinite, not always directly found in particulars that themselves can only reach towards its unveiling. Civitarese (2013b) following Grotstein, explains this in terms of a truth drive – a drive for truths to show themselves and be explored in communication with others. Bion recognised that while truth is needed to sustain the life force, lying is often used as a survival mechanism. It is through the gradual expansion of truths that the mind can grow. I have said earlier that I do not wish to trace the biographies of the theorists I have encountered, at least not in any depth. But the progress of Bion's thinking about truth and its pursuit in psychoanalysis is important. Ogden (2004), for example, points out a radical shift from an interpretative to an expansive stance in Bion's practice.

The experience of reading early Bion generates a sense of psychoanalysis as a never completed process of clarifying obscurities and obscuring clarifications, which enterprise moves in the direction of a convergence of disparate meanings. In contrast, the experience of reading Bion's later work conveys a sense of psychoanalysis as a process involving a movement toward infinite expansion of meaning.

(Ogden 2004, p. 285)

My own analysis, while conducted with a traditional Freudian analyst, led me to study Bion and the idea of the drive for emotional truth – an idea within me, even in my teenage years, yet articulated more fully and skilfully by him. It was just prior to my analysis that I first became involved with the Tavistock Group Relations perspective and the influence of Bion's work in this tradition (see Rice 1966; Shapiro and Carr 2012). I was asking myself more than ever what it was that made me the person I am, the person I am in the process of becoming. I was able to appreciate more fully the idea of myself as an instrument in my clinical, group and teaching roles. I wanted to find how to stand on the edge of that precipice that separates a mind that can think from the experience of a mind overwhelmed by no-thought.

What Grotstein refers to as Bion's "metapsychoanalysis" is primarily his theory of thinking developed from clinical experiences. This theory postulates the development of an apparatus of the mind for transforming emotions, sense impressions and immediate experience into thought and action, initially through the development of the alpha function; a function of transformation that tolerates the frustration of absence – the absence being experienced as a "no-thing" inside – and allows thinking the no-thing into a thought rather than an invasive hallucination (Bion 1962b, 1970; Grotstein 2007). Thinking develops as the infant learns to tolerate the sometimes absence of the breast – the first part object sustaining life and making a connection. For the infant, the "no-breast" (its absence) is a painful experience, and pain can be tolerated through the experience of a mother who, through her own "reverie", can accept the frustrations and fears of the infant, transform them in her own mind such that they are no longer anxiety provoking, and return them to the infant through her care, comfort and intuition. In this, he extends the ideas of his second analyst, Melanie Klein, on the concepts of projective identification and introjection (I explore intuition later in the chapter). The development of the alpha function creates what Bion calls a contact barrier.[1] This acts as a division between consciousness – with its capacity to think thoughts – and the unconscious that disguises reality and, with this disguise, can produce true dreams and other phenomena as described in psychoanalysis. The alpha function denotes a "situation of change from something that is not thought at all to something which is thought" (Bion, *Brazilian Lectures* Vol. 7, cited in Able-Hirsch 2016). So, it can be seen that the contact barrier forms a special kind of containment.

Bion's psychoanalytic work moved beyond the treatment of neuroses to a deeper examination of psychotic functioning – functioning devoid of adequate alpha functioning. Here, he enters new realms of psychic life and new ways of seeing emotional truths and their effects, claiming that there is a potentiality for psychotic functioning in all minds – the neurotic and psychotic parts of the mind existing throughout development. Psychotic functioning, he claims, is dominated by splitting off all parts of the personality that might be in contact with reality. Splitting and projective identification in psychotic functioning replace repression.

> The differentiation of the psychotic from the non-psychotic personalities depends on a minute splitting of all that part of the personality that is concerned with the awareness of internal and external reality, and the expulsion of these fragments so that they enter into or engulf their objects.
>
> (Bion 1967a, p. 43)

And,

> Where the non-psychotic part of the personality resorts to repression as a means of cutting off certain trends in the mind both from consciousness and from other forms of manifestation or activity, the psychotic part of the personality has attempted to rid itself of the apparatus on which the psyche depends to carry out the repression. The unconscious would seem to be replaced by the world of dream furniture.
>
> (Bion 1967a, p. 52)[2]

This attack on the apparatus essential for repression and the formation of the repressed unconscious – that is, on the formation or operation of a contact barrier – is a psychotic attack on links in and with reality, especially emotional reality. Instead of being transformed through thinking, emotion becomes intolerable. The possible links of emotion to thinking and reality become attacked. A kind of pseudo logic devoid of emotional truth emerges.

> These attacks on the linking function of emotion lead to an over prominence in the psychotic part of the personality of links which appear to be logical, almost mathematical, but never emotionally reasonable.
>
> (Bion 1967b, p. 109)

In writing this, I remember the father of a patient many years ago when I was working as a child psychotherapist. I was working with his son, who was brought to see me because of his anxious and aggressive behaviour. When working with children, I would occasionally also have sessions with parents, working primarily on their parenting roles, while at the time, in the 1970s and 1980s, in the clinics where I worked, a different therapist would see the parents more regularly as their patients. On this occasion, the father brought me a photo of a destroyed bird aviary, telling me that he had built it, but his 12-year-old son had destroyed it. He was agitated while showing me and put his face angrily and uncomfortably close to mine. I asked about the situation of the destruction and why he thought it had happened while also asking him to sit back in his chair. He gave me a detailed story and wanted to impress upon me that while he loved and cared for his son in every way possible, his son attacked everything he did. His story came out in spurts of alternating anger and despair. He wondered why his son, who loved the aviary, had destroyed it. My own feelings were that he was alternately attacking and pleading with me and that he expected me to retaliate. I still have a bodily memory of the shaking inside that I experienced.

Later, on seeing the mother, I learned from her a different story which I had no reason to doubt, especially through my own experience and intuitive feel from the father, and which was confirmed to me in our clinical meetings by her therapist. The aviary had been built by her husband, the father, but, she claimed, had also been destroyed by him in anger with his son. In his story to me, it seems this father had projected much of his anger and destructive feelings onto, probably into, his son. Together with the photograph, he had weaved a plausible story that was also emotionally unreasonable. I wondered about the attacks he had made on his own emotional life. I certainly felt at the time that he had wanted me to feel the fear, anger and despair that he had but was struggling to contain.

One might say that the psychotic part of the personality does not *have* an unconscious, rather it *is* an unconscious; an immediate expression of untransformed beta elements, hallucinations and primitive anxieties, sometimes dressed up in plausible rhetoric. But psychotic functioning is not a direct expression of the dynamic and repressed unconscious, as formulated by Freud, because in psychotic functioning such an unconscious has not been established. My patient's father had woven a lie into a fabricated reality. I couldn't say he was conscious of his lie; there was no indication of this. But neither was it unconscious in the Freudian conception. In Bion's terms, he had attacked and broken all links between his emotions, his thoughts and the reality of his son. It was the weaving of the broken fragments that had given him a new plausible and defensive story, where his son was the one doing the damage: the broken fragments being the dream furniture. Freud's major work on psychosis was his work on the Judge Schreber case, where he finds that the psychotic presentation is an attempt to reconstitute a world after it has fragmented (Freud 1911–1913). This work comes close to Bion's formulations, but Freud did not have the language of beta elements and the alpha function.

I also remember a young psychotic man who decided I was Chinese because my name was "Long", which he said was Chinese like "Wong". My obvious Caucasian appearance and my saying I was not Chinese made no difference. My name became a thing rather than a symbol. I only saw him briefly – he was arrested by police for having several offensive weapons in his room and was then treated by a psychiatrist. He had a whole background story about me with many seemingly logical links. His dominant emotion was one of a restless agitation. His emotional experience was not simply contained in how he moved and spoke but was also projected into his weapons, which he hid away. One is also reminded of so many conspiracy theories that have a life through social media: dispersed into a virtual world, picking up seemingly logical arguments to disguise the fear and hatred that they disembody.

More than many of his fellow analysts, Bion believed that psychosis could be treated through psychoanalysis. An emotional truth may take much time and pain to discover, and Bion pointed to the human urge to avoid such truths. He termed this a "hatred of experience", following Freud, seeing that psychological growth can only come from an engagement with the world of direct experience and its emotional links with its truths. He illustrates this clearly with examples (Bion 1967b) showing how the psychotic patient needs to move through the pain of finding themselves "mad" and tolerating this, moving then to gaining a stronger sense of reality. Emotional experience is more basic to humanity and human freedom than logical thinking, no matter how sophisticated and helpful the latter is and has been to human progress. All logic, in the end, is aimed towards human survival, even when serving psychological defences, because for Bion all thought is ultimately transformed emotion, and our emotional truths – that make us human in the real world – are at the basis of that survival. Emotion, claims Bion, is the vehicle for truth. Moreover, an emotional truth is not necessarily something forever, but can change and transform – a truth in transit (Horovitz 2007 in Bergstein 2019, p. 104), hence a transformation in those situations of growth through genuine communication, such as psychoanalytic engagement, or through love.

In working psychoanalytically, Bion understood and regarded sessions with his patients as dominated either by love, hate or knowledge (Bion 1962a, 1970; Grimalt 2022). These denote the key to the session with its unconscious communications, and he noted them as L, H or K and marked them with + and – signs to denote their emotional quality and strength. Knowledge indicates the epistemophilic instinct noted by Klein (Bott-Spillius 1988), who saw the root of the quest for knowledge in the child's interest in parental sexuality. However, notes Bion, much consciously achieved knowledge does not necessarily lead to a deeper emotional truth. This is too often avoided not only because of the pain involved in really recognising our deeper selves, but also because emotional truth is in the process of becoming/emerging (the evolution of O – ultimate psychic reality), not in being cognitively known (K).

Emotional experience and truth involve the internal psychic quality of the experience. This can only be reached beyond sensory experience and is difficult to put into words. Bion says,

> There are no sense-data directly related to psychic quality, as there are sense-data directly related to concrete objects.
>
> (Bion 1962a, p. 53)

And, he argues, psychic quality in this sense can only "become", it is not "known":

> I shall use the sign O to denote that which is the ultimate reality represented by terms such as ultimate reality, absolute truth, the godhead, the

infinite, the thing-in-itself. O does not fall in the domain of knowledge or learning save incidentally; it can "become" but it cannot be "known".

(Bion 1970, p. 26)

Bion's work stresses the need both to find one's emotional truths to grow as a person *and* to communicate not only what is readily communicable consciously but also what cannot be verbalised and is ineffable. Even beyond accessing our own emotional truths is the essential urge to communicate them to an "other" who recognises and accepts them (Bergstein 2019). Through intuitive processes, the analyst must find a way to "be" with the patient and together come towards the "O" of the session.

Speaking of the analyst, Bion says,

If he (sic) is able to be receptive to O, then he may feel impelled to deal with the intersection of the evolution of O with the domain of the objects of sense or of formulations based on the senses. Whether he does so or not cannot depend on rules for O, or O>K, but only on his ability to be at one with O.

(Bion 1970, p. 32)

In this, there is the idea of the unconscious as unknowable, only encountered by somehow being with; a kind of resonance or deep identification through becoming *with* the unconscious, which in moments of connection – shown by a dark beam – is glimpsed. And it is through this almost impossible communication of unspeakable experience that growth can occur because the infinite unconscious has been realised; made real if only fleetingly. Such an idea is so much in tune, if not identical with Schelling's *Weltalter* (Schelling 1942) that argues a deep will in the infinite to become, and hence to know itself through living beings. One senses in Bion the will for a deep truth to be expressed whether from an individual's emotional experience or from a group's need to grow through new ideas that may destroy their past complacencies, and the pain and defences in doing so.

Although acknowledging Freud's contention that consciousness is the sense organ of psychic qualities, this is not enough for Bion, and his theory of the alpha function is proposed as an alternative to what he sees as Freud's binary proposition of primary and secondary process thinking. The process of the alpha function transforms emotion into primitive thinking and allows for the formation of consciousness. I return to alpha functioning in due course. Just to say here that Bion has an interest in those aspects of emotional experience that could be transformed, called alpha elements transformed through the alpha process, and those elements that could not be metabolised, called beta elements. Suffice it here to again quote Bion:

I have proposed the theory that alpha-function, by proliferating alpha-elements is producing the contact-barrier, an entity that separates elements so that those on one side, are and form, the conscious and on the other side are, and form, the unconscious.

(Bion 1962a, p. 54)[3]

This is discussed further in the section titled Thoughts without Thinkers.

In his study of psychosis, Bion describes what he calls an inaccessible state of mind, different from consciousness and the unconsciousness of the dynamic repressed unconscious (here, we see him as heir both to Schelling and Freud). He suggests that this state of mind has never been conscious and is a mental state unexplored by the study of neuroses and repression. This is a psychic, possibly somatic unconscious, unable to be put into words without the transformation of alpha functioning – noted in his discussion of proto-mental phenomena.

Bion found that where a mind is dominated by psychotic functioning, the infinite is unbearable and psychotic symptoms occur. Psychotic functioning does not communicate in the usual way of using language. Words become things rather than symbols, and communication is by projective identification – just as happened with the young man I discussed earlier. When psychotic functioning is not dominating, even though present, the infinite is experienced as ineffable, mystical and reached only intuitively – through non-sensuous understanding. Psychic quality, its very nature, is reached through intuitive processes. Intuitive understanding is critical to Bion's psychoanalytic work. It is a deep apprehension of the emotional truth of oneself or another. He describes it as spontaneous and immediate, not thought through, not a subject of K.

> Bion conceives intuition as a holistic cognitive modality, which belongs to the whole system and allows us to get in touch with O, with what happens in the session and the "ultimate reality" of the patient's mind… insight implies an awareness of the logical relationships between a problem and an answer; in intuition there is only a rapid, sudden, feeling of coherence, without any logical, rational connection. It is a presentiment that is felt in the body, a flash of consciousness, which reveals the unknown and maintains the link with the invisible and the infinite.
>
> (Rugi, in Grimalt 2022; 10% and 54% into
> Kindle edition)[4]

In belonging to the whole system, intuition comes from both the conscious and unconscious parts of the mind. "Intuition has an essential role, it is a preliminary recognition of patterns, in the infinite and formless sea of our unconscious, from which we extract 'constancy', or as Bion says 'invariants'" (Gerber 2016). The intuition of the analyst, the receptive mother, in fact any receptive and observant listener, comes from the capacity for reverie – a kind of waking dream state. Like dreams, intuition is not easily remembered and must be worked on; it is transformed by the listener or observer. "The fate of this intuition is to contribute not to memory (which is part of knowledge) but to mental growth (which is an evolution of O)" (Caper 2016; 40% Kindle edition). To intuit, according to Bion, requires continuing discipline and vigilance lest it be interrupted by memory, desire and forced understanding – these states of mind interfere with linking to the unconscious. "The sacrifice of memory and desire is conducive to the growth of 'dream-like' memory which is a part of the experience of psycho-analytic reality" (Bion 1970, p. 71). Aspects of mental growth are not remembered in the normal sense of remembering but occur and are incorporated.

From his study of psychotic phenomena, Bion was convinced that the psyche needs not simply to express and protect itself but also to pursue truth to develop. While knowledge is often conscious, truth is rarely in the realm of conscious knowledge. For Bion, "O" is the ultimate truth, unattainable in its totality, and resides not in sensory knowledge and learning, but in a deeper non-sensory understanding of emotional experience. He uses terms such as "O" to indicate meaning that is unsaturated with past meaning and that can gain its own new meaning within his theorising.[5]

> Bion (1965, 1970) would frequently cite Milton's phrase, "the deep and formless infinite" in regard to his comments about "O". [6]...Bion's picture of the Unconscious, along with that of Winnicott and Matte-Blanco, conveys an ineffable, inscrutable, and utterly indefinable inchoate formlessness that is both infinite and chaotic – or complex – by nature. *It is what it is and is always changing while paradoxically remaining the same.* From this point of view, Freud's instinctual drives and Klein's paranoid-schizoid and depressive positions can be understood as secondary structures, strategies or filters, to assist the infant in mediating this chaos.
>
> (Grotstein 1997, p. 217)

Thoughts without Thinkers

Bion builds upon a statement within Freud's paper on the unconscious, which states:

> It is a very remarkable thing that the *Uncs.* of one human being can react upon that of another, without passing through the *Cs.* This deserves closer investigation.
>
> (Freud 1915, p. 201)

Bion does engage in this further investigation, for it is this phenomenon, considered incontestable by Freud, that indicates to Bion a system of thoughts independent of conscious thinkers. A thinking apparatus – the mind – is developed to think these thoughts.

As mentioned earlier, Bion stresses the intuitive capacity of the unconscious mind – hence the importance of the state of mind – reverie, being without memory, desire or the struggle for understanding. Psychoanalysts who use Bion's methods strive to work with their own intuition in reaching the unconscious minds of their analysands. "He (the analyst) must be open to reverie, and offer an observant, receptive presence in the continuous present of the session" (Grimalt 2016, chapter 1; 15% into Kindle edition).

While in his later theories, Freud had conceptualised the psyche primarily as consisting of structures – the id, the ego, the super-ego – Bion remained with Freud's earlier ideas of systems and their functions (Symington and Symington 2002), developing his ideas about the processes of thinking and coming to understand the truth in things. Taking the ways that we use language figuratively in relation to thought and emotion (e.g. chewing over an idea or not stomaching an experience), he explored the process of thinking in terms of digestive processes – incorporating or expelling thoughts as if they were good or bad food. He believed that the capacity to think grew from such bodily processes in order to think about the environment. Such a view is supported by biological scientists and is discussed in Chapter 10 on the unconscious in nature. Only more recently in our evolutionary history have we come to think about ourselves and our own thinking.

It is this idea of thought as an object and thinker as a subject that opens for us a new view of the unconscious process and communication.

Bion argues that transformations occur through the alpha function and this, as in dreams, is occurring all the time even when we are not asleep. He talks of the process of coming to think as a transformation. Freud named two modes of thinking: primary and secondary processes. Primary process thinking is driven by the pleasure principle with its drive to rid the personality of tension or what he called unpleasure. Secondary process thinking is attuned through the reality principle to take account of the world as experienced through the senses. Taking this as a basis, Bion explores the dynamics of the primary process and its transition to secondary process thinking, understanding this as a development rather than a dichotomy. As mentioned earlier, rather than primary and secondary process thinking to describe the different thinking in conscious and unconscious processes, he uses the ideas of the alpha function and the contact barrier to describe the boundary developed between conscious and unconscious and the thinking processes that occur.

Thinking develops as the alpha function organises an emotional experience into preconceptions. When such preconceptions match or "mate with" a realisation, a concept is developed. In a patterned way, "constant conjunctions" of thoughts begin to emerge and "selected facts" serve to centre these conjunctions within models or theories – a theory about what a certain experience means or about what name should be given to a class of objects, for example. When the alpha function is not present or able to function, the beta elements may dominate. These are the unsymbolised or undigestible thought elements, sometimes referred to as bizarre elements; for example, words that are experienced as things rather than symbols and may be ejected or spat out. They are somewhat like what the philosopher Immanuel Kant referred to as things-in-themselves, without an attendant symbolisation through readily communicable language.

> If alpha function is troubled and therefore inoperative, sense impressions as well as emotions remain untouched and become beta elements, which cannot be used to produce dream thoughts. Instead they are evacuated through projective identifications that discharge the mental apparatus from accretion of stimuli… they represent undigested facts.
>
> (Lopez-Corvo 2003, p. 43)

The boundary between conscious and unconscious is understood as a contact barrier: a kind of permeable membrane through which alpha elements may pass or be prohibited.

Remember the quote:

> I have proposed the theory that alpha-function, by proliferating alpha-elements is producing the contact-barrier, an entity that separates elements so that those on one side, are and form, the conscious and on the other side are, and form, the unconscious.
>
> (Bion 1962a, p. 54)

If, however, alpha functioning is not occurring, there may be an agglomeration of beta elements, and a beta-screen of unthinkable elements is formed. Only a thinker with alpha functioning can transform these elements into symbolised thought. However, beta elements may be communicated by the psychotic part of the personality or in primitive ways unconsciously (Lopez-Corvo 2003). A major way of this occurring is through projective identification.

Bion took forward Klein's ideas on projective identification. He introduced the ideas of container/contained whereby the container – mind – can accept projections and, through a process of reverie, is able to transform the projected material. In this view, projective identification can be regarded as a form of communication. The prototypical example of such communication is the projection of distressing experiences from infant to mother who, as container, through reverie and a capacity to think, can transform the distressing experience into an experience that is tolerable. This is then transmitted back to the infant through her behaviours, emotions, intuition and observations. In this extension of the concept of projective identification, the dynamics are between people, not simply an intrapersonal phantasy. As Clarke (2014, e-journal no pages) describes:

> For Bion, therefore, projective identification is part of the thinking process. Originally a procedure for "unburdening the psyche of accretions of stimuli", phantasy is projected into the container, and in a reprocessed

form projected back into the projector. The point is that bad or intoler-able feelings are transformed by the recipient and are made tolerable. Bion calls this process of transformation the "alpha function".

If, as Bott-Spillius notes, "all goes well", then the projector, the infant, eventually introjects this function of transformation and thus develops a means of thinking and tolerance of frustration.

The capacity to be a container and to transform projections through the alpha function and then provide a verbal response, Bion calls the "language of achievement" – "an intuitive language affording a transient glimpse of the fleeting evolutions of the patient's truth as reflected by the emotional expe-rience in the here-and-now" (Bergstein 2019, p. 37). However, in putting experience into words, something is lost.[7] A gap or caesura occurs, and the analyst/mother/container must be able to tolerate the frustration that occurs with this loss. And this is where unprocessed beta elements may be projected.

The function of containment is a complex function that is important for Bion's theory of thinking, described above. A container, such as a mind capa-ble of alpha functioning, may hold and transform its "contents" (Bion 1984).

Creativity and the Unconscious

For Freud, the return of the repressed was most healthily expressed in the process of sublimation. He saw the creative artist as steering a path between trauma and artistic creation. This linked creativity closely with unconscious processes. Such an idea is further expressed in the work of Kris (1952) and Ehrenzweig (1967), both of whom I read avidly. The artist is seen to move between regression and rationality; unconscious scanning and conscious focus-ing; playful free association and careful evaluation. But in Freud's conception, creativity is a solution to the problem of anxiety and repression rather than a direct expression of the unconscious. Perhaps a rather harsh critic in this regard, Whyte says,

> Freud neglected one of the most important, had nothing fresh to say about it, and seems only to have mentioned it in passing: (that is) the general character of the unconscious mental processes which underlie the appearance of novelty in all creation, imagination and invention.
> (Whyte 1960, p. 68)

Schelling's idea of the unconscious as a source of creativity is revived in the work of Bion. Bion's epistemology places unconscious processes at the heart of creativity. This is implicit in his naming the unconscious as infinite, with all possibility. The "artfulness" during symptom formation described by Freud is part of that creativity. The play of the primary process, with its free associations, underpins the possibility of new solutions. Moreover, the processes deline-ated by Bion in his clinical practice as he traces how emotional experience is transformed are essentially creative. The emergence of constant conjunctions and selected facts occurs in primary process thinking during reverie or during dreaming when the unconscious process has free rein.

Group and Societal Process

Bion's work on groups and social processes falls into two periods. The first in the 1940s led to a series of articles on group dynamics, brought together in the book *Experiences in Groups* (Bion 1961). The second period was in the late 1960s and beyond when his theory of thinking was being developed, and he wrote on ideas about the establishment (both the establishment of the mind and the idea of the establishment in society).

His work on group dynamics is best known for the idea of unconscious basic assumptions in groups. This established the idea that groups, as entities in themselves, had an unconscious, made from collusive yet unconscious agreements between group members. Following Freud's work on groups (Freud 1921), he understood that a high functioning group – what he called a work group – was organised into functioning roles, each pursuing a consciously held group purpose. Due to stress and anxiety, this work group might instantaneously fall into basic assumption mode to protect group members from the anxiety present. A basic assumption is an assumption held collectively and unconsciously by group members. Bion named three: basic assumption dependency (BaD), basic assumption fight/flight (BaF) and basic assumption pairing (BaP). BaD, for example, holds the assumption that the leader is dependable, all-powerful and the only person able to think and come up with ideas. This protects the members from a variety of anxieties such as competitiveness, fear of failure, vulnerability and helplessness. The leader, it is assumed, will always come up with the answers to any problems. The group then acts upon the assumption, often including the leader, who may unconsciously collude. Much has been written about these assumptions, and other basic assumptions have been named and explored since this work. I won't reiterate this except to say that these ideas have stimulated a vast literature on unconscious processes in groups and organisations, including work done on social defences against collective anxieties (see, for example, Menzies 1970; Armstrong and Rustin 2014).

The second period of work is discussed extensively in the book *Attention and Interpretation* (Bion 1970). Here, he deals with ideas of the group, institutions, their establishments and the ideas contained within. Although his particular focus is on the institution of psychoanalysis itself, these ideas are applicable to all social institutions and groups.

> In recent years there has grown up the use of the term Establishment; it seems to refer to that body of persons in the State who may be expected usually to exercise power and responsibility by virtue of their social position, wealth and intellectual and emotional endowment.… I propose to

borrow this term to denote everything from the penumbra of associations generally evoked, to the predominating and ruling characteristics
of an individual, and the characteristics of a ruling caste within a group.
(Bion 1970, p. 73)

Bion argues that groups, institutions, nations and minds alike have establishments that need and have "conventions, laws, culture and language" (Bion
1970, p. 63) in order to preserve their coherence and identity. But, he points
out, they also need exceptional individuals with new and creative ideas so that
the institution might develop and grow. Similarly, a mind needs new, perhaps
disturbing, ideas to grow and develop. These exceptional people and ideas he
names as the mystics (or geniuses) and the messianic idea. An example he gives
is the institution of religion being disturbed and shocked by Christianity – the
new messianic idea. Another might be the institutionalised mind having a set
idea changed by a new idea – many ideas in science fit this bill: the Copernican
Revolution, Darwin's ideas on evolution and Freud's psychoanalysis.

In his paper "Emotional Turbulence" (1976), Bion is at pains to demonstrate how, both at individual and societal level, there is a strong tendency for
humans to fill the gaps and caesuras in knowledge at the expense of real truth,
lest the turbulence of ignorance is felt. Such turbulence and the need to avoid
the feeling of ignorance lie at the basis of perversity that I discuss in organisations (Long 2008). Yet, if the turbulence can be tolerated, new questions
arise, and perhaps the experience gained will lead to transformations. Lies, he
says, need the thinker to hastily fill these gaps in K (presumed knowledge),
while the truth needs no thinker.

These formulations take us to Bion's creative ideas about containment.
As mentioned earlier, Bion utilises many biological metaphors in his work.
Here, he discusses the ways in which individuals and groups might relate to
one another. Three modes taken from ecological studies of how organisms
connect to one another are commensal, parasitic and symbiotic relations. In
commensal relations, two organisms – or in Bion's terms, two groups – live
alongside one another, each with little effect on the other. They simply share
an ecological niche – or in Bion's terms, a common environment. In parasitic
relations, one of the organisms or groups prospers at the expense of the other.
Nonetheless, the organism, its population or group must somehow stay alive
or continue to exist in order that the parasite can continue to benefit from it.
A description of such a relation is found in the philosopher Hegel's idea of the
master/slave relation. Although unequal and the benefits to one are greater
than to the other who appears to be dominated, the parasite and its host, at
least at the population level, need one another. The third symbiotic relation is
one of mutual benefit. For Bion, these three types of relations are psychological and can be applied to relations between groups or to relations between
ideas in the mind. One idea can live alongside another with no consequence;
or an idea might feed off and destroy other ideas; or ideas may enrich each

other. Similarly, with groups and the ways in which their members think and act.

Returning to the relation between the mystic and the establishment, he says,

> In the symbiotic relationship there is a confrontation, and the result is growth-producing though that growth may not be discerned without some difficulty. In the parasitic relationship the product of the association is something that destroys both parties to the association.
>
> (Bion 1970, p. 78)

He gives the example of a group dominated by envy, where the envy destroys all parties and belongs not simply to the individual but is also an unconscious function of the relationship.

One distinctive adaptation of Bion is found in the work of Italian psychoanalysts Ferro (2018, 2019; Levine 2022), Civitarese (2013a, 2013b) and colleagues. Ferro developed what is called Post-Bionic Field Theory. This takes Bion's ideas directly into the interpersonal and social space of the analytic session: all implicit in Bion.

> Ferro's Field Theory operationalizes Bion's concept of an analyst who is not the repository of "the truth" but is instead one who has the capacity to listen, to dwell in doubt, to utilize reverie, humor and play, and facilitate the transformation of previously unthinkable aspects of the patient's experience into articulatable mental elements such as pictorial images, thoughts and dreams.
>
> (Levine 2022, cover description)

Another is found in Lawrence's social dreaming (Lawrence, 1991, 2005, 2007; Long and Manley 2019). This is a method where participants share dreams, connections and associations in a social dreaming matrix in order to discover new thinking about social dynamics. In the matrix, the social content of the dreams assumes dominance rather than the personal meaning for the dreamer. Just as Ferro suggests that a psychoanalytic session might be regarded as a dream, so Lawrence and his followers examine a matrix of dreams as if it were a dream.

In concluding this chapter, I recognise how Bion's use of dreaming and reverie resonates with my interest in dreams – often shared at the breakfast table with my mother when I was a child – and how his use of biological metaphors – the digestive system as a metaphor for thinking; the relation of organism to environment; the modes of commensal, parasitic and symbiotic; and the idea of a group as a living system in an environment – all resonate with my thinking honed through my own studies in and love for ecology (see my interview in Sher and Lawler 2023). Bion has a deep understanding of the human mind as both lodged within and as a development from its animal beginnings.

But he also has an appreciation of the human need for self-understanding and the truths within. In his work is the recognition of a struggle between human animality and transcendence. He sees the need for humanity to grow towards its truths and through that to greater self-determination, that is, towards our free will as a collective. This is not an egoistic individual expression of will, but choice as part of being in the human group. And there are also glimpses of beyond – a transcendence to the infinite. What that is exactly, what he calls "O", is not so much able to be known as part of being and experiencing. I revisit the idea of transcendence in Chapter 11.

These ideas are of importance to group, organisational and societal thinking. There is an understanding that the "mind" is not a phenomenon directly commensurate with the individual brain but something within the collective. Biran's words in 1998 are still relevant to organisational as well as societal life:

> If we borrow this idea of Bion's and transfer if from the individual to the public, we will be able to discover whole "pockets" within society that operate under the influence of beta-elements. These elements are stored in the collective memory in their crudest form; they have not been digested, and time and experience leave no impact upon them. They express the inability to learn from experience and they are repeated over and over again – as, for example, in terrorist activity.
>
> (Biran 1998, p. 96)

How true for us in the world today.

Notes

1 The idea of contact barriers comes originally from Freud in his "Project for a Scientific Psychology" (1895) where he talks of "quality screens" as a first step to protection against external powerful stimuli (Freud S.E. 1, p. 306).

2 It should be noted that the dream furniture of the psychotic is not the same as the function of normal dreams; "he now moves not in a world of dreams but in a world of objects that are ordinarily the furniture of dreams" (Bion 1959, p. 51). This is a world where the links between objects, persons and thoughts have been attacked and destroyed.

3 This conceptualisation of the division between conscious and unconscious differs from Freud's initial theorising and also from that of Lacan. See P. Boxer (2017) "Bion, Lacan and the thing-in-itself" https://lacanticles.com/bion-lacan-and-the -thing-in-itself/. Boxer says "Thus while the end of analysis in Bion's terms was to be able to take up a relation to 'O', almost in the sense of a zen master, for Lacan the end of analysis was for the individual to be able to take up their particular symptom and live 'true to desire'". Bion theorises the transcendental. This, Boxer questions, believing a move to the empirical would be more suitable (https:// lacanticles.com/thoughts-on-bions-faith-in-o/). This will be revisited in Chapter 12.

4 For Bion, "O" is the ultimate truth, unattainable in its totality, and resides not in sensory knowledge and learning, but in a deeper non-sensory understanding of emotional experience.

5 Rugi (2016) traces this back to the influence on Bion of Whitehead's *Principa Mathematica*. He also notes the influence of Bergson's definition of intuition on Bion's formulation.
6 Grotstein argues that two aspects of "O" come from (i) pre-conceptions inherited through culture via the unrepressed unconscious (beta elements) and from (ii) the sense impressions of emotional experience, also beta elements (Grotstein 2007, p. 217).
7 This, I think, is where Bion comes close to Lacan. Both find a caesura or gap due to an inability to symbolise experience.

References

Able-Hirsch, N. (2016). 'Bion, Alpha-Function and the Unconscious Mind', *British Journal of Psychotherapy*, vol. 32, no. 2, pp. 215–225.
Armstrong, D. and Rustin, M. (eds.) (2014). *Social Defences against Anxiety: Explorations in a Paradigm*. London: Routledge.
Bergstein, A. (2019). *Bion and Meltzer's Expeditions into Unmapped Mental Life*. New York: Routledge.
Bion, W.R. (1959). 'Attacks on Linking', *International Journal of Psychoanalysis*, vol. 40, pp. 308–315.
Bion, W.R. (1961). *Experiences in Groups*. London: Tavistock.
Bion, W.R. (1962a). *Learning from Experience*, 3rd ed. London: Maresfield library, Karnac.
Bion, W.R. (1962b). 'A theory of Thinking', *International Journal of Psycho-analysis*, vol. 43, pp. 306–310.
Bion, W.R. (1963). *Elements of Psychoanalysis*. London: William Heinemann Medical Books Ltd. (Reprinted London: Karnac Books.)
Bion, W.R. (1965). *Transformations*. London: Maresfield.
Bion, W.R. (1967a). *Second Thoughts*. London: Karnac Books.
Bion, W.R. (1967b). 'Attacks on Linking', in W.R. Bion (ed.). *Second Thoughts*. London: Karnac. (Initially published in *International Journal of Psychoanalysis*, vol. 40, 1959.)
Bion, W.R. (1970). *Attention and Interpretation*. London: Tavistock.
Bion, W.R. (1976; 1987). 'Emotional Turbulence', in Francesca Bion (ed.). *Clinical Seminars and Other Works*, pp. 295–311. London: Routledge.
Bion, W.R. (1977). *Two Papers: The Grid and Caesura*. Edited by Jayme Salomao. Rio de Janeiro: Imago Editora.
Bion, W.R. (1984). *Transformations*. London: Karnac. (First published 1965.)
Biran, H. (1998). 'An Attempt to Apply Bion's Alpha and Beta Elements to Processes in Society at Large', in P. Bion Talamo, F. Borgogno and S. Merciai (eds.) *Bion's Legacy to Groups*. London: Karnac Books.
Bott-Spillius, E. (1988). *Melanie Klein Today: Mainly Theory*. London: Routledge.
Caper. R. (2016). 'Intuition and Science' in A. Grimalt (ed.). *Bion, Intuition and the Expansion of Analytic Theory*, Chapter 7. New York: Routledge Kindle Version.
Civitarese, G. (2013a). 'Bion's "Evidence" and His Theoretical Style', *The Psychoanalytic Quarterly*, vol. LXXX, no. 3, pp. 615–632.
Civitarese, G. (2013b). 'The Grid and the Truth Drive', in Philip Slotkin (trans.) *The Italian Psychoanalytic Annual*, pp. 91–114. MA Cantab. MITI.
Clarke, S. (2014). 'Projective Identification from Attack to Empathy', *Kleinian Studies e-journal*. www.psychoanalysis-and-therapy.com.

Duke, J. (2023). Where Do Words Come From? Unpublished PhD Thesis. University of Divinity Melbourne Australia.

Ehrenzweig, A. (1967). *The Hidden Order of Art: A Study in the Psychology of Artistic Imagination*. London: Weidenfeld and Nicolson.

Ferro, A. (2018). 'Bionian and Post-Bionian Transformations', *Romanian Journal of Psychoanalysis*, vol. 11, no. 2, pp. 47–56.

Ferro, A. (ed.) (2019). *Psychoanalytic Practice Today: A Post-Bionian Introduction to Psychopathology, Affect and Emotions*. London: Routledge.

Freud, S. (1895). 'Project for a Scientific Psychology', S.E. 1. https://www.encyclopedia.com/psychology/dictionaries-thesauruses-pictures-and-press-releases/project-scientific-psychology sourced [accessed 21 September 2023].

Freud, S. (1911–1913). 'The Case of Schreber', in James Strachey (ed.). *Papers on Technique and Other Works: The Standard Edition of the Complete Psychological Works of Sigmund Freud*, Vol. X11. London: Institute of Psychoanalysis and the Hogarth Press.

Freud, S. (1915). *The Unconscious, Vol XIV: The Standard Edition of the Complete Psychological Works of Sigmund Freud*, edited by James Strachey, pp. 159–204. London: Institute of Psychoanalysis and the Hogarth Press.

Freud, S. (1921; 1961). *Group Psychology and the Analysis of the Ego*. S.E. 69. 69–143. London: Institute of Psychoanalysis and the Hogarth Press.

Gerber, I. (2016). 'Bion and the Infinite Unconscious – an Intuitive Science', in A. Grimalt (ed.). *Bion, Intuition and the Expansion of Analytic Theory*. New York: Routledge Kindle Version.

Grimalt, A. (2016). 'Tribute to Pere Folch', in A. Grimalt (ed.). *Bion, Intuition and the Expansion of Analytic Theory* New York: Routledge Kindle Version.

Grimalt, A. (ed.) (2022). *Bion, Intuition and the Expansion of Psychoanalytic Theory*. London: Routledge, e-edition.

Grotstein, J.S. (1997). 'Bion's "Transformation in "O", the "Thing-in-Itself", and the "Real"', *Melanie Klein and Object Relations*, vol. 14, no. 2, pp. 109–141.

Grotstein, J.S. (2007). *A Beam of Intense Darkness: Wilfred Bion's Legacy to Psychoanalysis*. London: Karnac.

Kris, E. (1952) *Psychoanalytic Explorations in Art*. London: George Allen and Unwin.

Lawrence, W.G. (1991). 'Won from the Void and Formless Infinite: Experiences of Social Dreaming', *Free Associations*, vol. 2(Part 2), no. 22, pp. 254–266.

Lawrence, W.G. (2005). *Introduction to Social Dreaming*. London: Karnac Books.

Lawrence, W.G. (ed.) (2007). *Infinite Possibilities of Social Dreaming*. London: Karnac Books.

Levine, H.B. (ed.) (2022). *The Post-Bionic Field Theory of Antonino Ferro: Theoretical Analysis and Clinical Application*. London: Karnac.

Long, S.D. (2008). *The Perverse Organisation and Its Deadly Sins*. London: Routledge.

Long, S.D. and Manley, J. (eds.) (2019). *Social Dreaming: Philosophy, Research, Theory and Practice*. London: Routledge.

Lopez-Corvo, R.E. (2003). *The Dictionary of The Work of W.R. Bion*. London: Karnac.

Mancia, M. and Longhin, L. (2000, December). 'Kant's Philosophy and Its Relationship with the Thought of Bion and Money-Kyrle', *International Journal of Psychoanalysis*, vol. 81, pp. 1197–1211.

Menzies, I.E.P. (1970). *A Case Study in the Functioning of Social Systems as a Defence against Anxiety: A Report on the Study of a Nursing Service of a General Hospital*. London: Tavistock.

Ogden, T. (2004). 'An Introduction to the Reading of Bion', *International Journal of Psychoanalysis*, vol. 85, no. 2, pp. 285–300.

Rice, A.K. (1966). *Learning for Leadership*. London: Tavistock Publications.

Rugi, G. (2016). 'Intuition in Bion: Between Search for Invariants and Creative Emergence', in A. Grimalt (ed.). *Bion, Intuition and the Expansion of Analytic Theory*. New York: Routledge Kindle Version.

Schelling, F.W.J. (1811/1942) *The Ages of the World*. F.D. Wolfe Bowman Jnr. (trans.). New York: Columbia University Press.

Shapiro, E. and Carr, W. (2012). 'An Introduction to Tavistock-Style Group Relations Conference Learning', *Organisation and Social Dynamics*, vol. 12, no. 1, pp. 70–80.

Sher, M. and Lawler, D. (2023). *Systems Psychodynamics: Theorist and Practitioner Voices from the Field. Chapter 12: 'Susan Long'*, pp. 140–153. London: Routledge.

Symington, J. and Symington, N. (2002). *The Clinical Thinking of Wilfred Bion*. London: Routledge.

Whyte, L. (1960). *The Unconscious Before Freud: A History of the Evolution of Human Awareness*. New York: Basic Books.

5 Jacques Lacan – The Unconscious Structured Like a Language Is Structured (by Difference)

In common with Freud and Bion, Lacan is concerned with the truth of the human subject – a truth from the unconscious: a truth that is about what it means not to "give ground to one's desire" (Lacan 1992 [1959–1960], p. 321, 2002[1996]-c), a phrase that has been variously interpreted (Green 1995–1996) but mostly understood as living by that desire that constitutes one's subjectivity, not the wiles of the ego. While the subject in Bion is transcendental (Grotstein 2007), looking to a beingness before and beyond language – unconscious and yet not so much ethereal as grounded in emotional experience; Lacan's subject is deeply rooted as a subject of discourse; as unconsciously subjected to a lack or gap mediated by language and culture; divided in experience from a simple animality yet with, perhaps, enigmatic moments of being in relation to a *plus de jouir* (a more than) "jouissance", in which jouissance refers to embodied joy, literally beyond signification.[1] However, in common, both look to a complex unconscious following Freud, with some aspects able to become conscious, other aspects repressed beyond any accessibility to consciousness, the unconscious *per se* having a wider compass than the repressed unconscious.

This chapter continues the journey through the evolution of the idea of the unconscious, taken from the perspective of my own journey and understanding. I have chosen Bion and Lacan as stopping points on this journey through the unconscious because, among many psychoanalysts, they are the ones to have looked deeply into the madness of the psychotic mind, where the unconscious shows up in different ways from its unruly but somewhat tamed neurotic appearance.

While I argued in Chapter 4 that the unconscious articulated by Bion, to use his own terminology, is beyond containment, in this chapter I argue that the subject's relation to the unconscious for Lacan, to use his terms, is divided, with estranged components in mind space. We find here a conception of the relation to the unconscious that unpicks and examines the Freudian view of the mind and subjectivity, expanding and transforming its nascent but not fully conceived divisions into irreconcilable foundations of a divided subjectivity, or more correctly a divided mind because subjectivity is formed in the division. It is an unconscious whose truths can be experienced, if only partially, in the experience

DOI: 10.4324/9781003559818-5

of madness with its absence of socially constructed meaning. "We are all mad" (Jacques-Alain Miller).[2] Yet, we can manage to live in a world with meanings that keep us sane if at the same time we can paradoxically see that world as an illusion, an imagination. Introducing the idea of the "subject" as central rather than ego, self or person brings forward the importance of the relation to the unconscious. It is a subject not grounded in its own authority, but a subject, just as in Freud's account, subjected both to unconscious desire and to the demands of society, and in so doing subjectivity is split and desire forever unfulfilled.

While working two days a week in a child psychiatric outpatient area of a large hospital in the early 1980s, I was supervised by the Argentinian Lacanian-trained psychoanalyst, Leonardo Rodriguez. Besides personal supervision, he conducted lunchtime seminars that looked at child psychiatry from a Lacanian perspective. Here, I was introduced to the work of Jacques Lacan and Maud Mannoni's work with children. Later, I attended seminars with Leonardo and philosopher Russell Grigg at the then Prince Henry's Hospital in Melbourne. We slowly moved through *Écrits*, sentence by sentence. This informed my thinking during my PhD studies. I am grateful to them both for their help. Lacan's ideas spoke to me because of his attention to the structure of language, speech and the unconscious. I had been dissatisfied with the first years of my undergraduate studies with their strong focus on behaviourism and felt that this approach could in no way explain language. I chose to study the development of language in children for my master's thesis, and the work of Noam Chomsky (1957) began to satisfy my need to see something at a deeper level. Lacan helped me take this thinking further, especially in gaining the distinctions between the Symbolic, the Imaginary and the Real. These three registers of experience are referred to throughout this chapter, and their meaning is gradually articulated. The distinctions drawn in their delineation somewhat paralleled my thinking about the distinctions between role and person gained from the then Grubb Institute in London and my understanding of groups from Bion (see Long 1991). I formulated the idea that roles in a group acted as signifiers in signifying chains rather than being simply an expression of a static role description. For me, roles become structural positions in group space, in the group mind if you like, having meaning primarily in relation to other roles in particular systems; somewhat like words being positions in linguistic space, having meaning primarily in relation to other words in the same language – the difference.

Much of my understanding comes from Lacan's early writings; his later work I have struggled with more recently. Nonetheless, I can trace out some major ideas that have influenced me and given me some understanding of how he describes the unconscious. As I am writing more for a generalist audience than for a specialist in any one of the theories I present, my rendition here of Lacan's version of the unconscious is limited. His theorising is a vast body of work where each conception is intertwined with all others and the work as a whole. I simply want to bring forward some of the ways in which the Lacanian unconscious extends and reworks Freud's version.

The effects of language, both written and spoken, are central to Lacanian theory. Lacan says (Lacan 1977b, p. 85) "when you congratulate yourself on having met someone who speaks the same kind of language as you do, you do not mean that you meet with him in the discourse of everybody, but that you are united to him by a special kind of speech". Speech, he says, "always subjectively includes its own reply" (Op. cit., p. 85). We talk to each other in this way, each not only anticipating but also missing the other. Psychoanalysis is seen as the talking cure. Early in his career, Lacan locates the unconscious in speech, saying, "the unconscious is that part of the concrete discourse, insofar as it is transindividual, that is not at the disposal of the subject in re-establishing the continuity of his conscious discourse" (Lacan 1977e, p. 49). Here, he follows Freud's insights into the gaps in his patients' speech that led Freud to see the effects of the unconscious in these gaps. The written word can be different, attempting more clearly to follow the rules of grammar but still affected by the unconscious, as Freud shows through his analysis of slips of the tongue or pen and by all those defences of rationalisation. Both spoken and written words are subject to the unconscious intrusion of words that press to speak themselves and that express the language-like rules of the unconscious: that attempt to symbolise experience on the basis of difference. Such words may be expressed as symptoms if they cannot reach the spoken discourse.

In talking of language, I find as many do, that Lacan is difficult to read not only because of the introduction of new ideas and their translation from French, but mainly because of the ongoing allusions to his own vast reading of philosophy, literature, linguistics, as well as psychoanalysis – a reading that I cannot replicate or emulate – and allusions that I can rarely follow without long excursions beyond my initial wishes or attempts to glean something from him. Indeed, one must be a dedicated Lacanian scholar – perhaps in the way that one should be dedicated to any of the theorists I attempt to examine in this book if one hopes to understand and use – to enter that "special kind of speech" that would allow finding the "same kind of language" as his.

I will say here that I am not an accomplished Lacanian scholar, and as I write, I wonder about including this chapter and the challenge it presents me. Reading Lacan gives the image of an academic/intellectual who often expresses himself with contempt and high disdain, especially for what he regards as misguided psychology. This leaves me feeling annoyed yet sad because his ideas, once reached, are like bright gems in a dark cave and shouldn't be missed but might be. It perplexes me to be led down so many wandering paths of associated scholastic learning and I wish he would get more directly to his point. Moreover, the ways in which he describes a variety of his concepts change over time, making it hard to be definitive – such is the nature of the evolution of thought, and many interpretations of his theories abound.

He is often accused of intellectualising, to which he replies that this accusation is a defence against the work of discovering the truth in what he says. I don't deny the worth of discovering such truths. To enter his discourse is a labour that he means to give his readers, at times to avoid simple misreading.

But at a deeper level, the various allusions do make his writing an ongoing illustration of the metaphoric and metonymic processes that he discusses as structuring the unconscious. The seeming metonym of one Lacanian concept leading to another with rarely so much as a simple, everyday explanation in between, I reflect, is there to throw me, the reader (consciously or unconsciously I am unsure), deeply into the experience of what he is trying to explain, like Joyce's *Ulysses*. This can become an estrangement that I feel is somewhat overdone. However, just as Joyce wrote *Ulysses* as an immersion "in" rather than "of", Lacan also writes "in" but without so much poetry (excuse and bear with my own attempts at allusions). While Joyce writes the unconscious, Lacan is still writing about the unconscious. But then he is a clinician, and much of his writing is taken from his talking to other clinicians who at least attempt to speak his language, as well as to the intelligentsia of Paris. Nonetheless, I need to attempt to put his ideas more into my own words and to help my readers find a way into their own experience of Lacanian theory.

Lacan believed that Freud had been misread and misinterpreted over the years, particularly in his translation into English. In proposing a return to Freud's original texts, his (Lacan's) early seminars critiqued readings by the schools of ego psychology and object relations in particular, and although there are points of intersection between Lacan and Melanie Klein not often recognised (Ruti and Allen 2019), their views on the place and nature of the ego strongly differ. For Lacan, the ego is not the seat of truth, but is a false picture reflected from the mirror of others, a falseness that leads us by the nose (Lacan 1970, p. 138). Lacan was particularly interested in Freud's early writings and ideas that included Freud's formulation of the subject's relation to unconscious processes in his *Project for a Scientific Psychology*.

For Lacan, it is speech and the processes of symbolisation that mediate the way we take up our humanity, our subjectivity and our socialisation. But this symbolisation comes at a cost. To have established the means of symbolising means to have lost something in the process of taking up our being, an originating loss for which the caesura – the separation from the placenta during birth – is a metaphor.[3] This means of symbolising rests on a prior affirming of our being in relation to this loss through which symbolisation is initiated (Evans 1996, p. 17). The affirmation of this loss establishes a fundamental signifier that confers identity on the subject (Evans 1996, p. 119). Its foreclosure gives rise to psychosis. Thenceforward, while there is always a gap, a lack due to our being in relation to this originating loss, such a loss and the gap it leaves are in relation to this fundamental signifier, referred to by Lacan as the-name-of-the-father (Lacan 1993 [1981], p. 96; Zizek 1996; Lacan 2002 [1996]-a, p. 534 [640]; Lacan 1970 [1966], 1993 [1981], pp. 81–82, 2002 [1996]-b, p. 388).

This originating trauma takes place within the context of a family matrix through which speech mediates our relation to both our own and others' humanity. There is always a gap, a lack due to this. It is the trauma that language brings to humanity. Lacan says, "the essential part of human experience, that which is properly speaking the experience of the subject, that which causes the subject to exist, is to be located on the level of the emergence of the symbolic" (Lacan 1988, p. 219; personal discussion with Philip Boxer). This emergence, Lacan claims, is heralded by the child's subjection to language and the law as mediated by the family matrix. This, in turn, structures the experience registered through the Imaginary order, that order of the everyday experience of object relations. We are each given a name, a place in society and are entered into the medium of language as growing infants. The division in our relation of being as subjects comes most acutely during what Lacan calls "the mirror stage" when the growing child comes to find an image of self with which he/she identifies and with which he/she continues to identify in ever-growing moments (Lacan 1977a). To Lacan, this is an imaginary self – a misrecognition – because we have experiences that remain unspoken, unseen in the mirror, unidentified with in the image, and hence experiences of lack in relation to what he calls the Real. Finding an image of the self that feels whole rather than fragmented in experience is validated by the adult who celebrates or at least recognises this image (Ruti and Allen 2019, p. 11). "That's you in the mirror; that's you in the photo with mummy", and without words, "that's you in how I look at you". But it forms an ego that can become narcissistically grandiose.

The body is fundamental. It is the site of desire and what Lacan calls "jouissance" – a kind of overwhelming but fractured satisfaction of the drives. But also, it represents something for an "other" little "o"; at first, the mother. The body is not just a symbol in discourse, although it can act as such. It is not just a place where the ego resides, although it comes as that in illusion. It has deep experience also in the Real (Pavón Cuéllar 2009). So, what does Lacan mean by desire?

The nature of desire is in the subject's relation to the unconscious "O".[4] "Desire is the desire of the Other", argues Lacan:

> the only object is a metonymic object, object of desire being the object of the Other's desire, and desire always being desire for some Other thing, very precisely for what is lacking, a, the primordially lost object, insofar as Freud shows it to us as always having to be refound.
>
> (Lacan 2017 [1998], p. 7)

The desire of the Other O (a radically unconscious alterity) is something we can never really grasp. There is a "lack", something missing, inevitably missing in the transition to human subjectivity. Lacan names this as little a, "objet petit a", the object that takes the place of the lack – "object cause of desire". The relation to lack is not represented in the body image because it is missing, because it is radically unconscious and never to be made conscious. We come to desire actual "things", or their representation, through the relation to lack (not a thing) that comes to inhabit and infuse what we desire.

What Lacan brings to the idea of the unconscious is how it is created through the formation of the divided subject, taking up Freud's distinction between a transferential unconscious and a real unconscious.

Phillip Boxer says,

> A Lacanian understanding of the unconscious starts from Freud's three-way distinction between the conscious, the descriptively unconscious (a "below-the-surface"), and a radically unconscious.
>
> (Boxer 2022, p. 2)

In this, he refers to Freud's 1915 paper where the systems conscious, preconscious and unconscious were described; and where Freud refers to an unconscious not able to be accessed, which he (Boxer) names as the radical unconscious (Boxer 2022 and several personal communications); by others named as the real unconscious (Restivo 2013; Miller 2017) or the unconscious beyond meaning.

Boxer (2022) points to Freud's emphasis that not all the unconscious is inaccessible to consciousness and in addition that "below the surface of consciousness" not all is repressed. Boxer goes on to say that the individual is subjected to these two forms of the unconscious. That is, together they relate to the individual as a subject, but in different ways. First, the descriptive or transferential unconscious subjects the individual to the social (small o) other through the object relation (interpersonal relations). This is the basis of ego development in relation to an imagined or projected other exemplified in the mirror stage. The ego is captured by and subjected to its image of others and a projected image of self.

Second, the individual is subjected to a (Big-O) Other through the relation to the repressed and beyond that to the lack in, what Boxer calls, the radical unconscious. This Big-O is the realm of the Symbolic order. The Symbolic order is what underlies the small-s symbolic system of human symbols and laws that make community possible. Subjection to the Symbolic order is what makes us functioning individuals, the small symbolic system shaping the way we take up roles within a society. However, this subjection leaves the gap of what is lost; what is given up – the jouissance or pleasure beyond the law of the Symbolic order that remains in relation to Real lack.

But the relation to what is lost is ironically not so much lost as forfeited upon entry to the Symbolic order – the caesura that might be seen as entry to our humanity. Hence, this forfeit becomes the lack of the radically unconscious and forms the basis of desire – the Lacanian term for those wishes that are forever unfulfilled although always striven for (The Dangerous Maybe Website 2021). I return to this notion of desire later. I believe it finds conscious echoes in the grief felt for "what might have been" but can never be: an indescribable yearning at a spiritual level and a barely glimpsed gap (see Long 2000).

In his seminar series (1954–1955), Lacan asks: What is the subject? He answers that in the strict Freudian sense, it is the unconscious subject – the subject who speaks (Lacan 1988). This is the subject of the Big-O that is itself in relation to a radically unconscious lack. Hence his claim that the unconscious is the discourse of the Other. In his later seminars, Lacan notes that the

Imaginary (little-o), the Symbolic (Big-O) and the Real (beyond symbolisation) are linked together in a Borromean knotting that comes to represent the different forms of identification, through which the three registers are held in relation to each other by the subject (Lacan 2021 [1956-7]; personal communication from Philip Boxer).

So, who is this subject who speaks? What is it to be subject to discourse?

In *The Interpretation of Dreams* (1900), Freud stated that a dream could be understood like a picture puzzle or a rebus. In dream work, the unconscious dream thoughts are translated into dream content – the images in dreams. In chapter 6, Freud (who I quote at length) says,

> The dream-thoughts are immediately comprehensible, as soon as we have learnt them. The dream-content, on the other hand, is expressed as it were in a pictograph script, the characters of which have to be transposed individually into the language of the dream-thoughts. If we attempted to read these characters according to their pictorial value instead of according to their symbolic relation, we should clearly be led into error. Suppose I have a picture-puzzle, a rebus, in front of me. It depicts a house with a boat on its roof, a single letter of the alphabet, the figure of a running man whose head has been conjured away, and so on.
>
> Now I might be misled into raising objections and declaring that the picture as a whole and its component parts are nonsensical. A boat has no business to be on the roof of a house, and a headless man cannot run. Moreover, the man is bigger than the house; and if the whole picture is intended to represent a landscape, letters of the alphabet are out of place in it since such objects do not occur in nature.
>
> But obviously we can only form a proper judgment of the rebus if we put aside criticisms such as these of the whole composition and its parts and if, instead, we try to replace each separate element in some way or other. The words which are put together in this way are no longer nonsensical but may form a poetical phrase of the greatest beauty and significance.
>
> A dream is a picture-puzzle of this sort and our predecessors in the field of dream-interpretation have made the mistake of treating the rebus as a pictorial composition: and as such it has seemed to them nonsensical and worthless.

For Freud, then, the dream content is to be read as symbolic – a kind of speaking from the unconscious. He talks of it being like a rebus:

> A rebus communicates its message by means of pictures or symbols whose names sound like various parts of a word, phrase, or sentence. For example, a picture of a can of tomatoes followed by the letters UC and a picture of a well means "Can you see well?" In Latin, the word *rebus* means "by things"; *rebus* is a form of the Latin word *res*, which means

"thing". English speakers started using the word *rebus* for picture writing in the early 1600s.

(Merriam Webster Dictionary)

This idea of speaking from the unconscious is fundamental to Lacan's view of the unconscious (Lacan 1977b). While Freud talks of threads of associations – derivatives, more or less distanced from repressed material, and "trains of thought" coming into associative connections with repressed material (Freud 1915, p. 148), Lacan emphasises chains of signifiers in speech occurring both consciously and unconsciously. The shared idea of signifying links is evident.

Lacan adapts the work of linguists Roman Jakobson and Ferdinand de Saussure concerning the relation between the signifier and the signified in semiotics. Saussure denotes the sign as composed of a signified, for example, "a tree, or more correctly the concept of tree, and a signifier – the word 'tree'".

However, in Lacan's adaptation the relation across the bar of the signifier to the signified is to the unconscious. He inverts the Saussurian diagram with the signifier on top to illustrate its dominance. Let me explain. Like Freud, Lacan regards the subject's relation to unconscious processes to be manifest in the processes of speaking, both processes being structured by difference – the meaning of a signifier being an effect of its difference from other signifiers. A word, he points out, is not simply tied into what it appears to denote but gains its meaning through its links in a signifying chain of other words. The meaning lies in its difference. Words are understood through other words. This is different from a signifier merely indicating what is signified; that is, with a fixed meaning. For Lacan, "a signifier is that which represents the subject for another signifier" (Lacan 1977d, p. 316); and "no signification can be sustained other than by reference to another signification" (Lacan 1977b, p. 150). Words as signifiers hold their meaning (even if this is transitory) through their contrasting difference from other words. Hence, the aphorism: the unconscious is structured like a language is structured, that is, on the basis of difference. Man, not woman; child, not adult; mad, not sane. Moreover, meaning comes retroactively from the signifying chain, not from individual words. The meaning of words strung together by speech becomes evident retroactively at the end of a sentence, paragraph or narrative. This is what Freud pointed out about the utterances of his patients. I could only begin to understand what the father was saying about the aviary and indeed about his son, once the fuller narrative was given (see my anecdote in Chapter 4 on Bion). However, the retroactive attribution of meaning by a listener emerges from the way the listener organises the relations between signifiers as well as across the bars between signifier and signified, a meaning that may or may not correspond to that intended by the speaker. Communication is complex.

Lacan further applies the ideas of metaphor and metonymy (major processes in our use of language) to Freud's ideas of condensation and displacement in the primary process. A metaphor substitutes one concept with another and is thus for substitution; for example, she is as a rose without thorns. A metonymy

– the part standing for the whole – selects the part and is for association; for example, the Crown versus Smith. Thus, in the relation between the signifier and the signified (adapted from de Saussure), the metaphor involves a condensation of signifiers (e.g. what does a word like "rose" "mean"?) and metonymy a displacement of signifiers (e.g. what does the "Crown" stand for?).

Lacan's adaptation of the idea of the relation between signifier and signified from linguist Ferdinand de Saussure brings forward the idea that because the signifying chain depends not on fixed signifiers, signification or meaning lies within the ambiguities of the instability of signification. This, he describes as the result of the constant slippage of the signified beneath the signifier – a slipperiness that defies constant definitions (Lacan 1977b) and is implicated in associative chains of unconscious metaphor and metonymy. Meanings are, we might say, slippery. However, he does argue for stabilising points that not only hold the signifier and signified together but also hold the signifiers in relation to each other. It is through these points of stabilisation that the retroactive attribution of meaning becomes possible, such as the meanings created from the Oedipal configuration of a family matrix that stabilise the individual's position through the relations between father, mother and child and the necessary relations between these positions in society – that adhere to the incest taboo and the authority of this informing the generations. These points of stabilisation derive from the relation that the subject has to the fundamental signifier within the context of the family matrix, this being the reason that Lacan calls it "the-name-of-the-father"; a master signifier that holds signifying chains in place and whose absence he sees as fundamental to the psychotic structure (Lacan 1977c).

> In contrast to the stability of the relationship between signifier and signified in Saussure's structuralist conception of language, as Lacan puts it, there is "an incessant sliding of the signified under the signifier": a signifier leads only to another signifier, never to a signified. For Derrida, there is thus an inherent indeterminacy of meaning. However, sanity and communication depend on at least the provisional illusion of the stability of meaning. Lacan argues that there are anchoring points (*points de capiton*) in a discourse which make interpretation possible, albeit retrospectively.
>
> ('Slippage of Meaning' 2022)

As has been said, the relation of signifiers to one another occurs in a signifying chain. Conscious and unconscious signifiers become related to one another through metaphor and metonymy. Unconscious signifiers or meanings linked to the subject's desire become part of their utterances and behaviours. Lacan is interested in the subject more than the ego. The subject involves the unconscious, and it is the unconscious that pushes to speak.

> The signifying chain has only one destiny: to insert the subject's unconscious desire in the subject's utterances. Thus, it constitutes the design

and the weave of the speaking subject's psychic fabric. More generally, it
is involved in all psychic causality.

('The Signifying Chain' n.d.)

It is as if all that we utter, all that we communicate, how we behave, are
linked to our unconscious desire, even as we do not know or understand this:
not a surprising conclusion given Freud's work. Think of those situations
where something is said or done and what follows is a rationalisation of the
act rather than a recognition of its cause. Freud noted this when he analysed
the functioning of hypnosis. The hypnotised person obeys the commands of
the hypnotist outside the hypnotic trance. When questioned, a rationalisation
is produced, whereas we know that the real reason for the behaviour or utter-
ance is the hypnotic command. So, with many of our behaviours where the
true reason is from unconscious desire. This takes us back to the question of
freedom – so important to Schelling as the ultimate basis of subjectivity; the
freedom to choose between good and evil; perhaps between truth and illusion. In Lacan's case, however, this freedom is rooted in the ethical choices
each one of us makes in how we give ground relative to desire (Lacan 1992
[1959–1960], p. 321): What it is that unconscious desire wants of us is mediated by our relation to society.

As indicated earlier, Lacan understood the subject's relation to his/her
experience as being in relation to three registers that are inextricably bound
up with each other: the Imaginary, the Symbolic and the Real. Experience in
relation to the Imaginary is in terms of what we experience perceptually as a
contiguous space–time bounded reality. In simple terms, it is that register of
perceptions, images and thoughts that we think of as describing our everyday
reality: it is the realm of object relations. However, the terms in which we
experience this everyday reality are shaped by the relation to the Symbolic register, *the invisible order that structures our experience of reality* (Zizek 1996),
with its structuring of difference.

This shaping means that the relation to difference in the Symbolic register
mediates the ways in which we experience the Imaginary. The effects of our
relation to the Symbolic are most apparent in our relation to speech, as I indicated earlier, where the meaning of words or phrases as signifiers is defined
not so much by what they refer to (the signified), as by their difference to each
other and hence, in relation to what we are not saying.

For example, think about a dictionary where the words, signifiers, stand in
relation to one another in their difference from one another. A dictionary can
only give other words to define a word. It is a system of interrelated signifiers
and the differences between them. The signifier "father" can be used as an
example. For instance, the father in the Symbolic (the relation of father in the
family) shapes the experience of the father in the Imaginary. We experience
the father through perception or imagination – a happy or sad father; a hostile
or loving father – this experience is shaped by or given meaning to (contained

by) the relation to what "father" means as a difference within a family as an institution.

The subject's relation to the register of the Real is then a relation to that which disrupts the contiguous and bounded nature of the Imaginary and to that which escapes signification, falling beyond the Symbolic. Experience in relation to the Symbolic register is in terms of the chaining of signifiers in the unconscious, which may or may not be articulated in the subject's speech, hence the gaps in conscious free associations identified by Freud.

For Lacan, the Imaginary or interpretative unconscious (as he calls it) is a relation to the chains of signifiers that are not articulated in consciousness, yet could be. Thus, with the interpretative unconscious, unconscious signifiers do not stand rigidly for an object or idea in perception. The relation between the two may be changed according to the context of other unconscious signifiers.

As described earlier, Lacan describes this as the signifier "sliding" across the signified. This understanding of the unconscious leads Fazioni (2012, p. 5) to initially say "the unconscious is not the place of irrational instincts or our psychical inner coffer. It is a logical-dialectical system that is interpretable by the psychoanalyst as a literary text", that is: an unconscious that can be interpreted. But he goes on to argue that psychoanalysis is not simply a hermeneutic exercise. Following Lacan, it is an ability to "work with a subject without reducing the subject to his (sic) representation" (Fazioni 2012, p. 11). Pavon-Cuellar (2009) notes this as working outside of the usual behavioural, cognitive and discursive psychologies of general psychology.

> A Lacanian critical psychology must be in opposition to any psychological reductionist description of the subject: either behavioural, or cognitive, or discursive; either animal, or computational, or grammatical; either for predicting, or understanding, or explaining.
>
> (p. 48)

Lacan's notion of the Real moves us beyond hermeneutics. Inveighing into this picture is then the relation to the real unconscious (Restivo 2013 p. 40)[5] and the notion of "desire": Lacan's word for that which is familiar to readers of the Strachey translation of Freud is "wish", although desire holds more of the relation to the lost object that Freud theorised. The lost object arising from the caesura is that which cannot be repeated. It is not so much an actual object but a "virtual" object – echoing a lost jouissance constituted by gaps in the unconscious structuring of difference in relation to which the subject experiences the partial drives. Lacan identified these partial drives as oral, anal, phallic (the relation to signification), scopic (the gaze) and invocatory (the voice). The relation to the real unconscious is a relation to gaps in the unconscious structuring of difference itself.

As with Freud, in Lacan, the subject's relation to desire is a manifestation of the relation to these partial drives, with the complication that our ego misrecognises this relation as a demand; our relation to desire being defined more by what gets missed in the pursuit of satisfying these demands – a gap. Therefore, the relation to desire is shaped by the relation to the Symbolic that functions like the law – the law of the father in the Oedipal context. The ways in which desire manifests itself in the form of a demand are, therefore, a social concept originating in those places where the Imaginary's body and the Symbolic's organisation of difference intersect in everyday reality: Lacan describes these places as cuts in the ego's boundaries where the inside–outside difference in the Imaginary breaks down, and there is also a relation to a gap in the Symbolic – the erogenous zones, for example, the lips, the anus, the sexual organs and also the gaze and the voice.

Because these cuts in the ego's boundaries are shaped by the relation to the Symbolic, they are signifiers and not simply the body parts of everyday reality. They stand in the place of desire, representations of desire taking the form of demands that can never be fully satisfied because of their relation to what is lost in the unconscious – a loss that is not just repressed, but that is radically unknowable. (The indivisible remainder of Schelling acts as a metaphor for this loss rooted in German idealism; however, its basis is different from the understanding of the relation to the originating loss of the caesura in Freud and Lacan.) It is in relation to desire that the phrase quoted at the beginning of this chapter, that is, not to "give ground to one's desire" is variously interpreted. For some, it is seen as an imperative to do whatever one wishes (Green 1995–1996),[6] while to others it indicates staying with unconscious desire related to the law of the Symbolic.

Towards the end of his work, Lacan referred to the subject's particular relation to this original loss as the subject's sinthome. Lacan makes the point that in the work of being "true to desire" in relation to this sinthome, we inevitably betray ourselves as who we are. This, then, is the Lacanian understanding of the psychoanalytic ethic.

> There is no other good than that which may serve to pay the price for access to desire – given that desire is understood here, as we have defined it elsewhere, as the metonymy of our being.
>
> (Lacan 1992 [1959–1960], p. 323)

The sinthome here is not analysable in the sense of being a signifier – a symptom whose unconscious meaning can be revealed or deciphered – but is an expression of the subject's enjoyment of the unconscious (jouissance) apparent in the way the subject holds together the knot of the Symbolic, Imaginary and Real.

> The sinthome is what is left after going through the enigma of the formation of the unconscious and its repetitive and never-ending productions of meaning…The symptom has something to say; there is communication taking place on the level of the symptom…The symptom lives in the domain of the transference unconscious, whereas the sinthome is

a consistency detached from the production of meaning…on a certain consistency of jouissance.

(Restivo 2013, p. 157)

Ruti and Allen (2019) describe the sinthome as the fantasy that lies at the basis of the subject: an enigmatic core that is implicated in repetition compulsions because it is essentially uninterpretable.

Lacan has extended the idea of the unconscious through his distinctions between the registers of the Imaginary, the Symbolic and the Real and through his exploration of sexual difference and jouissance. While there is an element of the unconscious that can speak and be interpreted, there is also that which cannot be spoken; that is outside signification and can only be experienced through jouissance and its expression in sexuality and art (Restivo 2013).

I return for a moment to the beginning of my journey, to Schelling and the God who wished to be known through his own materialisation as other (Schelling 1942). I am reminded of the Book of Genesis: "In the beginning was the word". This is echoed by Lacan, who sees the beginning of subjectivity in the affirmation in relation to an original loss that gives rise to a fundamental signifier. However, from Lacan's perspective the Book of Genesis becomes more like a metaphor for the subject's formation. The human who experiences through and within the bound together realms of the Symbolic, the Imaginary and the Real, becomes a subject – subjected to each of these realms – through the advent of human culture and its supreme achievement: signification, language. At one time, Lacan claims, "the true anthem of atheism is not 'God is dead, but God is unconscious'", locating God in the big other "O". However, Dalzell (2022) traces Lacan's view to his later formulation of God as not in the Symbolic but in the Real linked to the jouissance beyond signification. This, Dalzell claims, indicates that Lacan does not put God in the idea of "Being" as the Romantic philosophers (including Schelling) do, but puts God beyond the word, beyond existence using the term *ek-sists* – totally unknowable, not even in any form; not the Imaginary God of projection into the father as the *subject-supposed-to-know* (that is the omniscient one) or the God of ultimate being in the unconscious. I introduce these ideas not to ascertain whether Lacan was a believer, an atheist as he claims or even a nuanced atheist as argued by Dalzell. Nor do I do it to interpret religion through a Lacanian lens as has been done many times, a recent example being Schreiber et al. (2019). I do it to locate his ideas of the unconscious in a line from Schelling.

What is critical in Lacan's theorising is the idea of "lack": that which is missing through gaining human subjectivity, in the move from the Real to the Symbolic. This is materialised in the Oedipal complex and its attendant castration anxiety. Lack comes into being through an affirmation of an original loss – something beyond words remains missing. The lack of the symbolisation that comes in place of this loss, while subject to a primordial signifier, also institutes desire. This is a kindred image to Bion's idea, despite large differences from Lacan in his theorising, that the act of containing through our use of words (conception), the result of the alpha function and Bion's contact barrier, leaves behind the chaos of beta space. I also see that while Bion talks of the unconscious as infinite, he also recognises the dynamic repressed unconscious of Freud, as does Lacan. All three – Freud, Bion and Lacan – refer to a complex unconscious with aspects beyond comprehension in human consciousness. Where Lacan differs from Bion is in the basis of the containing vertex, which for Lacan is rooted in the affirmation of being – in relation to an originating loss.

Lacan tells of human desire as being unending. If I am honest, I know that in my life I have desired and continue to desire many things – knowledge, to work well and successfully, prestige, material things, love – and I try at times to dampen those desires and stay content with what I have. But I do desire also to know my desire, as Lacan asks: an endless struggle that is life.

We can say that Lacan has, in many ways, made explicit that which is implicit in Freud's idea of the unconscious (Freud 1915b). But beyond that, he has helped us traverse the foundations of subjectivity. For Lacan, the subject is created through speech that also forever damns it. The freedom "to be true to desire" here is seemingly always beyond reach while at the same time appearing reachable. Our choice appears to be (if it could be called that) to live out our being somewhere in between being estranged (alienation in Lacan's terms) from our fundamental creaturely being through becoming civilised within an imaginary world of meaning, or living a madness of jouissance, beyond the strictures of taboo, sometimes becoming a living psychosis and facing fearful hell. A way between is to accept our estrangement and pursue meaning, knowing its illusionary and endless nature; perhaps finding moments of joy that, while experienced with full enjoyment in the body, are fleeting and barely grasped. This is a truly poetic vision. Perhaps its bleaker expression is intimated by Shakespeare.

> Tomorrow, and tomorrow, and tomorrow,
> Creeps in this petty pace from day to day,
> To the last syllable of recorded time;
> And all our yesterdays have lighted fools
> The way to dusty death. Out, out, brief candle!
> Life's but a walking shadow, a poor player,
> That struts and frets his hour upon the stage,
> And then is heard no more. It is a tale
> Told by an idiot, full of sound and fury,
> Signifying nothing.

> (Shakespeare's Macbeth)

While the love poems of John Donne perhaps express the fleeting joy of achieving meaning, and Blake's *Songs of Innocence and Experience* gives both the joys and woes of being a human subject, with Lacan we are left with the question of whether linking jouissance with signification leads to freedom or to the ultimate oppression, given the world we live in.

Notes

1 For Lacan, jouissance can be a restricted pleasure within the confines of the strictures of the Symbolic order and its laws – a phallic jouissance – or an unrestricted pleasure beyond such strictures. His theories on sexual difference locate masculine sexuality in the former and feminine sexuality with access to the latter.
2 Jacques-Alain Miller spent much time exploring the "structuralist" aspect of Lacan's teaching in its different facets until he switched to the late Lacan in 2005, culminating in 2007/2008 with his series of lectures at Paris 8 University under the title: *Tout le monde est fou* (we are all mad). See Gueguen (2013).
3 Schelling talks of the indivisible remainder, which Zizek (1996) interprets from his reading of the Lacanian position. Boxer challenges this, arguing that Zizek's understanding of Lacan is flawed. https://lacanticles.com/in-which-zizek-misreads-lacan/.
4 The Big-O (Other) of Lacan should not be confused with Bion's "O". While both are wanting to designate something about the unconscious, these concepts are quite different.
5 Restivo (2013) notes that it is in the later writing of Lacan that the idea of the real unconscious emerges.
6 Green, a former Lacanian disciple, argues that Lacan's later reprehensible behaviour towards patients was supported by an understanding of "being true to desire" as pursuing one's own selfish, egotistical wishes for the sake of jouissance. Maybe Lacan himself slurred his own meaning of the nature of desire and its expression. However, as I said in the introduction to this book, I will not pursue the interaction of concept with biography, no matter how compelling, and will have to rest with the notion that Lacan's meaning might be interpreted in different ways.

References

Boxer, P. (2022). 'How Are We to Distinguish a "Repressed Unconscious" from a "Radically Unconscious"?' *Lacanticles*. https://lacanticles.com/how-are-we-to-distinguish-a-repressed-unconscious-from-a-radically-unconscious/ [accessed November 2022].

Chomsky, N. (1957). *Syntactic Structures*. Berlin: Walter de Gruyter GmbH & Co., New York: Mouton and Co.

Dalzell, T. (2022). 'On the Death of God in Lacan – A Nuanced Atheism', *The Heythrop Journal*, vol. 111, pp. 27–34. https://onlinelibrary.wiley.com/doi/epdf/10.1111/heyj.13976

Encyclopedia.com. https://www.encyclopedia.com/psychology/dictionaries-thesauruses-pictures-and-press-releases/signifying-chain [accessed 28 October 2022].

Evans, D. (1996). *An Introductory Dictionary of Lacanian Psychoanalysis*. London: Routledge.

Fazioni, N. (2012). 'Unconscious and Subjectivity: Intersections between Psychoanalysis, Philosophy and Science', *Avello Publishing Journal*, vol. 1, no. 2 The Unconscious, pp. 1–17.

Freud, S. (1900). *The Interpretation of Dreams*. J. Strachey (trans.). Revised by Angela Richards 1976. Pelican Freud Library, vol 4. Harmondsworth: Penguin Books.

Freud, S. (1915a). *Repression*. S.E. vol. 14, pp. 141–158.

Freud, S. (1915b). 'The Unconscious', in J. Strachey (trans. and ed.). *The Standard Edition of the Complete Psychological Works of Sigmund Freud Volume XIV (1914–1916)*. London: Hogarth Press.

Green, A. (1995-6). 'Against Lacanism: A Conversation of Andre Green with Sergio Benvenuto', *The European Journal of Psychoanalysis*, no. 2. Against Lacanism. A conversation of André Green with Sergio Benvenuto – European Journal of Psychoanalysis (journal-psychoanalysis.eu) [accessed March 2024].

Grotstein, J. (2007). *A Beam of Intense Darkness: Wilfred Bion's Legacy to Psychoanalysis*. London: Karnac.

Gueguen, P.-G. (2013). 'Who Is Mad and Who Is Not? On Differential Diagnosis in Psychoanalysis', *Culture/Clinic*, vol. 1, pp. 66–85.

Lacan, J. (1970 [1966]). 'Of Structure as an Inmixing of an Otherness Prerequisite to Any Subject Whatsoever', in R. Macksey and E. Donato (eds.) *The Languages of Criticism and the Sciences of Man: The Structuralist Controversy*. Baltimore: Johns Hopkins Press.

Lacan, J, (1977a). 'The Mirror Stage as Formative of the Function of the I as Revealed in Psychoanalytic Experience' (Initially delivered at the 16th International Congress of Psychoanalysis, Zurich, July 17, 1949), in Allan Sheridan (trans.). *Ecrits: A Selection*, pp. 1–7. London: Tavistock Publications.

Lacan, J. (1977b). 'The Agency of the Letter in the Unconscious or Reason Since Freud' (First written 1957) in Alan Sheridan (trans.). *Ecrits: A Selection*, pp. 146–178. London: Tavistock Publications.

Lacan, J. (1977c). 'A Question Preliminary Any Possible Treatment of Psychosis', in Alan Sheridan (trans.) *Ecrits: A Selection*, pp. 179–225. London: Tavistock Publications.

Lacan, J. (1977d). 'The Subversion of the Subject and the Dialectic of Desire in the Freudian Unconscious', in Alan Sheridan (trans.) *Ecrits: A Selection*, pp. 292–325. London: Tavistock Publications.

Lacan, J. (1977e). 'The Function and Field of Speech and Language in Psychoanalysis', in Alan Sheridan (trans.) *Ecrits: A Selection*, pp. 30–115. London: Tavistock Publications. Taken from the report to the Rome congress in 1953.

Lacan, J. (1988). *The Seminar of Jacques Lacan Book 2 1954–55*. Jacques-Alain Miller (ed.). Cambridge: Cambridge University Press.

Lacan, J. (1992 [1959–1960]). *The Seminar of Jacques Lacan, Book VII: The Ethics of Psychoanalysis*. Jacques-Alain Miller (ed.). London: Tavistock/Routledge.

Lacan, J. (1993 [1981]). *The Seminar of Jacques Lacan Book III 1955–1956: The Psychoses*. Jacques-Alain Miller (ed.). London: Tavistock/Routledge.

Lacan, J. (2002 [1996]-a). 'The Direction of the Treatment and the Principles of Its Power', in Alan Sheridan (trans.) *Écrits: A Selection*, pp. 226–280. London: Tavistock Publications.

Lacan, J. (2002 [1996]-b). 'Response to Jean Hyppolite's Commentary on Freud's "Verneinung"', in Bruce Fink (trans.) *Ecrits: The First Complete Edition in English*. New York: W.W. Norton and Co.

Lacan, J. (2002 [1996]-c). 'The Subversion of the Subject and the Dialectic of Desire in the Freudian Unconscious', in Bruce Fink (trans.) *Écrits: The First Complete Edition in English*. New York: W.W. Norton & Company.

Lacan, J. (2017 [1998]). *The Seminars of Jacques Lacan Book V – Formations of the Unconscious 1957–58*. Cambridge: Polity Press.

Lacan, J. (2021 [1956–57]). Jacques-Alain Miller (trans.) *Book IV – The Object Relation 1956–57*. Cambridge: Polity.

Long, S.D. (1991). 'The Signifier and the Group', *Human Relations*, vol. 44, no. 4, pp. 389–401.

Long, S.D. (2000). 'Engaging the Task: A Socio-anaytic Discussion of Task Presence and Absense', *Socio-Analysis*, vol 2, no. 1, pp. 80–101.

Miller, J.-A. (2017). 'The Real Unconscious', *Lacanian Ink*, vol. 50, pp. 22–41.

Pavón Cuéllar, D. (2009). 'Untying Real, Imaginary and Symbolic: A Lacanian Criticism of Behavioural, Cognitive and Discursive Psychologies', *Annual Review of Critical Psychology*, vol. 7, pp. 33–51. http://www.discourseunit.com/arcp/7.htm

'Slippage of Meaning' (2022). https://www.oxfordreference.com/view/10.1093/oi /authority.20110803100511397 [accessed 27 October 2022].

Restivo, G. (2013). 'Jouissance and the Sexual Reality of the (Wwo) Unconscious', PhD. Thesis Auckland University of Technology. https://openrepository.aut.ac.nz /items/06299f4f-ba74-476e-a7b5-dce3b8f9fc7a

'The Signifying Chain' (n.d.). https://www.encyclopedia.com/psychology/ dictionaries-thesauruses-pictures-and-press-releases/signifying-chain

Ruti, M. and Allen, A. (2019). *Critical Theory between Klein and Lacan: A Dialogue*. New York: Bloomsbury Publishing.

Schelling, F.W.J. (1942). *The Ages of the World*. New York: Columbia University Press.

Schreiber, E., Schreiber, G., Avissar, S. and Halperin, D. (2019). *International Journal of Applied Psychoanalytic Studies*, vol. 16, no. 3, pp. 181–194. https://doi.org/10 .1002/aps.1603

The Dangerous Maybe Website (2021). https://thedangerousmaybe.medium.com/ lacans-borromean-knot-and-the-object-cause-of-desire-3fd580df80b [accessed 02 November 2022].

Zizek, Slavoj. (1996). *The Indivisible Remainder – On Schelling and Related Matters*. New York: Verso.

6 The Unconscious in Social Theory and Research

The twentieth century saw the widespread dissemination of psychoanalytic ideas, certainly in the clinic, but also in social theory. While clinicians continued to develop ideas about the unconscious through clinical practice, it was in the social arena that the concept underwent its more radical changes; or better said, where it was combined with a diverse range of thinking about unconscious processes other than strictly Freudian interpretations. The field of influence from psychoanalysis to other areas is broad, including especially sociology, anthropology, history (Levine 1978) and studies in feminism.

In this chapter, I limit myself to a consideration of some major twentieth-century ideas about the unconscious in society, taking a historical perspective and noting their continued influence. They are what influenced me at the time. Nonetheless, I recognise that psychoanalysts and social theorists have continued to explore the effects of unconscious processes in large systems. For example, the works of Volkan (2004, 2020), Boccara (2014), Scanlon and Adlam (2022), and Brunning and Khaleelee (2021) among many, look at the intergenerational, inter-group and ongoing social effects of unconscious processes. They are part of an ongoing tradition, and to trace their continuing work would require another book. I continue here with a historical perspective, looking at the roots of influence from the social sciences.

Many early social science references were initially complimentary towards the idea of the unconscious (Levine 1978). However, the social sciences, especially American sociology, have had a mixed attitude towards psychoanalytic ideas, especially the unconscious (Rabow 1983). Rabow argues that attempts at combining the two disciplines have often been thwarted by disciplinary chauvinism (ibid, p. 562) and a misunderstanding of psychoanalysis. Some attempts at integration have been more successful, especially in Europe, and work in the discipline of anthropology was, in the mid-twentieth century, perhaps more successful at accepting ideas of the unconscious, if not directly the Freudian unconscious (see, for example, Róheim 1950; Kluckhohn 1957; Levi-Strauss 1969; Robinson 1969). However, some radical and popular American sociologists took the unconscious to heart.

My PhD supervisor, Charles Langley, had done his PhD at Harvard and was always interested in social theory, an interest he shared with me. This

DOI: 10.4324/9781003559818-6

certainly broadened my interest in unconscious processes. I began to see applications of the idea in society.

One idea that has captured the interest of those coming after Freud and that requires the Freudian unconscious for its existence is repression (Freud 1915). Freud insisted that his term *Verdrangung* be translated as repression (Maddox 2006). Many social theorists take that meaning and link it to the idea of social and political repression. Maybe this is a completely different meaning to psychological dynamics; nonetheless, for Freud repression or *Verdrangung* is one of censorship and domination internal to the person. We can see how the social scientists adopted the Freudian idea of repression and linked it to domination. Freud himself drew analogies and metaphors between individual and social developments (Freud 1930). Repression, as perhaps the defence mechanism par excellence, is central to psychoanalysis and to the relation of the conscious to the unconscious (see Chapter 3 on Freud). It is a complex dynamic with vicissitudes of interaction with other defences and acts in quite individual ways under different circumstances (Freud 1915).

Freud did extend his ideas to group and social analysis, and it was from this thinking alongside his metatheory that most of the post-Freudian social theories developed; not all of them strictly psychoanalytic, however defined. And here, from a vast field, I refer to some of the ideas that have most influenced my thinking, while recognising that I am touching just a few strands in a vast fabric of research and thinking.

Whereas Bion and Lacan could be said to stay within the traditional psychoanalytic ethos, albeit with quite radical extensions and interpretations of the Freudian unconscious, many theories from the broader social sciences of the mid-twentieth century began to extend the meaning of unconscious processes away from the individual towards the social field. I am dealing here with this period of history. What is central is that there is a consideration of unconscious processes at societal and cultural levels. While this has become acceptable in the twenty-first century, it was in the twentieth century that some radical thinking emerged.

I explore three main traditional categories of approaches, although grouping these into categories does not do justice to the very rich differences within the categories.

1. The Neo-Freudians.
2. The Frankfurt School.
3. Social scientists, historians and anthropologists.

In my exploration across these categories, I have found: (i) differences in political position vis-à-vis psychoanalysis – by which I mean more conservative or more radical approaches; (ii) differences in philosophical and scientific as well as applied approaches; and (iii) whether or not the theorist is a clinician, field researcher or social scientist (or a mix of these) makes a difference to their approach to the unconscious.

For example, psychiatrist Harry Stack Sullivan, often considered one of the Neo-Freudians, remained conservative in his approach. He saw the unconscious as manifest in the symptomatology of psychiatric conditions at different stages of life and attributed many to problematic interpersonal relationships (Sullivan 1953). His focus on the importance of ego development, and the fact that he often refers to "covert processes" (Sullivan 1953, pp. 176–177) rather than the unconscious, places him among those whom Lacan, perhaps unkindly, scorned as trivialising psychoanalysis (Lacan 1970). As a clinician, Sullivan emphasises the importance of recurring patterns of interpersonal connections and behaviours, many of which are covert and require bringing to the attention of the patient. In Sullivan, we see an unconscious not deeply inherent in humans, but one created through destructive social interactions.

Conversely, Herbert Marcuse, avowedly a utopian visionary from within the Frankfurt School, was a political activist who believed that a hidden message within Freudian psychoanalysis, most often overlooked, was that Freud himself saw the unconscious as holding the answer to human freedom from political and economic domination by a repressive society (Marcuse 1969). In Marcuse, we see an unconscious inherent to humanity, waiting to be freed.

Perhaps both positions (and more) are implicitly in the Freudian unconscious, even in Schelling's unconscious. Both may be part of the rich tapestry that this concept of the unconscious brings us. In the history of this idea, these social thinkers move beyond the intra-psychic to the interpersonal and social constructions already there to be uncovered, remembering that Schelling and Freud talk of issues beyond the individual. That there are observable patterns of symptoms of the unconscious (the unconscious being always an inferred phenomenon, unable to be directly encountered) is not disputed. The nature of the unconscious and how it weaves its effects are always the points of dispute.

Neo-Freudians

The Neo-Freudians were named as such due to their basic agreement with Freudian ideas. However, they each had disagreements with classical psychoanalysis on different fronts. Depending on who you read, different theorists are included in this group. The main names are (i) during Freud's life, Adler, Rank and Jung and later (ii) Sullivan, Horney, Fromm and Erikson. Here, I will not discuss Jung, Rank or Adler. In my opinion, they are not Neo-Freudians. They are not reviving Freud in new ways as do the latter group, but broke with many Freudian ideas during Freud's life to form their own schools of thought. A major reason for their break with Freud was their disagreements with his emphasis on sexual instincts as the prime explanatory principle for the development of the psyche. Jung began to equate libido with general psychic energy (Maddox 2006, p. 96), and Adler, concerned with power, brought forward his ideas on the superiority complex. However, I return to Jung's formulation of the collective unconscious at a later stage.

The main avowed claims and impetus for the Neo-Freudians' differences with Freud were that they disagreed with what they felt was his overemphasis on the childhood sexual aetiology of personality and the importance of the instincts. Social determinations and influences, they believed, had been minimised. Erikson, for example, wished to demonstrate the influence of social factors from childhood through to later in life. He is well known for his work on the different stages in life from infancy until old age, showing how navigating different psycho-social concerns is vital for development throughout life (Erikson 1950, 1968). Horney, a German-born psychoanalyst who in adulthood moved to the United States, meeting and working with Fromm and Stack Sullivan, spoke of "basic anxiety" as fundamental to humans living in a hostile environment. Neurosis, she argues, is a somewhat normal response to social conditions. Strategies are developed that avoid this anxiety by moving towards, moving away from and moving against others (Horney 1946). She was an early critic of Freud's ideas on feminine sexuality (Horney 1967), arguing for the idea of male envy of woman's capacity to give birth.

Fromm developed the idea that personality was formed through two major needs: the need for freedom and the need for belonging (Fromm 1941). Although often considered with the other American Neo-Freudians, he fits better in the Frankfurt School and is discussed there. Harry Stack Sullivan, a highly influential American psychiatrist, is of interest for his work with schizophrenia, believing that sufferers could be worked with and that the condition was the result of disturbances in interpersonal relations, especially in childhood (Sullivan 1953). He regarded the social environment as critical to development, citing the work of George Herbert Mead and anthropologist Malinowski, and he collaborated with social scientists such as Edward Sapir, known for his work on the relation of language to culture (Sapir 1927; 1949).

Criticisms of the Neo-Freudians are that they moved away from the analysis of the instincts with a focus on the body to a focus on the ego, and although keeping to notions of the unconscious, did so superficially (for example, see Adorno's and Marcuse's criticism of Fromm and other so-called "revisionists" described in McLaughlin 1999; and criticism by Brown 1959). Otto Fenichel, a supporter of the politicisation of psychoanalysis who at first welcomed the ideas of social influence brought by these analysts, later became a strong critic through the International Psychoanalytic Association (IPA). His criticisms were based both on grounds of what he regarded as the unscientific theoretical revisions made by the Neo-Freudians and what he saw as their conservative politics, calling them "pseudo-leftists and psychoanalytic right-wingers" (Harris and Brock 1992, p. 611; Jacoby 1986). This criticism is perhaps unfair, as they each kept to ideas of the importance of the repressed unconscious with its links to social factors. And they did bring a much-needed focus on the social environment with links to other social sciences at a time in history when large social changes were taking place. Also, it is unfair to coalesce them together as if there were no real differences in their work and theories. Sullivan, for instance, kept strongly to Freudian ideas of the childhood aetiology of mental illness and the return of the unconscious in symptomatology (Sullivan 1953; McLaughlin 1999); while Fromm was interested in large social phenomena and objected to being put into such an ill-distinguished category as a Neo-Freudian. But controversy has never been new to the followers of psychoanalysis, and this was the time of flight for many analysts from Nazi Germany to America; political views were strong. Horney, for example, left the IPA.

Among this group of Neo-Freudians, Erich Fromm is perhaps of most interest to the study of the development of the unconscious as an idea, given his introduction of the term "the social unconscious". He became a central part of the Frankfurt School.

But before moving on, I should perhaps mention Wilhelm Reich, a student of Freud who developed the reading of emotional expression and studied the manifestation of the unconscious through an understanding of what he called vegetative or Orgone currents; Orgone energy being "discovered" from Reich's interest in the free energy of the orgasm (Simonian 2011). In contrast to Freud's depiction of the id energies (the instincts) as "a cauldron full of seething excitations" needing to be tamed (Freud in Robinson 1969, p. 24), Reich regarded these energies as wholesome, with the problem being a sexually repressed society (Robinson 1969). He attempted to carefully examine the way his patients held their bodies, how their musculature reacted and developed "character armour"; hence his naming it "character analysis". In an interview with Kurt Eissler in 1952 (edited by Higgins and Raphael in 1967), he says,

> Psychoanalysis, as you well know, works with words and unconscious ideas. These are its tools. According to Freud, as I understood him, as he published it, the unconscious can be brought out as far back as the *Wortvorstellungen* (verbal ideas) when the word images were formed. In other words, psychoanalysis cannot penetrate beneath or beyond the second or third year of life... Now character analysis developed the reading of emotional expression. Whereas Freud opened up the world of the unconscious mind, thoughts, desires and so on, I succeeded in reading emotional expressions. Until then we couldn't "read the mind". We could only connect verbal associations.
>
> (Reich in Higgins and Raphael 1967, pp. 1–2)

In the interview, he proceeds, perhaps improperly, to analyse Freud's personal emotions and physical symptoms in terms of his own extension of libido theory: vegetative or Orgone energy. This energy, he claims, is directly observable evidence of the unconscious.

As a student of psychoanalysis in the 1970s, I was told to avoid Reich as a crank: a believer in many unscientific practices. Jailed for refusing to obey a court order in association with his Orgone boxes and his claims about their effectiveness,[1] he died in prison. He is mentioned here because his ideas have informed many more recent practices in body therapies and bioenergetics. Whether or not these practices have sound foundations is not of concern here. But the idea of the unconscious as expressed through bodily phenomena persists. Certainly, in classical psychoanalysis the presence of hysterical conversion symptoms is strongly documented, and the physical manifestations of anxiety and depression are well known. But Reich's ideas of energy and body take the formulation of the unconscious much further away from its grounding in repressed ideation. For Reich, the unconscious is caught up physically in the bodily armour that defends against sensations and sexuality. Along with Marcuse (1955) and Brown (1959), he advocates for the reduction, even the abolition, of the repression of sexuality through changes in social restrictions. However, Brown sees Reich as misguided, not for his vision of a non-repressive culture, but because Reich becomes fixated on genital sexuality rather than the repressed forms of infantile sexuality and their instinctual expressions (Brown 1959, pp. 140–141).

Frankfurt School

> Originally located at the Institute for Social Research (*Institut für Sozialforschung*), an attached institute at the Goethe University in Frankfurt, Germany. The Institute was founded in 1923 thanks to a donation by Felix Weil with the aim of developing Marxist studies in Germany. After 1933, the Nazis forced its closure, and the Institute was moved to the United States where it found hospitality at Columbia University in New York City.
>
> (Internet Encyclopedia of Philosophy 2023)

This school of thought and research is now known as "critical theory",[2] and since the influence of Erich Fromm and encouragement by Horkheimer, has combined psychoanalytic thinking with Marxist ideas. Due to the influence of Fromm,[3] the school became increasingly devoted to empirical studies and the influence of psychoanalytic thinking on social change – perhaps culminating in the eyes of those psychoanalytic thinkers, in the study led by Adorno et al. (1950)[4] post the Nazi era – the authoritarian personality (1950). While the study of large social systems was the major interest of the Frankfurt School, this was a study of a personality type, not a study of the state of totalitarianism. Nonetheless, it has since had much influence on social psychology and personality studies, not least in the adoption of the F scale, a questionnaire aimed at identifying fascist thinking and associated personality traits (F scale; Adorno et al. 1950).

As with many schools of thought and research, the Frankfurt School split into two during its years in the United States. Horkheimer and Adorno, with their group, returned to Germany in the 1950s, although Adorno continued work in the United States from time to time.

My concern here is with the ways in which the Frankfurt School members conceptualised the unconscious. Marx had originally spoken of the consciousness of different classes, about themselves and their place in the world (Marx 1992; initially 1867). This has become known by Marxist students as "class consciousness", followed by the term derived from Marxist theory – "false consciousness": a state of being where the conscious mind is dominated by the ideologies of the dominant ruling classes. But false consciousness is not so much an idea of the unconscious as of a manufactured consciousness for the purposes of oppression; an oppression where the apparatuses of the state (and associated ideologies) both infiltrate the mind of subjects of the state and reproduce themselves within society in an ongoing way (Althusser 1970).

Much of the philosophy of the Frankfurt School lay in the analysis of society in terms of the dynamics of domination and the need for social change. Essentially, they were Marxists who wished to revisit Marxist ideas considering more recent societal changes, although how each member defined Marxism differed to a smaller or greater degree. Horkheimer led a group who were critical of the ways in which capitalism has led not to a more equitable society, but to one of division, inequalities, destructiveness and domination of the many by the few: that is, a repressive society (repression here being an aspect of social domination). Hence, the name critical theory which derives from dialectic thinking – the exposure of contradictions within; in this case, within advanced society – and from there to bring about change.

The Frankfurt School is using the idea of repression mostly in a different way from the Freudian idea of repression[5] applied in theories of psychopathology. Here, repression is equivalent to social domination. Such repression is linked to a lack of awareness of this by the socially repressed. The repressive forces are intimately linked into the social fabric. Unawareness understood as unconscious is different from the dynamic repression described within psychoanalysis. Or is it? How are they linked? The lifting of repression in its different and especially its destructive forms is regarded as central.

Erich Fromm

Erich Fromm was invited to the Frankfurt School by Horkheimer, who saw Freudian psychoanalysis as a way of attempting to understand why social domination had not led to widespread revolt and the collapse of capitalism.

Fromm blended the ideas of both Freud and Marx, creating a compromise between the Freudian emphasis on the unconscious, biological drives and repression (seemingly, the belief that character is determined by biology), and Marx's belief that people are a product of their society, particularly the economic systems therein.

> Fromm's theory was no mere derivative, however; he added the revolutionary concept of freedom to these deterministic systems, granting

people the ability to transcend the various determinisms described by Freud and Marx. To Fromm, freedom was central to human nature.
(Journal Psyche https://journalpsyche.org/
eric-fromm-social-unconscious)

Fromm sees the difficulty in freedom being its implications of individual responsibility and isolation. Humans attempt to escape from this, he argues, by joining with authoritarian systems in thoughtless conformity. Such systems attempt to aggressively destroy an "otherness" that is felt persecutory. But often this destructiveness is turned inward into self-destructive behaviours. These escapes from freedom are ultimately alienating, Fromm argues, as freedom is central to humanity (Fromm 1941). It is this unthinking, unconscious conformity that is the problem for the mass of the population.

Fromm shows some of the limitations of traditional psychoanalysis. McLaughlin (2017) illustrates this, saying,

> the great conceit of psychoanalysis is also its core night-mare, namely, that many clinicians operate in the belief (at least implicitly) that it is possible to heal the world without dealing head on, and in political and structural ways, with the enormous inequality, market fundamentalism, xenophobia, patriarchal structures, and militaristic and colonial-racist realities and histories that shape people's lives. It was Fromm's great contribution to psychoanalysis to challenge this obvious untruth.
>
> (McLaughlin 2017, p. 432)

In his joining of Freudian and Marxist ideas, Fromm coined the term "social unconscious", claiming that: "each society determines which thoughts and feelings shall be permitted to arrive at the level of awareness and which have to remain unconscious. Just as there is a social character, there is also a 'social unconscious'" (Fromm 1962, chapter IX p. 1). Chapter 7 looks more closely at the ideas of the social unconscious.

Herbert Marcuse

While Fromm had revised the Freudian idea of instincts to emphasise a social influence, Herbert Marcuse, a critic of Fromm in this regard, revisited psychoanalytic instinct theory, looking to both this and social influence as partial determinants of character. Marcuse accepts the Freudian idea of a repressed unconscious both at the individual and the societal level. While not abandoning much of Freudian psychoanalysis, he argues that there is a hidden trend. While Freud's picture is of a civilisation bought at the expense of instinctual pleasures, where the pleasure principle gives way to the reality principle and small gains in pleasure are found through sublimation (Freud 1930), Marcuse sees a crack in what he considers too pessimistic a view. He argues that Freud made it his task to bring forward the memories hidden in the unconscious

through psychoanalysis, and that even while describing the repressive functions of civilisation, he, Freud:

> upholds the tabooed aspirations of humanity: the claim for a state where
> freedom and necessity coincide. Whatever liberty exists in the realm of
> the developed consciousness, and in the world it has created, is only
> derivative, compromised freedom, gained at the expense of the full sat-
> isfaction of needs.
>
> Conversely, the unconscious, the deepest and oldest layer of the men-
> tal personality, is the drive for integral gratification, which is absence of
> want and repression. As such it is the immediate identity of necessity
> and freedom. According to Freud's conception the equation of freedom
> and happiness tabooed by the conscious is upheld by the unconscious.
> Its truth, although repelled by consciousness, continues to haunt the
> mind; it preserves the memory of past stages of individual development
> at which integral gratification is obtained. And the past continues to
> claim the future: it generates the wish that the paradise be re-created on
> the basis of the achievements of civilization.
>
> (Marcuse 1955, p. 3)

In bringing together Freudian and Marxist ideas as part of the Frankfurt
School, he attempts to demonstrate how instinctual life, unconscious due to
societal and institutional repression, can be released in a non-repressive social
order, an implication he believes is hidden in Freud's work.

> Marcuse's book *Eros and Civilization: A Philosophical Inquiry into Freud*
> is a response to the pessimism of Freud's *Civilization and Its Discontents*
> (1930 [1961]). Freud's book paints a bleak picture of the evolution of
> civilization as the evolution of greater and greater repression from which
> there seems to be no escape. The death and life instincts are engaged
> in a battle for dominance with no clear winner in sight. According to
> Marcuse, Freud fails to develop the emancipatory possibility of his own
> theory. Marcuse's task is two-fold. First, he must show that human
> instincts or drives are not merely biological and fixed, but also social,
> historical, and malleable. Secondly, he must show that repressive soci-
> ety also produces the possibility of the abolition of repression (Marcuse
> 1955: 5).
>
> (Stanford Encyclopedia of Philosophy 2024)

In his argument, Marcuse creates an extension of the idea of repression, naming his idea "surplus repression". In this, he distinguishes the biological basis
of the instincts from the social. *Basic repression* refers to the type of repression
or modification of the instincts that is necessary "for the perpetuation of the
human race in civilization" (Marcuse 1955, p. 35). This is necessary repression

and civilisation depends upon it (Marcuse 1979). Yet, Marcuse argues that society employs more repressive force than is necessary. *Surplus repression* refers to "the restrictions necessitated by social domination" (Marcuse 1955, p. 35). Surplus repression controls and shapes the instincts such that they meet the needs of a ruling class over and above the human need to survive. Moreover, this surplus repression unconsciously creates greater societal aggression (surplus aggression) in response (Marcuse 1977).

Taking Freud's notion of the reality principle, he states that the prevailing form of the reality principle is found in performance – within the forms of production following Marx.

> The performance principle, which is that of an acquisitive and antagonistic society in the process of constant expansion, presupposes a long development during which domination has been increasingly rationalized: control over social labour now reproduces society on a large scale and under improving conditions. For a long way, the interests of domination and the interests of the whole coincide: the profitable utilization of the productive apparatus fulfills the needs and faculties of individuals. For the vast majority of the population, the scope and mode of satisfaction are determined by their own labour; but their labour is work for an apparatus which they do not control, which operates as an independent power to which individuals must submit if they want to live. And it becomes the more alien the more specialized the division of labour becomes. Men do not live their own lives but perform pre-established functions. While they work, they do not fulfill their own needs and faculties but work in *alienation*.
>
> (Marcuse 1955, p. 45, quoted in Stanford
> Encyclopedia of Philosophy 2024)

Marcuse strives to capture the psychological processes underlying the acceptance of surplus repression, much as Zizek will do later in discussing the false promises deep within societal/political ideologies. His analysis sees highly sophisticated systems of domination that are in place through social institutions. Jauhiainen (2023) considers the complexity and intransigence of Marcuse's idea in current-day form:

> In the era of global capitalism, the main problem may no longer be the repression of subjects by their rulers, but a problem of an intricate, worldwide system of complex, systematic oppression. Western lifestyle presently relies on cheap, displaced labour. If oppressed factory workers refused to toil for the gratification of the privileged minority, the system of production and consumption would suffer significant losses. Likewise, if capitalism collapsed or the privileged minority decided they no longer

needed to constantly update their wardrobes and smart gadgets, many factory workers would lose their livelihood.

(Jauhiainen 2023 online article)

Humans are alienated without recognising their alienation, or perhaps even when recognising it as such, they are inveigled into it systematically. He recognises the advances of modern technology and the possibilities they offer for an equitable society, but deplores the actual direction taken as the processes of domination insidiously continue. This paradox, Marcuse sees as a basic question for the Frankfurt School's multidisciplinary group (Marcuse 1964, 1977). Despite technological advances and the increased liberal thinking of the Enlightenment and beyond, how is it that human destructiveness increases?

Bringing Freud to Marxist ideas, alienation for Marcuse is as much alienation from basic nature and its sexuality as from economic and political democracy. In looking to the instinctual basis of life, he distinguishes between true and false needs; the former being the realities of a good existence, the latter being indoctrinated through a repressive society; false needs are engendered to keep feeding ongoing production processes, themselves disguised as leading to new but false freedoms.

> The criterion for free choice can never be an absolute one, but neither is it entirely relative. Free election of masters does not abolish the masters or the slaves. Free choice among a wide variety of goods and services does not signify freedom if these goods and services sustain social controls over a life of toil and fear-that is, if they sustain alienation. And the spontaneous reproduction of superimposed needs by the individual does not establish autonomy; it only testifies to the efficacy of the controls.
>
> (Marcuse 1964, p. 10)

That economic and political repression has existed through history, he accepts and believes it necessary to understand why, when technology has reached a high degree of development, this issue of human alienation (from nature, from the liberation of thought, from the inequality of the distribution of resources) still occurs and perhaps grows. He saw the current society of his day – mid-twentieth century – as one where destructiveness and death instincts (Thanatos) dominate over life instincts (Eros). This occurs through a process of ideological, political and economic dynamics expressed through corporations and everyday life such as television and advertising. The working classes – the hope for revolution in early Marxism – have been incorporated into the social system of insidious domination. There is a "'voluntary servitude' (voluntary inasmuch as it is introjected into the individuals)" that justifies dominating social practices and institutions (Marcuse 1969, p. 15). What looks like greater democratic practices through dispersed shareholding and wider voting rights in Western governments – the promise of a more socialistic culture – is misleading (Marcuse 1977).

He states that the capitalist mode of production has had a profound influence not only on conscious thinking and attitudes but also on unconscious thinking. For example, he says that the ideologies of the dominant forces in society are so entrenched in language that it is difficult to articulate criticism in the readily understandable language of popular culture. However, he does see good literature as pointing a path towards liberation through the use of imagination. Moreover, claiming that societal repression has been primarily patriarchal repression, he looks to the feminisation of culture as a way forward (Marcuse 1977). Ever hopeful, he saw in the student revolts of the late 1960s the possibility of a rift with the establishment. His thesis is that by strengthening the life instincts, change for the better could be achieved.

Marcuse shows himself as a systemic thinker who identifies many of the societal problems still with us today.

Social Scientists and Historians

The theories discussed in this section are strongly linked to the idea of repression as enacted socially. Their proponents are critics, primarily of Western society, the growth of selfish individualism and, paradoxically, the loss of personal agency due to unconscious social determinism and social control, whether external or through an incorporated super-ego. In line with the radical ideas of Marcuse, Brown speaks of the possibilities of freeing libido from its societal repression. Slater sees Western societies leading to alienation and loneliness. While also uncovering these problems, Rieff argues that through a process of desacralisation, the basis for meaningful social relations is lost and aggressive impulses go uncontained. Through these theories, unconscious instincts and their expression are regarded as either too strongly repressed or not held in the right balance, with the implication that there is a good balance, if only we can find it. The theories discussed are just a sample of the thinking occurring mid-twentieth century: the time following World War II, the growth of women's liberation and the so-called sexual revolution. The unconscious becomes not so much a place to be feared as a social phenomenon to be explored.

Norman O. Brown

Following the transference ideas of Freud, Brown argues that the unconscious can only become conscious by being repeated. Hence the subtitle of his book *Life Against Death* being "the psychoanalytic meaning of history" (Brown 1959). Understanding historical events, even as they happen, is fraught (Stannard 1980). Much of the past is interpreted through the lens of present ideas. While individual therapy consists of analysing the repetitions exposed in neurotic symptoms – the return of the repressed – and bringing these to consciousness, Brown similarly regards culture as basically a return of the repressed for humanity, through time. Just as in the psychoanalytic encounter, the repressed becomes conscious through the repetitions in transference love or hate, Brown says, "repetition in real life is the pre-condition for re-establishing contact between consciousness and the unconscious" (Brown 1959, p. 145). This is established through transference as "an act of love" (Brown 1959, p. 146) and thus it may be said that the repressed unconscious becomes conscious through "projections onto the external world" (Brown 1959, p. 154).

> The repressed unconscious can become conscious only by being transformed into an external perception, by being projected. According to Freud, the mythological conception of the universe, which survives even in the most modern religions, is only psychology projected onto the outer world. Not just mythology but the entirety of culture is a projection. In the words of Spender, "The world which we create – the world of slums and telegrams and newspapers – is a kind of language of our inner wishes and thoughts".
>
> (Brown 1959, p. 170)

From here, he argues that culture is the result of the "repressed" as projected onto the world. Moreover, to gain insight into what is repressed, we must read it from that world.

> If we retain the original insight that reenactment is a prerequisite for gaining consciousness of the repressed unconscious, we must suppose that there is no direct channel of communication between consciousness and the repressed unconscious, with the result that the repressed unconscious energies must go out into external reality before they can be perceived by consciousness.
>
> (Brown 1959, p. 148)

In moving towards a position arguing for freeing Eros from the problematic repetitions of history, he explores what he sees as contradictions within Freud's ideas of Eros and Thanatos. For example, Freud, he says, inconsistently distinguishes between object-love and identification[6] (Brown 1959, chapter iv) and that in the Freudian view of mourning, the loved lost object becomes introjected and incorporated into the ego such that the subject identifies with the lost object, thus having the relation of both love and identification. Such is the fate of the brothers in the myth of the primal horde. Thus, for Brown, object-love and identification are two forms of eros based on the initial pleasures of infantile sexuality. Freudian psychoanalysis, he further argues, regards this infantile polymorphous perverse sexuality as maturing into adult genital sexuality, although the repressed trends continue to exist unconsciously. While Brown agrees that infantile sexuality is repressed, he regards this formulation as misguided because, he argues, genital sexuality is based on a negation of earlier forms rather than a maturation; it is a defence brought about by the strictures of the super-ego and culture.

Brown argues that life and death instincts propel their expression into the world and its cultures; a world that he defines as created by "the disease called man" (Brown 1959, chapter 1), noting how the instincts become both projected into, and repressed by, culture. Freud, he says, provides the answer of sublimation to the problems of culture's expression of destruction and sexuality. But for Brown, sublimation is not the answer but provides a further repression of the instincts, leading them into further subjugation: the ultimate defence against the instincts. I quote him here:

> The basic characteristic of sublimation is the desexualisation of sexual energy by its redirection towards new objects. But as we have seen desexualisation is disembodiment. New objects must substitute for the human body and there is no sublimation without the projection of the human body into things; the dehumanization of man is his alienation of his own body.
>
> (Brown 1959, p 281)

Whereas sublimation into artistic objects might, at times, be a somewhat satisfactory but limited solution, sublimation into the objects of greedy acquisition and power leads to destructive forces. Brown puts forward an alternative to sublimation: the abolition of repression in culture. He says,

> Human consciousness can be liberated from the parental (oedipal) complex only by being liberated from its cultural derivatives: the paternalistic state and the patriarchal god.
>
> (Brown 1959, p. 155)

Often compared with the work of Marcuse,[7] it must be noted that in this formulation of repression, Brown is referring to that repression common to humanity in the form of the Oedipal complex – the shaping of the psyche through subjection to the social restrictions embedded in the super-ego, not simply to political repression.

His argument is that there is a need to return to the sensuous body, the polymorphous sexuality of childhood – to a world where eros is in the lived relation to reality rather than in an attempted domination of reality. A perhaps impossible task, he understands human life as a continuous recreation (Brown 1966) and that history may not always have to be endless repetition.

No wonder that both the ideas of Brown and Marcuse became an underpinning for the student rebellions of the late 1960s and the counter-culture movement of the 1960s and 1970s. Brown's analysis, in turn, leads towards the relation of religion to the unconscious: a patriarchal god is part of the problem of societal repression. For Freud, the institution of religion is a defence against reality. An implication from Brown is that religious sentiment is derived from an externalisation of eros into a sublimated object; that Freud saw religion for what it was but was unable to find a way past this.

Philip Slater

Slater is another sociological thinker who takes the idea of unconscious dynamics into the social arena. His interest is in groups and their cohesive and regressive dynamics; in the libidinal connections in groups and their evolution (Slater 1966). He follows Freud insofar as Freud indicates that eros, or libidinal and life instincts, have the ultimate aim of bringing people together (Freud 1930, 1940). But he is not satisfied with Freud's descriptions of Eros and Thanatos, which seem to him too vague, and he renames them as libidinal diffusion and libidinal contraction: that is, libidinal impulses towards or away from others; more simply perhaps, the desire to be part of a collective and the desire to move away. He takes from Franz Alexander these impulses as trends towards greater and lesser organisations and thus argues for two different trends: libidinal diffusion as a movement towards group cohesion and libidinal contraction as a move away (Slater 1963). Examining three different types of libidinal withdrawal from groups, Slater names "social anxiety" as the response to the social regression involved (Slater 1963, p. 342). This anxiety becomes institutionalised in methods of social control that keep people in collectives, preventing a move away, or manage the tendencies for such social regression in socially approved ways – such as the acceptance of dyadic relationship withdrawals from the group to marriage and the creation of new families. Socialisation, he argues, is the way in which social control holds society together, against the pulls of social regression:

> What is insufficiently recognized is that the socialization process almost invariably guarantees that impulse control is not based entirely on the reality principle, but is firmly grounded in a socially manipulable, non-rational basis. Some of the ego's controlling functions must atrophy in order to permit the essentially competitive social institutions-whether in the ancient version of external authorities or the more sophisticated form of an internalized superego-to operate. For social control is more homogeneous, more consistent from person to person than individual, rational control. It permits a smooth predictability in the affairs of men.
> (Slater 1963, p. 346)

While the renaming of Eros and Thanatos, I believe, acts as a withdrawal from the dynamic power of these instincts and their unconscious manifestations that are broader than Slater's reformulations, his emphasis on the strength of attraction towards social life partially retrieves his work. For Slater (1970), humans have a need for dependency and community: as described above, this is a biological imperative at a libidinal level.[8] Taking a lead from Fromm's ideas in *Escape from Freedom* (Fromm 1941), which he cites in his own popular book *The Pursuit of Loneliness*, Slater examines American society, finding that its emphasis on individualism, competition and careerism is leading to psychologically isolated loners – a threat to both the people and the wider society. Although in this book he refers to libidinal repression as part of the picture, it is his work with groups that is more directly psychoanalytic. This, and his book *Microcosm: Structural, Psychological and Religious Evolution in Groups* (1966), indicate his emphasis on repression as a psycho-social phenomenon with unconscious dynamics operating at a social level.

This latter book influenced me during the 1970s when my own PhD studies were gestating, and I was studying student groups (Long 1992). It is based on Slater's study of small groups in a laboratory setting at Harvard, as well as training and therapy groups, somewhat akin to the therapy and study groups of Bion and those that formed the basis of academic small-group study (for example, Bennis and Shepard 1956; Hartmann and Gibbard 1974). Using the close study of group behaviour and dialogue, he traces the unconscious libidinal vicissitudes of developing group structures (as he says, in microcosm). Extrapolating to broader societal and religious themes – the deification of leaders, the revolt against dependency upon them, the symbolism of cannibalism, the importance of boundary and differentiation – he traces these as group developmental ideas in an evolutionary context. In particular, he takes Freud's story of the murder of the primal father, finding it a systemic rather than historical event:

> As we shall see, the correspondences between the group revolt and Freud's primal horde myth are quite elaborate, suggesting the possibility that the latter reflects a systemic process rather than an historical event.
>
> (Slater 1966, p. 4)

Referring both to his studies and to myths throughout history, the group, he says, can develop from unconscious collusion to conscious deliberative action.

> In order to increase consciousness, libido is invested in the leader or other individual (or subgroup) and then taken back. Such a person is not only permitted but encouraged to be narcissistic in ways that normally are negatively sanctioned. There seems to be a feeling that this withdrawal and hoarding of libido on the part of the leader will ultimately confer a boon on the collectivity...This seems to me to be one of the most essential meanings of the primal horde myth.
>
> (Slater 1966, p. 250)

This is a chilling analysis when applied to the rise of right-wing extremist politics in many countries in the twenty-first century. In reading Slater, we find the development of group consciousness emerging from initial unconscious collusion. He sees in human history the story writ large, of the tension found in smaller groups, between the need for community and dependency and that of autonomy. But especially his interest in how humans in groups can come to a true democracy. Much of this can be seen as heir to Freud's work on groups (1921, 1940) and Bion (1961) regarding the group as a whole having unconscious dynamics. His work demonstrates his strong belief in democracy despite, or perhaps because of, his critique that the United States has moved into more authoritarian ways of being (Slater 1992). His analysis of the evolutionary process of the creation of narcissistic leaders is relevant for the twenty-first century and how we today might learn lessons from this.

Philip Rieff

Philip Rieff (1966, 1979), also noting societal repression, felt that Freudian theory undermined the morally based repression that society requires to maintain civility and its high culture.

The super-ego contains the conscience, often harsh and unforgiving. In individuals, it is formed from strict imperatives – what Philip Rieff calls an interdictory authority; an authority of the parent, whose interdicts are experienced as harsh even if the actual parent is less stringent. Think of the infant who bursts into tears at a reprimand, perhaps given for its own safety – "don't touch that!" Rieff analyses the nature of authority in societies. Different forms of authority emerge in the overall system. The interdictory authority may be softened by a remissive authority. The remissive authority forgives the mistakes. It doesn't abolish the interdictory authority but ameliorates its harshness. However, challenging the interdictory authority is the more rebellious transgressive authority. This transgresses the interdicts and may, in turn, introduce new ones. Thus, there is a dance of authority. Some interdicts may become perverse. In the dance of perverse institutional interdicts and the individuals who take up either remissive or transgressive positions, the outcome is scapegoating – along the lines discussed by René Girard. The interdicts become harsh, the remissive position is taken by accomplices and the transgressive by the whistle-blower. In some sense, each of these roles needs the others for the dance to continue, as it must, and each is linked to conscience even if mistaken and harsh. This is like the dance of the bully, the victim and the saviour. And very often, the same people can take up different roles. The bully may become a victim, and the saviour a bully during relentless legal and political struggles.

But the super-ego also contains the ego-ideal. This is that part of the psyche that presents us with an ideal towards which we may strive, with which we would like to identify. While the primitive experiences of interdictory authority are ultimately tied to conscience and are about the dynamics of love and hate, the dynamics of the ego-ideal are about identification, belonging and a striving for meaning, attainment and industry.

(See 1959 commentary at https://www.commentary.org/articles/richard -peters/freud-the-mind-of-the-moralist-by-philip-rieff/.)

Christopher Lasch

I remember eagerly buying and reading Lasch's book *The Culture of Narcissism* (1980) because the title resonated strongly with me. The culture I was living in seemed to be becoming more selfish and less meaningful. Consumerism was growing, and I was feeling, and later wrote about, many of the issues of which he speaks (Long 1999). In the same vein as Rieff, Lasch argues that the "therapeutic" has infiltrated culture to such an extent that it is not seen for the dominating force that it has become.

> The psychoanalytic profession may have fallen on hard times, but a ther-apeutic sensibility is diffused even more widely than it was in 1966 when Phillip Rieff brought out his second book, aptly entitled *The Triumph of the Therapeutic*. Today the therapeutic has triumphed so completely that Rieff sees little hope of challenging it.
>
> (Lasch 1996, p. 219)

And it seems by this time in the late twentieth century, the idea of the uncon-scious in the sociological analysis of Lasch is more implicit than explicitly argued. It is clear that Lasch has read and agreed with much of Fromm, Rieff and Marcuse (Lasch 1977). The infiltration of unconscious conformism in a narcissistic consumerist society is basic to his ideas. No institution within Western society is seen unaffected: the family; academia; the arts; industry; reli-gion (or what might be left of it). Modernity is more than the "double-edged phenomenon"[9] of providing new comforts along with the increasing military and environmental destructiveness noted by Giddens (1990). Insidiously, the new rulers are "the elites" (Lasch 1996) who have control over multinationals, the media and marketing, leading to the production of desire. The erosion of true democracy is evident for Lasch.

> The general course of recent history no longer favors the levelling of social distinctions but runs more and more in the direction of a two-class society in which the favored few monopolize the advantages of money, education and power.
>
> (Lasch 1996, p. 29)

This seems prescient in the face of recent Western politics where splits between the "haves" and the "have nots" are evident.

Levi-Strauss and Structuralism

For Levi-Strauss, a French anthropologist, cultural structure (learned behav-iours and ideas) is an expression of the hidden structure of the human mind, not from some external reality. He is seen as the father of structuralism, a loosely defined movement within anthropology and other social sciences (Rossi 1973). According to de George and de George (1972), structuralism is a conviction that surface events and phenomena are to be explained by structures, data and phenomena below the surface. The explicit and obvious is to be explained by and is determined – in some sense of the term – by what is implicit and not obvious.

(p. xii)

These editors name Marx, Freud and de Saussure as foundational to the movement and note that the authors included in their book *The Structuralists from Marx to Levi-Strauss* while demonstrating this conviction, have never necessarily linked themselves together under the umbrella of structuralism (see also Ehrmann 1970). Foucault and Lacan, for example, deny being classed under this rubric. Nonetheless, the term and its general meaning have remained. Structuralism is concerned with the relations between, rather than within, individual components and shows the hidden structures beneath everyday living (see, for example, Sapir 1949).

Influenced by Freud, Marx and de Saussure, Levi-Strauss looks for codes that lead to unconscious structuring. Apparent reality, he argues, has a hidden dimension that requires decoding. In his thorough study of myths and their variants from different villages across different countries, he creates a way of discerning their structure, not from the surface appearance of the myth but from structurally analysing their content into constituent parts, much as linguists analyse language into constituent parts. And just as with language, a speaker does not have to have knowledge of the constituent parts of grammar or phonetics to be able to speak fluently, humans proceed to develop myths without conscious knowledge of their constituent parts, which they nonetheless produce time and again across cultures. He says,

The true constituent units of a myth are not the isolated relations but *bundles of such relations* and it is only as bundles that these relations can be put to use and combined so as to produce a meaning.

(Levi-Strauss 1955, p. 175)

He found myths from quite disparate parts of the world to have common structures (Levi-Strauss 1969), and finds that linguistic phenomena, as well as all other social phenomena, are "the projection, on the level of conscious and socialized thought, of universal laws which regulate the unconscious activities of the mind" (Levi-Strauss 1969, p. 28).

He has questioned the adequacy of the empiricist method insofar as it claims to reach reality only through sensory perceptions and rejects the phenomenological and existentialist methods insofar as they maintain that reality can be reached through our conscious experience without offering any guarantee against the illusions of subjectivity.

(Rossi 1973, p. 22)

Rossi claims this as a Kantian approach to the unconscious: saying that he – Levi-Strauss – works on the ideas of biological constraints to the structuration of the unconscious and sees the symbolic level of culture as unconscious. In this conceptualisation of unconscious activity, Levi-Strauss shares the perspective of an unconscious beyond conscious access put forward by Freud and Lacan. It is structured into the very constitution of humanity and becomes evident through a commonality (although not an absolute identity) between myth, language and music (Levi-Strauss 1969). It is not my concern here that the linguistics of Roman Jakobson and de Saussure[10] and the subsequent theorising of Levi-Strauss based on them have been subjected to much criticism, as indicated even when I was first reading (Leach 1970). My interest is in the impact that they had on the evolution of the idea of the unconscious as a deeply structural aspect of the mind. Tambun (2023), for example, argues that despite post-structural-ist criticisms, the theory of Levi-Strauss forms the basis of modern management theories, including Edgar Schein's popular theory of organisational dynamics, indicated by three levels of organisational culture, with the deepest uncon-scious level being underlying assumptions (Schein 2010). I would argue that, along with psychoanalytic ideas, the systems thinking of the structuralists has infiltrated much of modern systems psychodynamic theory, though I have not found much literature that acknowledges this directly. The influence is perhaps best seen in the work reported in the *Journal of Psychosocial Studies.*

This chapter has strayed down many paths, perhaps with too strong a focus on American mid-century formulations of the unconscious. Such was the influence of these authors on an Australian student in the mid- to late-twen-tieth century. The unconscious has taken a form derived from the Freudian idea – perhaps inherent in the work of Freud but not there elaborated – and now married to thinking about culture and society more broadly, especially the post–World War II hopes for a better future, and yet also despairs about narcissism, consumerism and a loss of meaning once found in religion. The therapeutic hope is regarded as somewhat misguided by many of these authors and is hijacked, they say, by the unconscious fabrication of desires: the thera-pists and clinicians just a part of this, providing band-aids for a sick society.

Early in my career as a psychoanalytic therapist, these authors disturbed me. I was keen to help children and families through therapeutic methods, but I also now more fully recognised the social conditions and structures that locked many into a dysfunctional life. Later, my work as an organisational consultant took cognisance of the social and cultural conditions that both contain and constrain organisation members. What place might free choice have with such conditions and structures, and what constraints are put on it, if it even exists?

Notes

1 Reich claimed that these boxes could cure many maladies, both physical and psycho-logical. The patient sat in the box and received "orgone radiation" (Robinson 1969).

2 The idea of critical theory using dialectic thinking relates not only to a critique of social practice but also more generally to discovering inherent contradictions in theory and ideology.
3 McLaughlin (1999) demonstrates the importance of Fromm, whose influence, he claims, tends to be written out of the history of the Frankfurt School due to a falling out between colleagues. Yet, Fromm conducted an early study of German workers and examined the idea of authoritarianism prior to Adorno's work.
4 Marcuse names Adorno a genius (Marcuse 1977).
5 Although one might argue that Freud's super-ego has a repressive function similar to the repressive societal forces noted by the Frankfurt School theorists, the Freudian view of history also notes such societal repressive forces (Freud 1930).
6 Freud's distinction between object-love and identification, fundamental to his analysis of groups (Freud 1921), is taken by Lacan (1970).
7 Brown says (1959, p. xii), "Herbert Marcuse's book *Eros and Civilization*, the first book, after Wilhelm Reich's ill-fated adventures, to reopen the possibility of the abolition of repression".
8 Slater echoes Wilfred Bion's idea of the "groupishness" of humans.
9 Noted on the back cover of his book (1990).
10 These linguists were also at the basis of the theories of psychoanalyst Jacques Lacan.

References

Adorno, T.W., Frenkel-Brunswik, E., Levinson, D. and Sanford, N. (1950) *The Authoritarian Personality*. New York: Harper and Bros.
Althusser, L. (1970 [1971]). 'Ideology and Ideological State Apparatuses: Notes Towards an Investigation', in Ben Brewster (trans.). *Lenin and Philosophy and Other Philosophical Essays*. Monthly Review Press. https://www.marxists.org/reference/archive/althusser/1970/ideology.htm
Bennis, W.G., and Shepard, H.A. (1956) 'A theory of Group Development', *Human Relations*, vol. 9, pp. 415–437.
Bion, W.R. (1961). *Experiences in Groups and Other Papers*. London: Tavistock Publications.
Boccara, B. (2014). *Socio-Analytic Dialogue: Incorporating Psycho-Social Dynamics into Public Policies*. Lanham, MD: Lexington Books.
Brown, N.O. (1959). *Life against Death: The Psychoanalytic Meaning of History*. Middletown, CT: Wesleyan University.
Brown, N.O. (1966). *Love's Body*, Revised ed. Oakland, CA: University of California Press.
Brunning, H. and Khaleelee, O. (2021). *Danse Macabre and Other Stories: A Psychoanalytic Perspective on Global Dynamics*. London: Karnac.
De George, R.T. and De George, F.M. (eds.) (1972). *The Structuralists*. Palatine, IL: Anchor/Doubleday and Co.
Ehrmann, J. (ed.) (1970). *Structuralism*. Palatine, IL: Anchor Books.
Erikson, E. (1950). *Childhood and Society*, 1st ed. New York: Norton
Erikson, E. (1968). *Identity, Youth and Crisis*. New York: Norton.
Freud, S. (1915). *Repression*. S.E. vol. 14, pp. 141–158. London: The Institute of Psychoanalysis and the Hogarth Press.
Freud, S. (1921) *Group Psychology and the Analysis of the Ego*. S.E. vol. 14, pp. 67–143. J. Strachey (ed.). London: The Institute of Psychoanalysis and the Hogarth Press.

Freud, S. (1930). *Civilization and Its Discontents*, S.E. vol. XXI, pp. 57–145. London: The Institute of Psychoanalysis and the Hogarth Press.

Freud, S. (1940). 'An outline of Psycho-Analysis', *The International Journal of Psychoanalysis*, vol. 21, pp. 27–84.

Fromm, E. (1941). *Escape from Freedom*. New York: Holt, Rinehart and Winston.

Fromm, E. (1962). *The Art of Loving*. New York: Harper and Row.

F scale – Oxford Reference oxfordreference.com/display/10.1093/oi/authority .20110810104941798 [accessed 4 September 2023].

Giddens, A. (1990). *The Consequences of Modernity*. Cambridge: Polity Press and Blackwell.

Harris, B. and Brock, A. (1992). 'Freudian Psycho-Politics: The Rivalry of Wilheim Reich and Otto Fenichel, 1930–1935', *Bulletin of the History of Medicine*, vol. 66, no. 4, pp. 578–612.

Hartmann, J.J. and Gibbard, G.S. (1974). 'Anxiety, Boundary Evolution and Social Change', in G.S. Gibbard; J.J. Hartmann and R.D. Mann (eds.) *Analysis of Groups: Contributions to Theory, Research and Practice*. San Francisco: Jossey Bass.

Higgins, M. and Raphael, C. (eds.) (1967). *Reich Speaks of Freud: Wilhelm Reich Discusses His Work and His Relationship with Sigmund Freud*. Ottowa: Library of Congress.

Horney, K. (1946). *Our Inner Conflicts: A Constructive Theory of Neurosis*. Abingdon: Routledge.

Horney, K. (1967). 'The Distrust between the Sexes', *Feminine Psychology*, pp. 107–118. W.W. Norton.

Jacoby, R. (1986). *The Repression of Psychoanalysis: Otto Fenichel and the political Freudians*, Revised. Chicago: University of Chicago Press.

Jauhiainen, I. 'The Performance Principle as a Tool to Desublimate the Drives in a Repressive Civilization: An Examination of Marcuse's Performance Principle Theory, and How Repressive Civilisation Deals with Individual Citizens' Natural Drives', *Academia.edu*. https://kingston.academia.edu/IrinaJauhiainen [accessed 11 September 2023].

Kluckhohn, C. (1957) *Mirror for Man*. New York: Premier Books, Fawcett Library.

Lacan, J. (1970) *Ecrits: A selection*. Alan Sheridan (trans.). London: Tavistock Publications.

Lasch, C. (1996). *The Revolt of the Elites and the Betrayal of Democracy*. New York: W.W. Norton and Co.

Lasch, C. (1977). *Haven in a Heartless World: The Family Besieged*. New York: Basic Books.

Lasch, C. (1980). *The Culture of Narcissism*. London: Sphere Books Ltd.

Leach, E. (1970). *Levi-Strauss. Fontana Modern Masters*. London: W.M. Collins and Co.

Levine, D.N. (1978). 'Psychoanalysis and Sociology', *Ethos*, vol. 6, no. 3, pp. 175–185.

Levi-Strauss, C. (1955). *The Structural Study of Myth. Journal of American Folklore*, vol. LXV11, pp. 428–444.

Levi-Strauss, C. (1969). *The Raw and the Cooked: Introduction to a Science of Mythology 1*. English Translation: London: Harper and Row and Jonathon Cape Ltd.

Long, S.D. (1992). *A Structural Analysis of Small Groups*. London: Routledge.

Long, S.D. (1999). 'The Tyranny of the Customer and the Cost of Consumerism: An Analysis Using Systems and Psychoanalytic Approaches to Groups and Society', *Human Relations*, vol. 52, no. 6, pp. 723–743.

Maddox, B. (2006). *Freud's Wizard: Ernest Jones and the Transformation of Psychoanalysis*. London: John Murray.

Marcuse, H. (1955). *Eros and Civilization: A Philosophical Enquiry into Freud*. Boston: Beacon Press.

Marcuse, H. (1964). *One-Dimensional Man: Studies in the Ideologies of Advanced Industrial Societies*. London: Routledge and Kegan Paul.

Marcuse, H. (1969). *An Essay on Liberation*. Harmondsworth: Pelican Books.

Marcuse, H. (1977). 'Interview with Bryan Magee: Manufacturing Intellect', *YouTube*. https://www.youtube.com/watch?v=0KqC1lTAJx4

Marcuse, H. (1979). 'Interview with Helen Hawkins', *YouTube*.

Marx, K. (1992). *Capital*. Harmondsworth: Penguin Classics. (Translated from *Das Kapital* [1867].)

McLaughlin, N. (1999). 'Origin Myths in the Social Sciences: Fromm, the Frankfurt School and the Emergence of Critical Theory', *The Canadian Journal of Sociology/ Cahiers Canadiens de Sociologie*, vol. 24, no. 1, pp. 109–139. https://doi.org/10 .2307/3341480

McLaughlin, N. (2017). 'When Worlds Collide: Sociology, Disciplinary Nightmares, and Fromm's Revision of Freud', https://www.researchgate.net/publication /318829292_When_Worlds_Collide_Sociology_Disciplinary_Nightmares_and _Fromm's_Revision_of_Freud [accessed 27 June 2024].

Rabow, J, (1983). 'Psychoanalysis and Sociology', *Annual Review of Sociology*, vol. 9, pp. 555–578.

Rieff, P. (1966). *The Triumph of the Therapeutic: Uses of Faith After Freud*. New York: Harper and Row.

Rieff, P. (1979). *The Mind of the Moralist*, 3rd ed. Chicago: University of Chcago Press.

Robinson, P. (1969). *The Freudian Left: Wilhelm Reich, Geza Roheim, Herbert Marcuse*. New York: Harper and Row.

Róheim, G. (1950). *Psychoanalysis and Anthropology; Culture, Personality and the Unconscious*. Madison, CT: International Universities Press.

Rossi, I (1973). 'The Unconscious in the Anthropology of Claude Levi-Strauss', *American Anthropologist*, vol. 75, no. 1, pp. 20–48.

Stanford Encyclopedia of Philosophy. https://plato.stanford.edu/entries/marcuse/ [accessed 3 September 2023].

Sapir, E. (1927/1949). 'The Unconscious Patterning of Behavior in Society', in E.S. Dummer (ed.). *The Unconscious: A Symposium*, pp. 114–142. New York: Knopf.

Sapir, E. (1949). *Selected Writings of Edward Sapir in Language, Culture and Personality*. Oakland, CA: University of California Press.

Scanlon, C. and Adlam, J. (2022). *Psycho-Social Explorations of Trauma, Exclusion and Violence: Unhoused Minds and Inhospitable Environments*. London: Routledge.

Schein, E. (2010). *Organizational Culture and Leadership*. 4th ed. New York: Wiley.

Simonian, S. (2011). 'Freud's Unconscious and Wilhelm Reich,' *The Journal of Psychiatric Orgone Therapy* (psychorgone.com) [accessed 4 September 2023].

Slater, P.E. (1963). 'On Social Regression', *American Sociological Review*, vol. 28, no. 3, pp. 339–364.

Slater, P.E. (1966). *Microcosm: Structureal, Psychological and Religious Evolution in Groups*. New York: Wiley.

Slater, P.E. (1970). *The Pursuit of Lonliness: American Culture at the Breaking Point*. Boston: Beacon Press.

Slater, P.E. (1992). *A Dream Deferred: America's Discontent and the Search for a New Democratic Ideal*. Boston: Beacon Press.

Stannard, D.E. (1980). *Shrinking History: On Freud and the Failure of Psychohistory*. Oxford: Oxford University Press.

Stanford Encyclopedia of Philosophy (2024). https://plato.stanford.edu/entries/marcuse/#PsyUtoVis [accessed 6 March 2024].

Sullivan, H.S. (1953). *The Interpersonal Theory of Psychiatry*. New York: W.W. Norton and Co.

Tambun, T. (2023). 'Claude Levi-Strauss and Structuralism: A Philosophical Journey, Then Arriving in Post-structuralism', https://www.linkedin.com/pulse/claude-l%C3%A9vi-strauss-structuralism-philosophical-journey-tambun/ [accessed 25 June 2024].

Volkan, V. (2004). *Blind Trust: Large Groups and Their Leaders in Times of Crises and Terror*. Charlottesville, VA: Pitchstone Publishing.

Volkan, V. (2020). *Large-Group Psychology: Racism, Societal Divisions, Narcissistic Leaders and Who We Are Now*. London: Karnac.

7 The Social Unconscious

This chapter introduces the idea of a social unconscious and considers some of its implications. In doing this, the perplexing question of the nature of the "mind" is necessarily confronted, more so when the idea of a social mind is invoked than when an individual mind is discussed, because we tend to think of the mind as an individual possession. This chapter questions such a colloquially held belief.

Given the constraints – biological and social; conscious and unconscious – placed on human development of both the body and mind, my position has grown to be one of discerning emergence as a critical phenomenon, barely able to be explained. Here, I accept that the mind is a transcendent psychological state, interdependent with, but not equivalent to, its physical substrate – the embodied brain and nervous system. The tricky question of how it can be regarded as a "social" phenomenon has had to be encountered by those discussing a social unconscious. Whether consciousness and the unconscious occur at both individual and social level, or whether they are indeed one and the same but distributed in different patterns, is a question that lies at the core of the idea of a social unconscious. I approach this question on occasion throughout the chapter. I conclude with the warning that working with the social unconscious, as with unconscious processes in individuals, requires training because as researchers and practitioners we are necessarily "pulled into" the dynamics involved.

As Doran (2017) says, the unconscious is the cornerstone of psychoanalytic theory. But contrary to general opinion, and as this book outlines, Freud with psychoanalysis did not discover the unconscious, but rather creatively discovered a way, through free association, to access at least part of what is the unconscious. Moreover, just as the idea of the unconscious has a long history (Long 2016), even dating back to antiquity but more formally articulated and discussed in the nineteenth century, so too, perhaps an idea of a social unconscious may predate its modern iteration. Certainly, a type of equivalent to the idea of a collective mind might be found in older indigenous cultures, at least insofar as group and tribal identities are concerned and links made with the land where the idea of being "as one" with the cosmos occurs (for example, Duran 2023). Nonetheless, we might conjecture that Jung's formulation of

DOI: 10.4324/9781003559818-7

the collective unconscious heralds attempts to see the Western idea of the unconscious as a phenomenon beyond the individual mind. Jung believed that we are born with unconscious primordial signs and images, inherited from past generations which he names the archetypes. These he saw as common to all humans in all cultures; for example, the archetypes of the Persona, Shadow, Child or the Wise Old Man. They are most often expressed in dreams and in cultural symbols, and form the core of a collective unconscious (Jung 1991).

The Freudian perspective on unconscious processes in groups is different. Freud regarded Jung's work on the collective unconscious as dabbling in the occult and broke with him following his (Jung's) publication of ideas about the non-sexual aspects of libido. Freud's approach to group phenomena is first strongly articulated in his 1921 short book *Group Psychology and the Analysis of the Ego*. Here, he notes the importance of the leader. In a psychological group, he argues, each group member identifies with the leader or the leading idea of the group through what he calls the ego-ideal. The ego-ideal is that part of the psyche that registers ideal aspects – what a person admires and desires to be like. The leader of a cohesive group is thus situated in the place – the psychological space – of the ego-ideal. Freud likens this identificatory process to the processes of hypnosis and falling in love, where the hypnosis or infatuation leads to the hypnotist or desired one being put in the place of the ego-ideal. Because in the group each member identifies with the leader, they have this identification in common and hence identify with one another in their egos. This forms the basis of group cohesion. This theory does not privilege a social unconscious, but we could say that there is an unconscious process through identifications that bind the group and that is shared by its members.

Freud later adds his myth of the primal horde – a presumed historical event that was repeated in primitive times where the tyrannical father or leader of the pre-human horde is eventually attacked and killed by his sons (Freud 1913). In remorse, each son (group/horde member) internalises a different aspect of the former father, and hence role differentiation in the horde is initiated. Taken from Darwin's idea of the horde, Freud himself regarded the myth as speculative, and it was discounted by many later anthropologists. Nonetheless, it continues his ideas on identification as a basis of group dynamics.

Although later group and organisational researchers and theorists have accepted or rejected different aspects of Freud's theory, some elements remain. Systems psychodynamics (Gould 2006; Sher 2013; Lawler and Sher 2023) keeps the idea of task (the leading idea) as central to group cohesion and regards the leader as a personification of task, or at times of anti-task, such as when the leader or central person initiates group defences, or the group falls prey to unconscious collusive dynamics (Redl 1942; Armstrong and Rustin 2015). Mature work groups in this tradition are seen as having differentiated roles (compare the differentiated roles of the brothers in Freud's myth) with members in touch with reality (Bion 1961). Similarly, many of Jung's ideas are employed in group and organisational work. The introversion/extraversion continuum has become popularised in the much-used (perhaps overused, even abused and simplified) Myers–Briggs Personality Type Indicator (Myers et al. 1998), and the archetypes are especially employed in narrative research in organisations (see, for example, Olssen 2000).

Two Streams of Thought about the Social in the Unconscious

In the mid-twentieth century, two streams of Western thought developed independently that are related to the idea of shared unconscious processes. One is what can be called the Bion/Tavistock tradition of group dynamics and group relations; the other is the tradition of group analysis founded by S.H. Foulkes but influenced by Erich Fromm. The latter tradition specifically uses the term "social unconscious", while the former does not. However, the Bion/Tavistock tradition conceptualises and uses ideas about unconscious processes that are shared in groups and social systems. Both traditions incorporate systemic ideas and see the unconscious operating beyond the individual.

Wilfred Bion examined the states of mind that occur in groups, finding a collusive group phenomenon that he named an assumption group (Bion 1961; Stokes 1994). Within each psychological group of people (meaning a group with a common purpose as compared with an aggregate of people) is a basic assumption that the members hold in common. This assumption is held at an unconscious collusive level and signals a fear or hatred of learning, together with an escape from learning in the face of a real world and its anxieties. The consciously operating work group may be derailed by this assumption group in one of its many forms. Bion named three forms – dependency, fight/flight and pairing – each of which holds its own beliefs, essentially to defend the group from associated anxieties. Other basic assumptions have been named since this work (Lawrence et al. 1996; Schneider and Shrivastaval 1998; Hopper 2009; Chattopadhyay 2019). Moreover, Bion seemed to attribute them to the inherent "groupishness" of humanity while also regarding them as affected by development (Bion Talamo, Borgogno and Merciai 1977). It could be said that the group basic assumptions indicate a form of social unconscious, although Bion did not name them that way and became more interested in what he termed proto-mental phenomena underpinning the assumptions. This proto-mental system hypothesised by Bion (1962) occurs where the mental and physical are not differentiated (Morgan-Jones 2009). While this is the case in early infancy, it persists throughout life and is especially prominent in psychotic thinking where the alpha function of thinking "thoughts" has not developed. He says that the basic assumptions might be considered as defences against proto-mental thoughts. Although not made by Bion, a link here might be with the Jungian idea of thoughts and images (archetypes as an instance) regarded as unconsciously inherited through culture.

Following this tradition, known as the object relations tradition incorporating the work of psychoanalysts such as Melanie Klein, Donald Winnicott and Wilfred Bion, the theory of social defences against anxiety should be mentioned (Jaques 1955; Menzies-Lyth 1988; Long 2006; Armstrong and Rustin

2015). The research in this area sees social systems as tacitly or unconsciously developing cultures and structures that defend their members from the anxieties and other unbearable emotions raised by the nature of the tasks undertaken. In Menzies-Lyth's (1988) iconic research, the culture of nursing in a public hospital was shown to institute a system of procedures and a work culture that defended against intimacy in nurse–patient relations. Such intimacy could, and often did, give rise to unwanted sexual arousal or fears of death. However, the defences so constructed are often the cause of further organisational stress, as Menzies-Lyth found. Social defences are resistant to change or modification, despite themselves producing discomfort, due to their collective dynamic of initially removing immediate anxieties and deeply felt fears, and because they become deeply entrenched in technical systems and procedures, beyond psychological collusions. I believe that the dynamics involved here are comparable to those underlying the unconscious entrenchment of repressive processes in social institutions, as described in Chapter 6. Since Menzies-Lyth's work, social defences have been examined in many different industries (Armstrong and Rustin 2015).

The Bion/Tavistock tradition, so called because it was taken up and developed by the Tavistock Institute of Human Relations and the Tavistock and Portman Trust – later to become internationally accepted in many similar organisations around the globe – has developed an idea of unconscious processes in groups and social systems most strongly from a psychoanalytic and systems conjunction. In many ways, we can see it as moving from the psycho- to the social: the person dynamics to the system. From this tradition has emerged the theory and practice of group relations, notably developed through the practice of group relations conferences, where members of a conference explore the conscious and unconscious dynamics within and between different groups in the here and now of the conference experience as a temporary organisation (Rice 1965; Aram, Baxter and Nutkevitch 2015).

However, the idea of a specifically named social unconscious comes from a different direction. This is the second tradition that I point towards. The term social unconscious came initially from within the Frankfurt School, described in Chapter 6. In his joining of Freudian and Marxist ideas, Erich Fromm coined the term "social unconscious", claiming that "each society determines which thoughts and feelings shall be permitted to arrive at the level of awareness and which have to remain unconscious. Just as there is a social character, there is also a 'social unconscious'" (Fromm 1962, 2019, chapter IX p. 1).

As described in Chapter 6, the Frankfurt School (Horkheimer and Adorno 1947 [2002]) used the idea of repression seemingly in a quite different way from the Freudian idea of repression. Here, repression is also equivalent to social domination. Such repression is linked to a lack of awareness of this by the socially repressed. The repressive forces are intimately linked to the social fabric. Such unawareness, understood as unconscious, is different from the dynamic repression described within psychoanalysis. Or, at least, it seems so at first glance. However, as the idea of the social unconscious is explored, it appears that by taking a systemic perspective – seeing both the individual and the social as systems in themselves – dynamic repression is acting in both systems. This perspective requires a shift from the idea of the "mind" as exclusively individual to an idea of the mind as social (see, for instance, Harre 1984; Long 1992). The idea of a group or social mind is a contentious issue and depends on how the mind is conceptualised. Hopper, who defines and uses the term social unconscious, does so purely as a basis for the discussion of cultural and communicational constraints (Hopper 2003, p. 128), arguing that social systems do not have a mind. My position is that the "mind" is always social and individuals each incorporate and embody just part of this metasystem (Long 1992, 1999; Dalal 2001; Long and Harney 2016).

Such a systemic perspective is taken up by group analytic psychotherapy founded by S.H. Foulkes (see Foulkes 1964). This form of group therapy makes interventions to the group as a whole, conceptualised as having an unconscious mental field across all members. Foulkes states:

> When a group of people, by which for our purposes I mean a small number of persons, form intimate relationships, they create a new phenomenon, namely, the total field of mental happenings between them all...The point I wish to stress is that this network is a psychic system as a whole network, and not a superimposed social interaction system in which individual minds interact with each other. This is the value of thinking in terms of a concept which does not confine mind, by definition, to an individual.
>
> (Foulkes 1971, p. 224)

I have previously looked at differences between the Foulkesian formulations and those of Bion, saying,

> While his (Foulkes) description of the unconscious matrix of "mental happenings" that is a property of the group rather than the individual, resonates with Bion's ideas of a proto mental matrix, (both had ideas of the group-as-a-whole) Foulkes differs from Bion. He disagrees with what he considered as Bion's idea of the transference of the internal dynamics of the person onto the group. Instead, he refers to a social unconscious that consists of social contexts that are generally not detected. He regards the community as the primary focus and that the inner processes of the individual are internalisations of the forces operating in the group.
>
> (Long 2016, p. 75)

This puts the community or social field as primary. Individuals emerge "as the result of developments within the community" (Foulkes 1964, p. 109). Because individual dynamics are regarded as internalisations of contextual issues, ideas within the Foulkesian paradigm of boundaries, within individuals, between individuals and around the group as a whole must be re-examined. During communications within the group, the unconscious social matrix is active so that these boundaries are crossed and infiltrated. For example, in a therapy group, a symptom of one patient may be expressed by another patient who hitherto did not display that symptom, or one person may be unconsciously chosen to "hold" thoughts and feelings rejected by others in the group. This has echoes of Freud's contention that the unconscious of one person can communicate with the unconscious of another (Freud 1915). However, whereas Freud does not extend this idea more fully, Foulkes provides an explanation of this through his idea of the group matrix.

Foulkes (1964) saw the group as operating on at least four levels simultaneously:

1. The *current level* where the group is regarded as representing the community with its values, ideas and opinions.
2. The *transference level* where the group is seen to represent the family – a level of mature object relations, with the leader often representing parental authority.
3. The *projective level* – a level of bodily and mental images – where the group as a whole may represent a body or different bodily parts.
4. The *primordial level* where primitive collective and cultural images may predominate.

In articulating these levels, Foulkes incorporates earlier ideas from a social systemic perspective in a systematic way, whether or not this was his intent. The group matrix incorporates Jungian ideas of a primordial collective unconscious, extends Freud's notion of unconscious communication, includes ideas of projection and introjection developed within the object relations school of psychoanalysis and echoes Fromm's insistence on the dominance of social institutions, their repressive functions and the structuration of the individual. In all this, the communal level is seen as predominant. Weinberg (2007) argues that although Foulkes does not include the social unconscious as one of his four levels, in analysing situations through the social unconscious, all levels should be examined and are implicit in Foulkes' work.

It might be argued that the matrix described by Foulkes is his version of a "group mind" without the complexity of the use of the word "mind," which, as I have indicated, tends to be seen colloquially as pertaining to the individual only.

> Foulkes has given us the powerful transindividual concept of group matrix, within which the structures of the group form and reform. Additionally, he has given us a view of structural regression that does not rely on developmental constructs. It postulates the primary importance of the group viewed as a community within which the representations of interpersonal relations, of intrapersonal object relations and of primordial phantasy all have a place.
>
> (Long 1992, p. 39)

The problem of a separate individual mind is always present in theories that postulate the incorporation of the mind from the social with the presence of transpersonal experience. In his later thinking, Foulkes distinguishes the foundational matrix from the dynamic matrix. This differentiation allows for a description of (i) the inner matrix of the individual – the foundational matrix built from ongoing past cultural and linguistic experience, and the foundation of the personality – to be separated from (ii) the dynamic matrix emerging from the group as it progresses; hence saving the idea of the individual mind.

Following Foulkes, the idea of the social unconscious has been developed primarily through the group analytic network. Hopper (2003), for instance, talks of "the unconscious constraints of social systems on individuals and their internal worlds, and, at the same time, the effects that unconscious fantasies, actions, thoughts and feelings have on social systems" (p. 126). The concept of the social unconscious, according to Hopper, refers to the existence and constraints of social, cultural and communicational arrangements of which people are

> unaware insofar as these arrangements are not perceived (not known) and if perceived are not acknowledged (denied) and if acknowledged are not taken as problematic (given) and if taken as problematic are not considered with an optimum degree of detachment and objectivity.
>
> (Hopper 2003, p. 127)

This view of the social unconscious differs from the traditional psychoanalytic idea of the unconscious in two prominent ways. First, it stresses unawareness at a social level rather than through a deeply individually repressed unconscious (although it might be argued that some aspects of the superego imply this). This lack of awareness is regarded as distributed through the social fabric and is introjected at the individual level. It shows up not simply in the behaviour of persons but also in the institutions within society such as the law, in market economies, the family, education and cultural expression and observation. Second, it talks of unconscious thoughts and feelings, whereas Freud (2015) initially argued that affects are not repressed; rather, associated ideation is repressed – an idea taken up throughout Lacanian theory. Despite these differences, Hopper argues that the unconscious includes (i) ideas that people were once aware of but are no longer aware of (compare the Freudian idea of repression); (ii) ideas and phantasies that persons were once only partially aware of and are no longer aware of – for example, phantasies experienced pre-language or primordial phantasies (compare Klein's ideas of infantile pre-linguistic phantasy); and (iii) what he terms the "dynamic non-conscious" – ideas that can only become barely conscious and are never really directly experienced. Here, he refers to the "unthought known", an expression about the unconscious taken up by Christopher Bollas (Hopper 2003, p. 127). Hence, his move from describing the personal to the social unconscious seems primarily to be one of acknowledging social constraint, lodged in social institutions, as a primary influence in the matrix discussed by Foulkes and

Anthony (1965) and encultured into individuals. This introduces a sociological lens alongside a psychoanalytic perspective and reminds us of the work of Althusser, the French philosopher who examined the ways in which ideologies constantly show up in social apparatuses and their practices, then lodge into private psychology. The social unconscious, beginning with Fromm, thus includes the ways in which culture embeds ideas in the populace without much awareness that this is occurring. An example of this is provided recently by Joy (2011) who notes "carnism" as a socially embedded cultural belief in an imperative to eat animals (sentient beings).[1]

> Fromm, Foulkes and Hopper take the idea of the unconscious and centre it in the idea of social unawareness. This concept of the unconscious refers not to simple ignorance but adds an almost wilful non-acknowledgement of social and cultural issues that are harmful to work and wellbeing. As with other group and social perspectives on the unconscious, it shares in the idea of collective denial and of turning a blind eye. But it adds a political dimension. The social unconscious implies on the one hand a possible attitude of detachment from the common good. On the other hand, it includes reference to those impediments to social justice that lie in inequalities of information. This is a different dimension from orthodox psychoanalysis in thinking about unconscious dynamics. These dynamics are no longer simply transposed from the psychodynamics of the "person" onto the larger systems of social and organisational dynamics, however valid and helpful that may be. The social system with its politics and ethics are now an integral part of an idea of the unconscious.
>
> (Long 2016, pp. 76–77)

This becomes more evident in other developments from within the group analytic field where authors and researchers have taken the more radical implications of Foulkes' conceptualisations. Dalal (2001) argues for an understanding following the later Foulkes. He distinguishes what he calls orthodox Foulkes from a later radical Foulkes. The orthodox Foulkes retains the idea of a personal unconscious as well as a social unconscious as if they are two different systems. The radical Foulkes has only one unconscious, argues Dalal, "and it cannot be other than impregnated with the social" (p. 542). The argument here states that the social/individual dichotomy is falsely based on the habit of seeing and conceptualising bound states rather than ongoing processes. There is no beginning to the chicken and egg dilemma of biological and social being because the interaction of the two is an ongoing process and has been throughout evolution. To separate them and look at how each interacts with the other in some sort of efficient causation is false thinking. This false thinking, Dalal attributes to many developmental theories in psychoanalysis and, he argues, leads to what looks like a rift between set inheritance and sociological influences; a war between human nature and society; a war that he argues is falsely conceived.

Foulkes was concerned with the ways that different individuals and sub-groups communicate in the social matrix. Further to this, using the work of Elias and Matte-Blanco, Dalal (2001, pp. 549–553) argues for the centrality of power dynamics in the social unconscious. It is power, he claims, that influences the communication channels in groups and between groups.

> We were able to see that the contents of the social unconscious varied depending upon where an individual was located in the field of power-relations, and that this in turn had a significant effect not only on self-esteem, that is, how individuals thought about and experienced themselves but also how this structured the kinds of relations these individuals could have with others in their vicinity.
>
> (Dalal 2001, p. 554)

Power relations and power differentials affect subjective experience and, in this view, construct and structure the social unconscious (Dalal 1998). This perspective echoes ideas from Foucault in his analysis of discursive power and communication (Foucault 1970; Geyer 2017). In Foucault's view, it is those who hold entry to and control the processes and outcomes of societal discourses who have power in social and cultural situations.

Although a major use of the idea of the social unconscious has been in the clinical practice of group analysis (Hopper 2003), it has also been used in understanding social dynamics at a broader level in society and its organisations (Wilke 2019). One line of work has been in understanding transgenerational trauma at a societal level and trauma in organisations (Hopper 2012; Wilke 2016). What is embedded in the institutions and histories of different cultures becomes embedded in unconscious processes of communication across generations and within organisational life, as is seen in studies within and beyond the disciplines of group analysis and group relations (Volkan 2001, 2014; Boccara 2013, 2014; Volkan, Scholz, and Fromm 2023). Not all these studies specifically note the idea of a social unconscious, but one might say it is implied. The analysis of "chosen traumas" and "chosen glories" in country and cultural contexts, for example (Volkan 2001), speaks of narratives that become embedded in the institutions and consciousness of whole peoples and transmitted in everyday behavioural patterns, many of which are tacit and unwittingly practiced. This is perhaps the Freudian preconscious in individuals rather than a repressed unconscious. But given that the social unconscious has been identified as unawareness of such cultural and communicational arrangements, or if brought to mind they are denied; or given that the social unconscious has also been linked to societal repression in a more political sense, such cultural transmissions can well be regarded as unconscious processes.

This conceptualisation and tradition of the social unconscious, from Fromm through to Wilke and Dalal, has a political and sociological basis. We can say it moves from the sociological to the individual incorporation of social phenomena at an unconscious level.

The Associative Unconscious

Freud uncovered unconscious processes (Freud 1915), including what he called primary process thinking, discerned when people are allowed to free associate – that is, to freewheel from one thought to another without any conscious attempt to censor their thinking. Freud discovered repressed ideation through an examination of blocks to this process – when conscious associations dry up. In psychoanalysis, then, the mind is a field of associations, many unconsciously linked. How, then, can associations be examined in a social field, in the social unconscious?

In his book *Reassembling the Social*, Latour (2005) argues that the idea of social has become used as if it relates to a stabilised set of affairs rather than the ongoing processes that better describe society. Manley (2018, 2019) notes these processes as a network of associations. Explanations of social phenomena – he states following Latour – interrupt the flow and can never be absolute. They are, perhaps, working hypotheses that themselves can only be a part of the flow; interruptions to be useful for a point in time.

Returning to the difficulty of a social "mind", it can be argued that the flow of associative thinking between interacting people can be regarded as a field of interaction: conscious at points in human interactions at times, but existing as a field unconsciously. This is the social matrix referred to by Foulkes; the rhizome referred to by Deleuze (Deleuze and Guattari 1988): that is, a network without a centre.

Together, Maurita Harney and I (Long and Harney 2016) name this unconscious matrix the associative unconscious:

> Here then is a formulation of the unconscious as a mental network of thoughts, signs and symbols or signifiers able to give rise to many thoughts, impulses and images.
>
> (p. 8)

> The associative unconscious is the infinite of human thought in all its possibilities.
>
> (p. 10)

> Each individual holds only a part of the vaster whole.
>
> (p. 11)

Using Peircian philosophy and the psychoanalysis of Bion, we understand this as a field of actual and potential associations and links within a psychological field, not restricted to individual minds. Just as language is part of a social fabric, not "belonging" to any one individual but able to be accessed and used, so is the vast associative unconscious: sometimes consciously accessed, at least in part; sometimes influencing thinking without conscious apprehension. It is a field from which hypotheses are drawn, whether in everyday activities or in scientific abductive logic (Peirce 1992–1998). No one individual can "hold" the whole in mind, and there are processes that prevent access: repressions; domination and political influences; physiological and chemical interferences; that some associations and ideas are not ready to be thought; that we don't have the technical or other expertise to think some thoughts. But the social field is ongoing and interactive, and the potential for new thinking is ever present. The field of the social/associative unconscious is a field of primary process thinking without a sense of time or linear logic. It is only once accessed, that secondary process thinking may be applied and sense-making attempted – at least for a moment in time when it might serve a purpose. These ideas have some congruence with the post-Bion field theory of Ferro (2018). When working with groups, or even in individual sessions, I find myself in reverie attending to an unconscious field between members of the group or between myself and my client, accessed through our associations. Only recently have I had a client say that our sessions together are like dreams, experienced and taken in loosely in the moment, elusive to grasp and sometimes lost, with fuller meaning only discerned later on reflection. It is the experience in the moment that is transformative; sense-making and memory come later. In Bion's terms – a transformation in "O" rather than in knowledge (K).

Implications of the Social Unconscious

Given that the social unconscious/associative unconscious can be considered an associative, rhizome-like matrix, accessed only in part by any one individual or small grouping, it follows that to access its richness, communications between people and groupings need to be as open as possible. This is especially important for the cross-disciplinary and cross-cultural work needed to approach today's global and wicked problems such as climate change, species loss and global pollution by plastics and other industrial waste. To this end, societies and organisations, including multinational conglomerates, need to understand those unconscious forces that prevent such co-operations. The dynamics of social defences, intergroup rivalries, unconscious collusions, basic assumptions and scapegoating of individuals and outgroups all need attention by societal leaders, alongside the more conscious negotiations attempted between groups and larger societies. Human motives and emotions that prevent two-way open communication will always be part of our nature and can't be wished away. Greed, narcissism, desire for power, and fears, anxieties, hubris and anger are examples that lead to the denial of realities and either excessive or inadequate risk-taking (Hirschhorn 1999; Long 2008; Long and Sievers 2012). Hopefully, as a species, humans can learn to better contain and restrict these through communal agreements, regulation and, at times, good will: most of all through a deeper understanding of their dynamics.

I have previously noted some of the processes that might be taken up in organisations to mitigate against unconscious perverse dynamics (Long

2019). I reproduce them here where "societies" might well be substituted for "organisations":

1. Organisations need to be aware of the emergence of unconscious and perverse dynamics. Pride in the organisation is motivating, but blind pride without recourse to the reality of performance is problematic and leads to narcissistic denial of problem areas. Reality checks across all functions are necessary. The maximisation of shared information minimises the chances of one part of the organisation having knowledge that acts against another part of the organisation. Processes for transparency and a culture of acceptance rather than blame avoid the need for cover-ups.
2. Ingroups and outgroups form naturally, quickly and quite unconsciously in an organisation based on personalities, roles, functions, hierarchical levels, power dynamics, locality and so on. These then affect decisions due to an unconscious bias that favours members of the tribe. There should be opportunities for cross-fertilisation where real tasks are undertaken across tribes.
3. Creative and innovative organisations access the associative unconscious of their cultures by creating reflective spaces and non-critical listening of all ideas. Judgment can come later when final decisions have to be made.
4. It needs to be recognised that although roles are differentially authorised for decision making, the information needed for those decisions is spread throughout the organisation at all levels. This information may not be available to decision makers because of organisational, contextual or societal constraints about who unconsciously is enabled to think what.
5. Misuse of situational power and its subsequent normalisation are not only distressing to individuals but also lead to misinformation for the organisation through fear and lack of trust. Consciously formulated checks and balances are required. This includes building into the organisation those democratic processes that allow for all voices to be heard and considered when making important decisions. This is not only important for the health and creativity of individual members, but it also allows for all the information that is needed for decisions to become available from the associative unconscious.
6. Organisation members need to be aware of the anxieties present in their work and sensitive to the organisational structures and cultures that act as defences against these anxieties. Only through open exploration in a safe environment can these be surfaced and prevented from becoming destructive.

In working with the social unconscious, whatever the tradition, the researcher, activist or consultant must recognise that they too will be pulled into its dynamics. This does not involve a way of escaping the dynamic or being aloof from it, but understanding and being sensitive to it. Then, it might be helpful to remember that working with groups and organizations requires the capacity to be pulled into the group's psyche and to re-emerge with a deeper understanding of the struggles our clients face and we with them.

(Petriglieri and Denfeld Wood 2003, p. 342)

This requires not simply training in an intellectual understanding of social unconscious processes but training in an approach to unconscious dynamics with the capacity to work sensitively and to contain and work with the unconscious projections involved (see, for example, Shapiro and Carr 1993). An ethical stance is required.

The idea of a social unconscious with a social "mind" appears at first as counterintuitive, mainly because our way of thinking puts individual persons as central and individual minds as a given. But the perspective of the individual mind as the centre of thinking has to change just as the Copernican Revolution changed thinking about the universe. While Freud showed how unconscious thoughts could overthrow the conscious so-called rational ego, Bion, Foulkes and those who follow argue for the centrality of an unconscious social field of associative and connective thinking. This social and associative unconscious becomes embedded in the very fabric of our institutions (family, law, education, industry) and is thus passed from generation to generation. Our freedom as a species is integrally linked to our understanding and experience of this unconscious.

Note

1 Joy's work was introduced to me by Margo Lockhart whose PhD thesis examines how people talk to each other about what they eat.

References

Aram, E., Baxter, R. and Nutkevitch, A. (eds.) (2015). *Group Relations Work: Exploring the Impact and Relevance within and Beyond Its Network*. London: Routledge.

Armstrong, D. and Rustin, M. (eds.) (2015). *Social Defences Against Anxiety: Explorations in a Paradigm*. London: Routledge.

Bion Talamo, P., Borgogno, F. and Merciai, S.A. (eds.) (1977). *Bion's Legacy to Groups*. London: Karnac.

Bion, W.R. (1961). *Experiences in Groups*. London: Tavistock Publications.

Bion, W.R. (1962). *Learning from Experience*. London: Karnac.

Boccara, B. (2013). 'Socioanalytic Dialogue', in S.D. Long (ed.). *Socioanalytic Methods*, pp. 279–300. London: Karnac.

Boccara, B. (2014). *Socio-Analytic Dialogue: Incorporating Psychosocial Dynamics into Public Policies*. Lanham, MD: Lexington Books.

Chattopadhyay, G. (2019). 'The Sixth Basic Assumption BA PU (Basic Assumption Purity/Pollution)', *Socioanalysis*, vol. 21, p. 17.

Dalal, F. (1998). *Taking the Group Seriously: Towards a Post Foulksian Analytic Group Analytic Theory.* London: Jessica Kingsley.

Dalal, F. (2001). 'The Social Unconscious: A Post Foulkesian Perspective', *Group Analysis*, vol. 34, no. 4, pp. 539–554.

Deleuze, G. and Guattari, F. (1988). *A Thousand Plateaus.* London: Continuum.

Doran, C. (2017) 'Rage and Anxiety in the Split Between Freud and Jung', Humanities, vol. 6, no. 3, p. 53. https://doi.org/10.3390/h6030053

Duran, B. 'American Indian Belief Systems and Traditional Practices', University of Oklahoma. http://www.wellnesscourts.org/files/Duran%20-%20American %20Indian%20Belief%20Systems.pdf [accessed 8 March 2023].

Ferro, A. (2018). 'Bionian and Post-Bionian Transformations', *Romanian Journal of Psychoanalysis*, vol 11, no. 2 pp. 47–56.

Foucault, M. (1970). *The Order of Things.* London: Tavistock Publications.

Foulkes, S.H. (1964). *Therapeutic Group Analysis.* London: George Allen and Unwin.

Foulkes, S.H. (1971). 'The Group as Matrix of the Individual's Mental Life', in S.H. Foulkes (ed.). *Selected Papers: Psychoanalysis and Group Analysis. 1990.* London: Routledge.

Foulkes, S.H. and Anthony E.J. (1965). *Group Psychotherapy: The Psychoanalytic Approach.* London: Maresfield Library.

Freud, S. (1913). 'Totem and Taboo', in J. Strachey (ed.)., S.E. vol. 13, pp. 1–164. London: Hogarth Press.

Freud. S. (1915). *The Unconscious*, S.E. 14 pp. 166–204. London: Hogarth Press.

Freud, S. (1921). *Group Psychology and the Analysis of the Ego*, S.E. vol 69, pp. 69–143. London: Hogarth Press.

Fromm, E. (1942). *Fear of Freedom.* London: Routledge and Kegan Paul.

Fromm, E. (1962 [2019]). *The Art of Loving.* New York: Harper Perennial; Anniversary edition.

Geyer, C. (2017). 'The Social Unconscious in Action: Linking Theory to Group Work with Young Adults', *Group Analysis,* vol. 50, no. 2. https://journals.sagepub.com /doi/10.1177/0533316417702265

Gould, L. (2006). *The Systems Psychodynamics of Organizations: Integrating the Group Relations Approach, Psychoanalytic and Open Systems Perspectives.* London: Routledge.

Harre, R. (1984). 'Social Elements as Mind', *British Journal of Medical Psychology*, vol. 57, pp. 127–135.

Hirschhorn, L. (1999). 'The Primary Risk', *Human Relations* vol. 52, no. 1, pp. 5–23.

Hopper, E. (2003). 'The Social Unconscious in Clinical Work', in *The Social Unconscious: Selected Papers*, pp. 126–161. London: Jessica Kingsley.

Hopper, E. (2009). 'The Theory of the Basic Assumption of Incohesion: Aggregation/ Massification or BA I:A/M', *British Journal of Psychotherapy*, vol. 25, no. 2, pp. 214–229.

Hopper, E. (ed.) (2012). *Trauma and Organizations.* London: Routledge.

Horkheimer, M. and Adorno, T. (1947 [2002]). *Dialectic of Enlightenment: Philosophical Fragments.* E. Jephcott (trans.). G. Schmid Noerr (ed.). Stanford, CA: Stanford University Press.

Jaques, E. (1955). Social Systems as a Defence Against Persecutory and Depressive Anxiety, in M. Klein, P. Heimann, E. Money-Kyrle (eds.) *New Directions in Psychoanalysis*, pp. 478–498. London: Tavistock Publications.

Joy, M. (2011). *Why we Love Dogs, Eat Pigs and Wear Cows: An introduction to Carnism*. Newbury Port, MA: Conari Press.

Jung, C.G. ([1959] 1991). *The Archetypes and the Collective Unconscious*, 2nd ed. R.F.C. Hull and H. Read (trans. and ed.). Princeton, NJ: Princeton University Press.

Latour, B. (2005). *Reassembling the Social*. Oxford: Oxford University Press.

Lawler, D. and Sher, M. (2023). *Systems Psyhodynamics: Innovative Approaches to Change, Whole Systems and Complexity*. London: Routledge.

Lawrence, W.G., Bain, A. and Gould, L. (1996). 'The Fifth Basic Assumption', *Free Associations*, vol. 6, no. 1, pp. 1–20.

Long, S.D. (1992). *A Structural Analysis of Small Groups*. London: Routledge.

Long, S.D. (1999). 'The Tyranny of the Customer and the Cost of Consumerism: An Analysis Using Systems and Psychoanalytic Approaches to Groups and Society', *Human Relations*, vol. 52, no. 6, pp. 723–727.

Long, S.D. (2006). 'Organizational Defences Against Anxiety: What Has Happened Since the 1955 Jaques Paper?' *International Journal of Applied Psychoanalytic Studies*, vol. 3, no. 4, pp. 279–295.

Long, S.D. (2008). *The Perverse Organisation and its Deadly Sins*. London: Karnac.

Long, S.D. (2016). 'The Transforming Experience Framework and Unconscious Processes: A Brief Journey Through the History of the Unconscious as Applied to Person, System and Context with an Exploratory Hypothesis of Unconscious as Source', in S. Long (ed.). *Transforming Experience in Organisations: A Framework for Organisational Research and Consultancy*, pp. 31–106. London: Routledge.

Long, S.D. (2019). 'The Unconscious Won't go Away: Especially in Organisations', *Organisation and Social Dynamics*, vol. 19, no. 2, pp. 218–229.

Long, S.D. and Harney, M. (2016). 'The Associative Unconscious', in S.D. Long (ed.). *Socioanalytic Methods: Discovering the Hidden in Organisations and Social Systems*, pp. 3–22. London: Routledge.

Long, S.D. and Sievers, B. (eds.) (2012). *Towards a Socioanalysis of Money, Finance and Capitalism: Beneath the Surface of the Financial Industry*. London: Routledge.

Manley, J. (2018). *Social Dreaming, Associative Thinking and Intensitives of Affect*. Switzerland: Palgrave Macmillan.

Manley, J. (2019). 'Associative Thinking: A Deleuzian Perspective on Social Dreaming', in S.D. Long and J. Manley (eds.) *Social Dreaming: Philosophy, Research, Theory and Practice*. London: Routledge.

Menzies-Lyth, I. (1988). 'The Functioning of Social Systems as a Defence against Anxiety', in I. Menzies-Lyth (ed.). *Containing Anxiety in Institutions*, pp. 43–85. London: Free Association Books.

Morgan-Jones, R. (2009). 'The Body Speaks: Bion's Proto-Mental System at Work', *British Journal of Psychotherapy*, vol. 25, no. 4, pp. 456–476.

Myers, I.B., McCaulley, M.H., Quenk, N.L. and Hammer, A.L. (1998). *MBTI Manual (A Guide to the Development and Use of the Myers-Briggs Type Indicator)*, 3rd ed. Palo Alto: Consulting Psychologists Press.

Olsson, S. (2000). 'Acknowledging the Female Archetype: Women Managers' Narratives of Gender', *Women in Management Review*, vol. 15, no. 5–6, pp. 296–302.

Peirce, C.S. (1992–1998). *The Essential Peirce, Volume 2: Selected Philosophical Writings (1893–1923)*. The Peirce Edition Project (ed.). Bloomington: Indiana University Press.

Petriglieri, G. and Denfeld Wood, J. (2003). 'The Invisible Revealed: Collusion as an Entry to the Group Unconscious', *Transactional Analysis Journal*, vol. 33, no. 4, pp. 332–342.

Redl, F. (1942). 'Group Emotion and Leadership', *Psychiatry*, vol. 5, pp. 573–596.

Rice, A. K. (1965). *Learning for Leadership: Interpersonal and Intergroup Relations*. London: Routledge.

Schneider, S. and Shrivastaval, P. (1988). 'Basic Assumption Themes in Organisations', *Human Relations*, vol. 41, no. 7, pp. 493–516.

Shapiro, E. and Carr, W. (1993). *Lost in Familiar Places: Creating New Connections Between the Individual and Society*. New Haven, CT: Yale University Press.

Sher, M. (2013). *The Dynamics of Change: Tavistock Approaches to Improving Social Systems*. London: Routledge.

Stokes, J. (1994). 'The Unconscious at Work in Groups and Teams: Contributions from the Work of Wilfred Bion', in A. Obholzer and V. Roberts (eds.) *The Unconscious at Work*, pp. 19–27. London: Routledge.

Weinberg, H. (2007). 'So What is this Social Unconscious Anyway?', *Group Analysis*, vol. 40, no. 3, pp. 307–322.

Wilke G. (2016). 'The German Social Unconscious: Second Generation Perpetrator Symptoms in Organizations and Groups', in E. Hopper and H. Weinberg (eds.) *The Social Unconscious in Persons, Groups, and Societies, Vol. II: Mainly Foundation Matrices*, pp. 61–81. London: Karnac.

Wilke, G. (2019). *The Art of Group Analysis in Organisations: The Use of Intuitive and Experiential Knowledge*. London: Routledge.

Volkan, V. (2001). 'Transgenerational Transmissions and Chosen Traumas: An Aspect of Large-Group Identity', *Group Analysis*, vol. 34, no. 1, pp. 79–97.

Volkan, V. (2014). *Animal Killer: Transmission of War Trauma From One Generation to the Next*. London: Routledge.

Volkan, V., Scholz, R. and Fromm, M.G. (eds.) (2023). *We Don't Speak of Fear: Large Group Identity, Societal Conflict and Collective Trauma*. Oxfordshire: Phoenix Publishing.

8 Unconscious in Organisations

This chapter brings me to a consideration of the unconscious in organisations – a study that I have undertaken for the last 40 or so years through research, consulting, coaching, and teaching. I can neither attempt to fully condense my thinking in this area, nor to summarise all the influences that have come from a multitude of scholars, theorists, practitioners, and consultants, many of whom are members of the International Society for the Psychoanalytic Study of Organisations (ISPSO), an organisation where I have been a member since 1994. Also of great influence has been the Group Relations community spread throughout the world and referenced earlier. The reader can examine the many books and articles written by authors within the field covered by ISPSO, organisational dynamics and Group Relations. Here I write about some of the main ideas related to unconscious dynamics in organisations that now influence my work in organisational research and consultancy (see also Long 2008, 2019a; Lawler and Sher 2023). So, the chapter is not so much about describing theories as articulating the way I work – all the time with thoughts about unconscious dynamics.

My basic stance is from a systems and psychodynamic or socioanalytic perspective that recognises a deep interrelatedness between structure and culture, form and process, cognition and emotion. The enquiry is about the difference between appearances and what lies behind or beneath the accounts that organisation members give and the behaviours they exhibit, the emotional life of the organisation, the joys and fears, the anxieties and how these are dealt with or left to fester. It is about the unconscious processes within and between the organisational roles, sub-groups, groups, the organisation-as-a-whole and its context: those processes that can be inferred from observed interactions within the organisation yet are not articulated by its members or in its accounts. Many unconscious processes are inferred from examining patterns, outlying behaviours and surprising incidents; those observations that are outside what one normally expects and can easily be overlooked. This is the inferential process of abductive logic (Peirce 1958; Ginzberg 1983; Long and Harney 2013).

When I explore such dynamics, my practice is guided by the belief that such an exploration is best done collaboratively with the organisation, recognising

DOI: 10.4324/9781003559818-8

that such collaboration must involve a variety of organisation members repre-senting a multitude of dynamics. The perspective or valency is different from the positions of board members, company executives, managers, professionals, and workers, as are the resources available to each of these roles, including the resources of power and authority. Collaboration is important because it is through a process of thinking together and exploring the emotions present in both researcher/consultant and organisation members, that any light can be thrown on those influences from the unconscious (its effects) that take the organisation unawares. But in this I must be aware that I may be "seduced" or drawn into collusive emotional stances or beliefs, organisational defences or even perverse dynamics (Long 2008) even though, if I am aware, such seductions may be useful data (Mersky 2001). Paying attention to my own responses and actions, plus working with others to minimise my assumptions and biases, is important. Heavy in my memory are the times when this has hap-pened, although the direct learning from the experience has been invaluable. Both the systems psychodynamic formulations of the Bion/Tavistock tradi-tion and the Foulksian group analytic ideas of unconscious matrix guide me, as discussed in the chapter on the social unconscious. Also, my early work as a psychoanalytic psychotherapist has proved a strong foundation, albeit along-side the recognition that group dynamics are not wholly equivalent to person dynamics.

I have been guided over the past 15 or so years by the framework – "The Transforming Experience into Authentic Action in Role Framework", short-ened to the "Transforming Experience Framework" (TEF) (Long 2016). In particular this helps me to look at the structural element of role together with the thoughts and emotions that taking up a role gives or puts into the role holder or leaves the role holder holding and experiencing on behalf of other roles, and how this becomes central to the experience within an organisation – whether a family, a large corporation, a government department or not-for-profit organisation. The different spheres of experience discerned by the framework – the experience of being a person, of being in a role, of being in a system, being in a context and the experience of Source (a deep purpose or belief, for example, of God or humanity or life as creative) – help me to see the different influences both conscious and unconscious on overt experience that are not simply "me" or ego-driven, but come from beyond personal psy-chology. An example that is always helpful is to distinguish between "person" and "role" because role is always in relation to other roles in the system, while persons may be best seen in relationships. The idea of being "in relation to" means that the people in the roles don't have to know one another or meet. Their roles are held together and influenced by the third position of the overall system. I don't personally know the prime minister of Australia but my role as a citizen holds me in relation to that role. This view led me to see the role as a particular instance of a signifier in a signifying chain of roles that together make a system (Long 1991) the idea being instigated by my reading of early Lacan (Lacan 1977).

So, I will proceed with a series of small vignettes from organisational work. These I will have to disguise, except where material has been published with the consent of the organisation and its members. Often the work looks to hidden collusive dynamics and how these become embedded in work processes and structures. Often illusions and delusions have developed, and these need to be uncovered. Many organisational consultations make only small steps in making unconscious motivations and strategies conscious and thus amenable to conscious decision-making. This is because of the power of entrenched behaviours and their satisfaction of embedded desires individually and collectively. Also there is a strength in the repetition compulsion of past dynamics.

Vignette 1 – Finding Hidden Assumptions and Their Unconscious Influence

The project was in the justice area, and my team (myself, John Newton and Jane Chapman) interviewed and observed many prison officers across a range of jails in the state. We also spoke to prison governors, social workers, education officers and other ancillary professionals working in the prison system. Working with a project steering group from the justice department, many staff members in the field dispersed across the countryside associated us with what they referred to as the "pointy heads" from head office and may have been at first reluctant to speak. It had taken quite some time to get regional prison officer representation on the steering group – this itself indicating a distancing between head office and regional workers. However, by listening carefully to what the regional personnel had to say, and faithfully recounting their views in our reports, we gained trust. In fact, by our going to regional jails, most at some distance from the city, and listening during interviews, these staff members willingly took part in the research. This done, even though in the first instance when we arrived at a facility, a senior officer would gather some prison officers together and say "you, you, you and you go with these people and speak to them". So much for research volunteers! However, we soon came to the view that it was a rare occasion that such staff members found anyone interested in how they saw their roles and the experiences they had in those roles. As a result, the interview material was most informative and rich.

The project was examining the change in role that many officers found themselves in. It was a change from a primary custodial role to a case management role. As one officer put it, "you used to lock them up and throw away the key and now we have to talk to them, ask how they are and help them". No mean task with little training.

The focus of this vignette is on a particularly interesting dynamic where in one prison different areas competed for the prisoners' time. Usually, a prisoner's sentencing would involve conditions that particular programmes be mandated to be undertaken during the period of incarceration. This might include, for instance, psychological programmes such as violence management. In addition, educational programmes are offered to aid the prisoner toward rehabilitation – many prisoners having few employable skills and many with minimal work ethic. There was also an industry function producing simple chairs. The education and programme officers appeared to be competing with the industry officers for prisoner time and had not collaborated by setting mutual timetables and goals. Why was this? It seemed a simple thing to do.

As part of the project, we were conducting role analyses with pairs of role holders (see Long, Newton and Chapman 2006 where an extensive description of the method is given). This followed an organisational cultural analysis where we found several rifts or schisms between various functions. Role analyses were conducted with role holders across these rifts. One was between the programme and industry functions as described above. It was during these sessions that role holders came to encounter and learn in some depth about the experience of the other in their role, in their pair. This was often a revelation, as it was for education and industry officers. It was not that they didn't know about the role and tasks of the other, at least to a seemingly workable degree. But gaining a closer understanding of the experience, anxieties, frustrations and hopes of the other in their role led to the possibility of greater co-operation between the functions. A hypothesis here was that the different officers held untested hidden assumptions (Vince 2019) about the experiences and especially the intents of the other. In the role analyses such assumptions were challenged and more co-operative working relations began to occur. The mutual role analyses across many rifts worked similarly. This was not simply a matter of staff members getting to know one another better – a simple socialising function. It was a matter of different role holders in the system coming to understand the systemic pressures, physical and emotional, on the roles involved, the task-based and anti-task pulls on the roles, and their connectedness to one another in the overall system purposes. The unconscious dynamic seemed to be driven by the assumption that roles in areas other than one's own were not to be trusted. Perhaps this spilt over from the traditional mistrustful relations between prisoners and prison officers – a parallel process dynamic.

The project used a collaborative action research model. But beyond typical action research, we used ourselves as instruments to better understand the dynamics involved. For example, the project engendered strong emotions in each of us although each felt a different predominant emotion. These were fear, revulsion, and prurient curiosity. On further exploration with prison governors, these three emotions came forward as primary for many prison staff. Our own interactions as a research team were also helpful in understanding the dynamics within the system, and we would spend time reflecting on these.

Uncovering the hidden assumptions and the use of ourselves as instruments in discovering parallel processes allowed us to develop working hypotheses about the state of the system during role changes and in turn to support the staff members through developing appropriate communication channels and content.

Vignette 2 – Power Relations Introjected into Organisation Processes and Structures

I have written about this situation previously (Long 2016) but I think it is a good illustration of how organisational structures and processes get established reciprocally through the dynamics of power relations. This vignette highlights the way in which power relations become integrated into a socio-technical system and further influence those dynamics.

In a hospital research project studying the uptake of new technology, the relations between various professional roles and their functions were examined. During interviews we heard of "the surgeon personality" a role stance that led to surgeons being seen as distanced, aloof, and often abrupt. This was told to us not only by other medical staff but also by a couple of surgeons.[1] The role itself calls for speed of surgery, a clinical and focused state-of-mind, with the capacity to cut into human flesh with a steady hand and little of the emotion that many would have in so doing. In the last twenty or so years, the distancing of medical staff from patients has undergone change with patient choice about treatments being discussed more openly and doctors being seen as expert advisors rather than solely being seen as the authority who knows and decides all. Surgeons are highly regarded for their skills and in the history of medicine are amongst the first healers (Friedenberg 2009).

The system required that patients with a variety of tumour indications were first seen by the surgeon, who then could make a diagnosis with the help of medical imaging and other tests. The surgeon would then refer the patient to other specialist practitioners for treatment following surgery or following a diagnosis that surgery was not needed; the many different specialists being in quite different departments, each of which might be needed to treat the patient. In this process the surgeons held the keys to a referral system and thus held informal power alongside their authority for task. Whether the historical place of the surgeon, his/her skills and the role personality led to this place of power, or whether the place of power in the system reinforces the so-called role personality is most likely due to a complex non-linear systemic causality. But the resulting dynamic is introjected into the processes and procedures that take place in the hospital and in relations with patients. On the one hand, it introduces much-needed order and hierarchy into an anxiety-provoking system of processes dealing with cancer patients, who already have anxiety about their condition, and clinical staff who must deal with this anxiety and are also subject to vicarious trauma. On the other hand, the process leads to other discomforts. (For example, in this research many patients said they had to undergo numerous repeated embarrassing examinations because each new specialist needed to examine for themselves, and some of these patients had severely advanced tumours.) The whole system might be seen as a defence against anxiety (Armstrong and Rustin 2015). Amelioration of the anxieties in this research was to some extent provided through the incorporation of a "cancer nurse" into the clinics. This role allowed for some integration of both patient and clinician experience, although the number of such positions was few, perhaps due to historical and even continuing relations among nursing and medical roles.

Although this project took place many years ago, my subsequent research and consultancy work in hospitals show these still to be complex organisations with many personal and social defences against the anxieties associated with the work and the risks involved in tending to human lives. Often in a context of limited resources, staff members adhere to overall strict hierarchical cultures yet with small cohesive localised departmental teams. It is as if the overall culture is one of intense bubbles of co-operative work in a more hostile sea of demands from a central management itself facing demands from the wider culture – resourcing, community need, risk mitigation and meeting targets. This leads to many hospitals consisting of sometimes competing silos with limited communication between them. While strict hierarchies help support clear accountability, their defensive function in protecting staff members from anxieties about risks often leads to a culture of blame and hence further anxieties and self-protective measures that can become anti-task.

Vignette 3 – Perverse Dynamics

I became interested in studying perverse dynamics since studying perversion through working with a Lacanian psychoanalyst in the early 1980s. Later in the work with the justice system, I conducted research in a sex-offender prison, and although the research was on the changing role of prison officers, stories of perverse crimes and the nature of dealing with the offenders through therapy programs were discussed. I began to think about systems as sometimes being themselves perverse and looked for indications in several case studies (Long 2001, 2008). I found five major indicators of a perverse system:

I)   A narcissistic culture where personal gain is paramount and runs against the common good.
II) Psychological denial is a major dynamic – in cases of wrongdoing this is both known and not known at the same time (much like a prisoner I encountered in the sex-offender jail who both knew of his crime yet denied it almost in the same breath, perversely believing his own fabrications.)
III) Accomplices are involved in collusive cover-ups. (This may include large institutional collusions, such as found in institutional child or elder abuse.)
IV) Employees are treated in an instrumental manner.
V)   The perverse dynamic becomes self-perpetuating.

While the many high-profile institutional cases that I study in my book (Long 2008) demonstrate how perverse practices and cultures come to permeate a whole system, smaller instances of perverse practices can creep into otherwise well-functioning organisations. If not caught, they can become the thin edge of the wedge.

In a not-for-profit a senior manager was embezzling money. This manager was well liked and had been part of the organisation for many years – a person devoted to the cause of the organisation. Following the uncovering of the crime, the other senior managers decided to deal with the issue themselves rather than call in the police. There had been suspicions and doubts about the situation for some time. But there was the quite misguided deep belief that nothing like this could ever happen in the organisation. This, they argued, was an aberration rather than a realistic possibility.

The manager was dismissed and much of the money recovered. Organisation members were swamped with horror, sadness and grief at the loss of the well-liked manager and the abuse of trust. Many different views and perspectives emerged. The manager's situation was discussed. Was the embezzlement in any way justifiable given the personal situation of the manager? Had this manager always hidden their true self? Should the police have been involved? What did this mean about their organisation? I was consulted to help work through organisational grief.

I am not saying in this case the organisation as a whole was perverse. In many ways the members were perhaps simply deluded in their blind trust of all, with no possibility of internal risk entering their thoughts or strategies. But the indications in this situation were that a narcissistic attitude had grown in the manager concerned insofar as he stole for his own benefit monies meant for a community service, and that for some time other organisation members had known yet could not let themselves acknowledge the problem. Moreover, following the dismissal, members and the board had colluded in their minds, at least officially, that this was not a criminal offence but a kind of mishap that could be dealt with internally. My concern was that the values of the organisation with their implicit denial of the possibility of internal wrongdoing, and a kind of blind forgiveness without consequences would continue to put them in jeopardy. Moreover, the grief could not be worked through under such conditions. Reparation requires that there is acknowledgement of harm done (Long 2021). All this required long discussions, self and organisational exploration and a review of organisation values and how to put them realistically into practice.

The methods involved here are well beyond the diagnosis of a problem. They require working through the thoughts and feelings of participants. For Freud, the working through involves true remembering. Just as in modern methods of trauma therapy,[2] Freud noted the importance of remembering the facts of the patient's past before change could occur (Freud 1914). Such remembering stands in opposition to the unconscious repetition of defences in word or action. Working through is a nuanced way of developing and understanding mutative interpretations. These are not simple pronouncements by the therapist (or organisational consultant). They are meaningful insights generated through the interaction of analyst and analysand. They are insights that are in the mind, the body, and felt through the emotions. The working through is not an intellectual exercise, but a deep coming to new ways of being. The work of reparation following organisational traumas involves such a working through.

Vignette 4 – Unconscious Dynamics Internalised in Roles and Their Interrelations

A collaborative action research project examined the many roles within the pioneering inter-group project that is a Drug Court.[3] This project looked at ways to increase collaborative efforts between the many roles having an interest in the court. The first drug court was instituted in Miami, USA, in 1989. There are now more than 3,400 drug courts in the USA and in 20 other countries, including Australia. They are based on the idea of therapeutic jurisprudence and the belief that imprisonment is not the answer to drug-related crime.

Two major purposes of the drug court are:

1. Reduction of drug-related crime and protection of the community (case management focus).
2. The provision of Drug Treatment Orders (DTO) that support the well-being of programme participants in order to meet the previous aim (treatment focus).

Drug court team members necessarily have two lines of management: one through their "home" or departmental organisation and one through their drug court; the home organisations often have quite different and sometimes conflicting interests in the offences and offenders that the court faces, leading to confusion for the role holder who has such dual reporting lines. The "home" organisation roles range across police prosecutors, legal aid lawyers, department of justice case managers, social services social workers and drug treatment providers, housing officers, and the judiciary. The complexities for collaboration and team cohesion are multiple. For example, collaboration between police prosecutors, defence lawyers and social workers in the Drug Court team includes making careful and fine discernments about how the information needed to represent the offender and the purposes of the court in aiding rehabilitation for the offender and protecting the community. Yet, in order to do its work effectively and efficiently the team has to have a high level of collaborative capability. The research benefited from the commitment of the staff to further develop the role collaborations that faced many challenges considering their traditional backgrounds. Their commitment to the therapeutic goals of the court was evident.

Through interviews, observations and role plays, our research team, together with staff participants, discovered many hidden assumptions built into drug court roles and their understanding and expectations of other roles. Many of these became apparent during a role play where drug court staff took up the roles, other than their own, of players in an improvised court scenario. When a person trained in a particular institution is introduced to work in an interorganisational context with a new role, the move into the purposes and demands of the new role must be faced, often with some stress. And conflicts with the internalised "in-the-mind" purposes and demands of the "home" organisation are often present. This is over and above the usual conflicts between personal and role demands (Long 2016). Such role conflicts must first be brought to light, and while some aspects of the conflict are obvious, many are hidden and unconsciously affect the taking up of the new role. Once brought to light, they may be worked through – no easy task, especially because they are supported by socio-technical procedures. The challenges, however, are not simply to the person's ability to take up a role, although this can appear to be the issue. This may be deceptive. The organisational structures involving induction and training, work processes, agreements and procedures are different in each of the separate "home" organisations, and these most often lie at the basis of role conflict.

Vignette 5 – The Creative Power of the Unconscious

Mostly work for organisational consultants occurs when an organisation is found to have problems. That is perhaps why most of the literature on the unconscious dynamics of organisations has a focus on their problematic darker side, on the hidden thoughts and their realisations that surprise us because they spring from what we don't wish to see. The history of the unconscious as an idea has also though, a thread of ideas about its creative potential. This is especially clear in Schelling, Bion and Jung.

A consulting assignment with an inpatient psychiatric institution involved me staying in residence over a six-day period. I conducted many individual interviews and made observations of the work in meetings and group discussions, both large and small. On my last day there I provided a detailed report of my "cultural analysis" of the organisation along with recommendations for working with the dynamics encountered. I felt this was a necessary part of my contract with them. It was for discussion with all staff members. Although my own experience, thoughts, and emotions over the time that I had been deeply immersed there were used as background data to formulate my working hypotheses – using myself as an instrument alongside the data from interviews and observations – something of the quality of the organisational culture was missing from the formal report.

I decided to write a fable drawing on my inner Jonathan Swift. In the fable I named myself as a visiting anthropologist from the other side of the world and wove in my various experiences. For instance, I described coming to my accommodation in the middle of the night – to an empty house ablaze with lights and all curtains open. I felt exposed and vulnerable, totally unsure of what was outside and who could see in. Perhaps this paralleled how new patients or even new staff members might feel when coming to the facility for the first time. I drew on my own resources, and I drew the curtains. The fable went on to talk of the organisation as a tribe, and I described how I encountered their rituals and patterns of behaviour, some highly creative and containing, some more hidden and unspoken. My own travels through their spaces and processes were sometimes humorously described. Other times I illustrated the challenges they had given me. In this I could also summarise the content of the interviews - what the tribe had said to me.

In a large meeting the staff accepted and worked with the fable far more than the formal report, which I presume was taken in more fully at a later time. The mixture of analogy and humour stimulated much discussion. I believe that my fable brought forward many unconscious dynamics in a mostly palatable way. And staff were able to develop and formulate their own recommendations.

I had spent quite a few hours the night before my last day there writing my report. The evening before that I had had a disturbing dream concerning the work, and it was still resonating with me. The dream had a sort of fairy tale feel to it. Not a Disney fairy tale but more like a Brothers Grimms' tale or one prior to the sanitising of fairy tales. Children prefer the scary tales that then offer a resolution to altogether sweet tales with no scary parts. They give insight into the unconscious and recognition of a barely accessed truth. I was about to go to bed with the dream still knocking at the door of my brain when the idea of the fable came to me. It was my resolution to the disturbance of my dream. I sat down and wrote its 2,800 words then and there. I thanked the creativity of the unconscious for helping me put into a story the many strands that the organisational culture had brought to me. I could then take it to the staff for further creative work.

Further Uses of Methods That Explore the Unconscious in Organisational Work

While my vignette above shows the influence of dreams on an individual in a system, dreams can bring forward meaning for a collective. In a post-Bion environment, Gordon Lawrence brought forward the theory and practice of Social Dreaming (Lawrence 2005, 2007).[4] This was influenced by Jungian perspectives as well as by Bion and psychoanalyst Charlotte Beradt's collection of dreams during the 1930s Nazi era in Germany (Beradt 1968). She demonstrated how the social context permeated the dreams of her patients. In social dreaming, dreams are recounted by participants who also make associations and connections to the dreams. This is done in a matrix setting where participants are seated so as not to directly face each other (in a snowflake formation) to encourage a kind of dreamlike state of reverie. The aim is to discover social meaning through attention to the dreams (Armstrong 2023; Long and Manley 2019). Practised in an organisational context within the containment of a bounded project, aspects of the associative unconscious present in the organisation can be discovered along with unconscious collective desires, fears and defences (see Lawrence 2010 for many case examples).

Working with participants in writing workshops, I have used social dreaming to help unlock the deep purposes within their writing projects, whether academic writing, prose or even reports. The workshops are residential, and a small temporary community of authors is established. Through associations and connections to the dreams presented to the matrix, these authors come to gain greater confidence in their writing, its purpose and execution. This is done within the ethos that written work comes not only from the authors but also from their cultures and, in a sense, from all those who attend to and read that work, notwithstanding the issue of copyright in the law.

I have more recently come to understand dreams as anticipatory in the sense that they, along with the dreamers, hold and act on anticipations of the future. This is neither teleological nor predictive, but an actualisation of anticipations. And, just as humans are anticipatory, so are larger systems. Organisations hold a history, anticipations and hopes and the organisational culture with its associative unconscious can be understood as calling forward the dreams of its members, in a sense, commissioning the dreams. That is my hypothesis (Long 2019b).

Other socioanalytic methods, including drawings, social photo-matrices, role analysis and listening posts, have been used in organisational work (Long 2013; Stamenova and Hinshelwood 2018). These methods bring forward, through associative work, unconscious meaning. Borghi et al. (2021) for example worked with social dreaming to examine the experiences of prison workers in Italy, finding several themes that illuminated that experience. I use work role drawings (Nossal 2013) and role biographies (Long 2016) both in consulting and coaching. Associations to these can bring forward not only themes in work roles and systems but also contain anticipations of the future (Long 2019b).

Notes

1 It should be noted that this is regarded as a "role personality" and is not intended to describe the persons in the role. Persons may or may not also have such a personality.
2 Trauma is also recognised as a psycho-social phenomenon. It is important for communities too, to remember rather than reenact the traumas and prevent the re-traumatisation that so often occurs in racism, homophobia, wars and all processes and dynamics that involve excluded persons (Scanlon and Adlam 2022).
3 This research was done through the National Institute for Organisation Dynamics Australia (NIODA) and was supported and funded by the Department of Justice in Victoria. The research team included Prof. Susan Long and Dr Nuala Dent.
4 For a description of the method see https://www.tavinstitute.org/wp-content/uploads/2019/05/The-Practice-of-Social-Dreaming-Guiding-Principles.pdf and Long and Manley 2019.

References

Armstrong, D. (2023). 'The Practice of Social Dreaming', https://www.tavinstitute.org/wp-content/uploads/2019/05/The-Practice-of-Social-Dreaming-Guiding-Principles.pdf [accessed 10 June 2024].

Armstrong, D. and Rustin, M. (2015). *Social Defences Against Anxiety: Explorations in a Paradigm*. London: Routledge.

Beradt, C. (1968). *The Third Reich of Dreams*. Chicago: Quadrangle Books.

Borghi, L., Cassardo, C., Mingarelli, E. and Vegni, E. (2021). 'The Relevance of Social Dreaming for Action Research: Exploring Jail Workers' Unconscious Thinking of the Changes in the Prison Organization', *Research in Psychotherapy, Psychopathology, Process and Outcome*, vol. 24, no. 2, p. 542.

Freud, S. (1914). *Remembering, Repeating and Working Though*. S.E. vol. 12, pp. 147–156.

Friedenberg, Z. (2009). *Surgery over the Centuries*. Great Shelford: Janus Publishing Co.

Ginzburg, C. (1983). 'Clues: Morelli, Freud, and Sherlock Holmes', in U. Eco and T.A. Seboak (eds.) *The Sign of Three: Dupin, Holmes, Peirce*, pp. 81–118. Bloomington: Indiana University Press.

Lacan, J. (1977). *Ecrits*. London: Tavistock Publications.

Lawler, D. and Sher, M. (2023). *Systems Psychodynamics: Voices from the Field*. Chapter 12. London: Routledge.

Lawrence, W.G. (2005). *Introduction to Social Dreaming*. London: Karnac.

Lawrence, W.G. (ed.) (2007). *Infinite Possibilities of Social Dreaming*. London: Karnac.

Lawrence, W.G. (ed.) (2010). *The Creativity of Social Dreaming*. London: Karnac.

Long, S.D. (1991). 'The Signifier and the Group', *Human Relations*, vol. 44, no. 4, pp. 389–401.

Long, S.D. (2001). 'Organisational Destructivity and the Perverse State of Mind', Plenary paper delivered at the Annual Meeting of the International Society for the Psychoanalytic Study of Organisations (ISPSO) Paris.

Long, S.D. (2008). *The Perverse Organisation and Its Deadly Sins*. London: Karnac.

Long, S.D. (ed.) (2016). *Transforming Experience in Organisations*. London: Karnac.

Long, S.D. (2019a). 'The Unconscious Won't Go Away – Especially in Organisations', *Organisation and Social Dynamics*, vol. 19, no. 2, pp. 218–229.

Long, S.D. (2019b). 'Dreaming a Culture', *Socioanalysis*, vol. 21, pp. 59–70.

Long, S.D. (2021). 'Repairing the Damage: Wishful, Defensive or Restorative?' *Organisational and Social Dynamics*, vol. 21, no. 1, pp. 28–39.

Long, S.D. and Harney, M. (2013). 'The Associative Unconscious', in S. Long (ed.). *Socioanalytic Methods*, pp. 3–22. London: Karnac.

Long, S.D. and Manley, J. (eds.) (2019). *Social Dreaming: Philosophy, Research, Theory and Practice*. London: Routledge.

Long, S.D., Newton, J. and Chapman, J. (2006). 'Role Dialogue: Organizational Role Analysis with Pairs from the Same Organization', in J. Newton, S. Long and B. Sievers (eds.) *Coaching in Depth: The Organisational Role Analysis Method*, pp. 95–112. London: Karnac.

Mersky, R. (2001). 'Falling from Grace – When Consultants Go Out of Role: Enactment in the Service of Organizational Consultancy', *Socioanalysis*, vol. 3, pp. 37–53.

Nossal, B. (2013). The Use of Drawing as a Tool in Socioanalytic Exploration, in S. Long (ed.). *Socioanalytic Methods*, pp. 67–90. London: Routledge.

Peirce, C.S. (1958). *Collected Papers of Charles Sanders Peirce* Volumes I–VI (ed. by C. Hartshorne and P. Weiss), 1931–1935, and Volumes VII–VIII (ed. by A.W. Burks).

Scanlon, C. and Adlam, J. (2022). *Psycho-Social Explorations of Trauma, Exclusion and Violence: Un-Housed Minds and Inhospitable Environments*. London: Routledge.

Stamenova, K. and Hinshelwood, R. (eds.) (2018). *Methods of Research into the Unconscious: Applying Psychoanalytic Ideas to Social Science*. London: Routledge.

Vince, R. (2019). 'Institutional Illogics: The Unconscious and Institutional Analysis', *Organization Studies*, vol. 40, no. 7, pp. 953–973.

9 Neuropsychoanalysis and the Unconscious

The idea and meaning of the unconscious have become ubiquitous, unbounded and borderless. It now sits within the process of modern advertising with implicit messages conferring desired attributes on the consumer beyond the actual utility of the product or service being offered: a process of unconscious association. It is in the language of "unconscious bias", a pre-determined attitude gained unwittingly and speedily before consciously encountering a person or situation – deemed to be present in workplaces unless guarded against (Ikiseh 2021). It lies at the basis of psychotherapy, whether in the form of individual depth psychology where the return of the repressed in symptoms is examined through attention to the transference; in family therapy where one family member unconsciously becomes a symptom for the family system; and even in behaviour therapy, overtly antagonistic to ideas of the unconscious, yet where behavioural patterns are discerned as repeated without conscious recognition. It is linked to systemic processes in groups and organisations so that role holders are understood to behave in ways that are determined by hidden unconscious cultural dynamics.

While the past chapters of this book have been primarily concerned with the way that different psychoanalytic and social writers and practitioners of the twentieth, reaching into the twenty-first century, have defined and theorised the unconscious, this chapter approaches some ideas taken from the neurosciences. For instance, Eisold (2010) describes a "new unconscious" as informed by developments in cognitive psychology, neuroscience, systems thinking and research into emotions. Hassin, Uleman and Bargh (2012) in the abstract of their edited collection say:

> Unconscious processes seem to be capable of doing many things that were thought to require intention, deliberation, and conscious awareness. Moreover, they accomplish these things without the conflict and drama of the psychoanalytic unconscious. These processes range from complex information processing, through goal pursuit and emotions, to cognitive control and self-regulation.
>
> (p. 1)

DOI: 10.4324/9781003559818-9

These are the views from cognitive neuroscience, focused primarily on perception and cognition. The unconscious here is an "out of awareness" function where perceptions, decisions, reactions and even intentions occur almost automatically in response to environmental conditions. Such an approach has become popular, perhaps primarily because it appeals to a positivistic scientism that appears rigorous in the eyes of today's "evidence-based" empirical psychology. Some, however, see the domination of the study of consciousness by the neurosciences as problematic, McVeigh (2024) naming this theoretical predominance as tyrannical because it emphasises the physical "hardware" of the body over the "software" of culture.

While the psychoanalytic idea of a repressed unconscious is different from the cognitive neuroscience idea, the unconscious is also being explored in terms of neuropsychological functions. Carhart-Harris and Friston (2010), for instance study the physical neurological substrates of secondary and primary process thinking, examining the functional organisation of intrinsic brain networks and the secondary process as described by Freud. They describe "the phenomenology of primary process thinking" where they, "reviewed evidence that it can be observed in certain non-ordinary states and cite studies indicating that these states share a common neurophysiology" (p. 1281).

Arguing that new ways of understanding the unconscious from current ways found in psychoanalytic object-relations thinking are needed, Detel (2021) attempts to categorise different aspects of the unconscious between what he calls the non-mental control elements of mental states and processes – which include neuronal activity and unconscious body schemata – and the mental unconscious. In the mental unconscious, he includes the psychoanalytic ideas of a repressed and non-repressed unconscious, but also what he describes as meta mechanisms whose process, structure and functions unconsciously operate as ground to this mental unconscious.

> This picture of the unconscious clearly departs from traditional views of the unconscious. For example, it abandons the still common way of talking about the operations of the ego, superego, and id. There are no instances or even substances in the soul that "do" something or "perform" a certain activity by their own power. Rather, functional mechanisms run on the basis of certain triggers, but their functions are not always free of contradictions and can come into conflict.
>
> (Detel 2021, p. 3)

Berlin (2011) reviews several articles that explore what she refers to as "a revival and re-conceptualisation of some of the key concepts of psychoanalytic theory…the processes that keep unwanted thoughts from entering consciousness" (Berlin 2011, p. 5) and concludes that we still know little about the processes that foster or allow interchanges between conscious and unconscious thinking. While Fertuck (2011) believes that we will only learn more through individual case analysis rather than pursuing ideas of repression or dissociation more generally.

> No doubt these and other developments in neuroscience will tell us more of what Kahneman (2011) calls "thinking fast"; the sort of thinking that occurs automatically below the level of consciousness and greatly influences conscious reflections, and conscious determinations (named as "thinking slow") that take more time. Much of the experimental work that Kahneman cites gives the impression that our conscious reflections are but justifications or rationalisations for what we initially decide unconsciously in a reflexive manner, based on learning and experience as well as instinct (an idea familiar to psychoanalysis).
>
> (Long, 2016, p. 94)

Again, this is a vast domain of theories that I can only touch at the edges; those edges being where neuroscientific ideas touch depth psychology approaches.[1] The idea of the unconscious is hard to navigate in these waters. But just as Derrida (1978) argued, its meaning, as with any word or concept, can never be nailed down in an absolute way but is dependent on the words and concepts that surround it, from which it differs and where it is located: in the context of specific theories. For those who wish to use it to inform practice and theory, the idea must be continually revisited and carefully defined lest it becomes stale and meaningless – spread unthinkingly into everyday parlance, or trapped within a false context, stripped of any truth that might be found through its articulation.

One revisitation is being undertaken by the links between neuroscience and psychoanalysis. For example, the journal *Neuropsychoanalysis* describes itself as providing "an arena for integrating the explosion of neuroscientific insights into existing psychoanalytic theories and models, and for enriching behavioural and cognitive neuroscience, neurology, neuropsychology and related fields with the dynamic perspectives of psychoanalytic thought and practice" (*Neuropsychoanalysis* 2023).

Before examining more recent developments though, I want to visit a book that influenced me back in the 1980s and 1990s. It is "The Origin of Consciousness in the Breakdown of the Bicameral Mind" by Julian Jaynes. It was perhaps naïve of me to think I could write about the unconscious without encountering a deeper examination of consciousness, and now I find this is inescapable. The Stanford Encyclopedia of Philosophy outlines multiple theories of consciousness (2014) and states that perhaps multiple theories are needed because of the many kinds of consciousness identified by scholars. I will investigate Jaynes' work (Jaynes 1976), influential and controversial when it was published and still with impact (see Kuijsten 2022; McVeigh 2024; and the Julian Jaynes Society julianjaynes.org) because it does lead to the psychoanalytic neuropsychology of current times. I avidly read the book because it brought together my many interests in language (especially the work of Noam

Chomsky and language development that I studied for my master's thesis), literature, history and neuropsychology, and moreover, he writes about complicated concepts in an engaging manner. At that time, as I have mentioned earlier, I could not accept a psychology dominated by behaviourism that did not take language structure and development seriously. In Jaynes, I found a researcher who believed that language was the foundation for the sort of consciousness that we have. Challenging to read and with ideas that seem counter-intuitive to the contemporary reader, it warrants a place in the evolution of the idea of the unconscious.

Initially, as mentioned earlier, it is important that consciousness is carefully defined. There are many denotations and assumptions about what is meant – just as with the unconscious – some of which are just rough everyday notions, for instance, that consciousness is simply awareness or being awake. Jaynes makes his definition clear, and this gives us insight into what he considers unconscious. He is clear that much of our action is done unconsciously, automatically, reactively if you like. He introduces us to the notion of consciousness as an internal mind space that includes an analogue "I". In his definition, consciousness is an "operator not a thing or repository and it is intimately bound up with volition and decision" (Jaynes 1976, p. 55). It is something akin to what we might call self-consciousness. "Subjective conscious mind is an analogue of what is called the real world. It is built up with a vocabulary or lexical field whose terms are all metaphors or analogues of behaviour in the physical world" (Jaynes 1976, p. 55). And this analogue consciousness (including an analogue "I" and a metaphorical "me") is not a simple perceptual imprint or memory storage. It is not reactivity or a copy of experience. It is not necessary for concept development or even for learning. Each of these, he meticulously argues, differs from consciousness. Consciousness is a metaphor for our behaviour. Take, for example, the analogue "I". This is a metaphor for the physical body and its behaviours, but more so. It is not a simple replica, but an internalised experience linked to the body, yet surpassing physical and time limitations in imagination. It can introspectively explore a "me" that thinks and feels. It can narrate its own various experiences and the experiences of the created "me" and observations of others, and through these capabilities the "I" experiences mastery of its own destiny with a sense of freedom of choice. For Jaynes, consciousness brings with it the experience of free will.

He builds his argument around consciousness as having developed through the human acquisition of language based on metaphor and association.

> When we consciously think of *a* tree, we are indeed conscious of a particular tree, of the fir or the oak or the elm that grew beside our house, and let it stand for the concept, just as we can let a concept word stand for it as well. In fact, one of the great functions of language is to let the word stand for a concept, which is exactly what we do in writing or speaking about conceptual material.
>
> (Jaynes 1976, p. 31)

Before language, he argues, there was no consciousness in this sense of a reflective inner mind space, and no capacity for introspection through an "I". There was awareness, perception, reflexivity, memory, learning, even rough-hewn concepts and all the automatic and learned behavioural responses we have today. But as creatures subject to language and metaphoric association, we do have an operative inner mind space or interiority. This we tend to locate in our heads behind our eyes, although some past cultures have located it elsewhere, and in some psychotic disturbances, it gets located externally and visits as a hallucinatory experience. Indeed, he examines the vestiges of what he names a bicameral mind in modern-day experience; one such hangover being found in hypnotism – of particular interest because of the Freudian move from hypnosis or mesmerism into psychoanalytic methods using free association: this latter being a method that we might say from a Jaynesian perspective fits with the idea of an internal mind space rather than a method relying on the authority of the external voice of the hypnotist.[2] In hypnotism, the voice of the hypnotist, says Jaynes, becomes the centre of the process and the subject must focus all consciousness on that voice.

> If the subject is not able to narrow his consciousness in this fashion, if he cannot forget the situation as a whole, if he remains in the consciousness of other considerations, such as the room and his relationship to the operator, if he is still narratizing with his analogue "I" or seeing his metaphorical "me" being hypnotized, hypnosis will be unsuccessful.
>
> (Jaynes 1976, p. 387)

Having introduced us to the idea of consciousness, Jaynes looks to its biological substrate in the brain and to its historical emergence. Working with evidence from the two sides of the brain (left and right hemispheres), their structures and functions, he studies the language centres of the brain in these different hemispheres. He argues, using the evidence from research into brain anatomy and function, that the area of the brain that links to language in the non-dominant right hemisphere (parallel to Wernicke's area in the left hemisphere, responsible for much of language structure and understanding) was more active in pre-linguistic or early linguistic humans. He names the earlier organisation of the brain as Bicameral.

The bicameral organisation engages the right brain language function and words are heard as if from outside – just as in what we now call hallucinatory experience. Without inner reflective space, linguistic "thought" comes not from what feels like the inside but from outside. What might such experience be like where a voice from the outside guides and commands? This, claims Jaynes, is the experience of the gods commanding and deciding found in early religion. From here, Jaynes employs extensive and compelling evidence from ancient literature such as the Iliad and the Old Testament in support of his theory.

Such is the bicameral experience prior to modern human consciousness. Using the example of driving a car with constant unconscious reactions to the driving environment and with consciousness somewhere else, perhaps in conversation or listening to music, he says:

> I am related to a world I immediately obey in the sense of driving on the road and not on the sidewalk. And I am not conscious of any of this. And certainly not logical about it. I am caught up, unconsciously enthralled, if you will, in a total interacting reciprocity of stimulation that maybe constantly threatened or comforting, appealing or repelling, responding to the change in traffic and particular aspects of it with trepidation or confidence, trust or distrust, while my consciousness is still off on other topics. Now simply subtract that consciousness and you have what a bicameral man would be like.
>
> (Jaynes 1976, p. 85)

All this until something unexpected happens. For the modern mind, consciousness is quickly switched to the situation. For bicameral man, argues Jaynes, such consciousness is not present. He or she waits to hear from the voice – most often experienced hallucination-like but understood as from the gods – in order to act.

There is an extensive period of history during which the bicameral mind was established and later moved to a mind with consciousness (an inner mind space with an introspective and analogue "I"). This is of considerable importance to Jaynes. How did the conscious mind as we now experience it come into being? Jaynes hypothesises that the advent of giving proper names to individuals heralded a culture requiring more organised law. Any previous hallucinated voices of linguistic communication now became personalised, and gods were created with distinct hierarchical authority to identify these voices. Much later, due to increases in new challenges to which the god voices could not consistently respond, humans had to rely more heavily on making decisions themselves from identifying the inner voices as their own. In effect, the increasing complexities of human culture, especially the complexities of living in cities, led to consciousness – the inner mind space where we talk to ourselves and narrate events. It is important to note that Jaynes is not talking about a change in brain form or structure but about development of function. For Jaynes, consciousness is a culturally learned phenomenon not an evolutionary biological development, having more to do with "sociopolitical arrangements than neurological structures" (McVeigh 2024, p. 5). Although Jaynes does distinguish between the two, one might argue that culture itself is an evolutionary adaptation and Jaynes can be read that way when he says that it is groups that evolve (Jaynes 1976, pp. 126–127). The question of how biological and cultural evolution are complexly intertwined is itself a conundrum.

The argument is too extensive to condense here, and it is not my task now to judge the veracity of, or problems with his analysis. The reader can find much of this on the Julian Jaynes website. Suffice to say that Jaynes learned languages of the antiquities to study their texts and made intense investigations into anthropology and archaeology. My interest lies with his conception of consciousness and unconsciousness, especially in extending the definitions of these. In his work, the unconsciousness of habitual and responsive behaviour rather than a repressed unconscious leads into the modern perspectives in neuropsychoanalysis.

Before leaving Jaynes, though, it seems worth saying that much of the psychoanalytic unconscious could be conceptualised as a special part of Jaynes' idea of consciousness. Although repressed, we might consider that the Freudian unconscious has a mind space with an analogue "I". It is just that for many defensive reasons, it is a separated mind space from the available space for introspection. In this mind, the instincts transformed as drives can have representation, and these may become fully conscious. However, the id function of what Boxer (2022) calls the radically unconscious – that which is inherent and cannot be accessed – could be understood by Jaynesian analysis as part of the bicameral organisation of mind; deeply inherent and pre-linguistic. I don't want to push this comparison too strongly or too far because both are part of complex extended theories and certainly not identical. But throughout the exploration of the evolution of the idea of the unconscious, there are places where different theorists and thinkers come across the same or similar phenomena for which they wish to give explanations. Moreover, since Jaynes' initial work, definitions of consciousness have become more nuanced. In the extensive area of the neurosciences, the search for the nature of consciousness continues. I stress again, the need to consider the definition being chosen during any such search, because there are many and varied definitions.

It is perhaps the work of Mark Solms and his associates that moves the idea of the unconscious, with a psychoanalytic flavour, most solidly into the field of neuroscience and starts to investigate those elusive links between the unconscious and consciousness alluded to by Berlin (2011). Solms, the first to use the term "neuropsychoanalysis" takes us back to the question that puzzled Schelling and the philosophers, and scholars such as Jaynes, more so than the idea of the unconscious. This is the question of consciousness. He names it, following Chalmers (1996) and others, "the hard problem of consciousness" (Solms 2018, p. 2), which poses the question of how we have the subjective experience of consciousness. As Berlin (2011) says, echoing some of what Jaynes said almost fifty years before, "unconscious processes appear capable of doing many things previously thought to require deliberation, intention and conscious awareness such as processing complex information and emotions, goal pursuit, self-regulation and cognitive control" (p. 20). Fertuck (2011) agrees, stating that "unconscious processes are more adaptive, smarter and survival oriented than previously assumed by psychoanalysis" (p. 46). If then such processes are carried out unconsciously, in the sense of being out of awareness, why do we have conscious self-awareness, decision-making and subjectivity? And how do these come about?

And, here again, we must be clear about how consciousness is being defined. Challenging the idea of consciousness being produced by the cortex, Solms' affective neuroscience cites the impetus for consciousness (not necessarily self-consciousness) as an effect of the old brain – the reticular activating system at the top of the brainstem. This neural system is responsible for consciousness, is neither cortical nor perceptual, but is affective. It registers internal states (hunger, fear, arousal) rather than external perceptions. Arousal is activated when a need is unmet and thus consciousness is seen as linked to survival in meeting needs. When internal states favour survival, they are felt as good. Perception is not conscious but feeling adds to perception and makes it conscious (primary consciousness). Predictive models reduce surprise and the need for consciousness – they allow automatic responses.

Solms (2018) initially challenges some long-held beliefs inherited from the Cartesian perspective on mind and body distinction, one of these being that brain processes somehow cause or directly give rise to subjectivity. Solms answers that there is a dual aspect: both body and mind as manifestations of "something" other than these independently; that there is no direct causative link between physiology and psychology. What then is this "something"? He argues that subjective conscious experience is beyond simple or even complex cognitive function. He is also clear that, as described by Berlin and Fertuck, most physiological and even many cognitive functions are unconscious; we don't feel or experience them. I might add, this is unless we train our consciousness to specifically focus on them as do some Yogis or subjects under biofeedback conditions. Even then the training is to maintain or influence the function rather than become directly conscious of it.

Solms goes on to ask:

Why is experience left unexplained, even when we have explained the performance of all the relevant cognitive functions in its vicinity?

(2018, p. 3)

He comes to the answer, that consciousness arises and lies with feelings; with emotions.[3] He locates the beginnings of consciousness in the Extended Reticular-Thalamic Activating System (ERTAS) located in the upper brainstem. This activates alertness and gives rise to the subjective feeling of consciousness. Cortical or cognitive consciousness, thinking, may follow, being influenced by the sensorimotor cortex (Solms 2013a; 2018). Moreover, Solms quotes evidence that describes when the cortex is removed or not present, as in some animal studies (ugh! My personal response) or with some unfortunate children born without a cortex, consciousness and affect are still present. This, it should be noted, is consciousness in the form of alertness and receptivity. There is no way of knowing if any self-reflection is occurring. It is when the ERTAS is damaged that consciousness is lost.[4] While contending that consciousness and subjectivity are not synonymous, he says:

> The arousal processes that produce what is conventionally called "wake-fulness" constitute the experiencing subject. In other words, the experiencing subject is constituted by affect.
>
> (Solms 2018, p. 6)

This is the primary emotionally experiencing subject who can then consciously respond to perceptual and cognitive representations and think about them. "The secondary (perceptual and cognitive) form of consciousness is achieved only when the subject of consciousness *feels* its way into its perceptions and cognitions, which are unconscious in themselves" (Solms 2018, p. 6). Subjectivity, that which arises from a self-organising function in the brain then finds a place for thinking. Kundstadt (2013) says, "If I understand Solms correctly, he is arguing that affect allows ideational consciousness to create the structured space needed for thinking, not that affect supports the meaning of the thinking process, which, in fact, it may distort". This space needed for thinking is what we colloquially think of as a mind.

Further to his argument is an explanation of how conscious decisions, predictions and actions are taken. In this he translates Freud's idea of the pleasure principle into neurological and physiological terms and discusses the function of homeostasis – or "preferred states" in the language of self-organising systems – regarding survival.

> The fact that self-organizing systems must monitor their own internal states in order to persist (that is, to exist, to survive) is precisely what brings active forms of subjectivity about. The very notion of selfhood is justified by this existential imperative. It is the origin and purpose of mind.
>
> (Solms 2018, p. 10)

His language here is of "active subjectivity", implying a more passive subjectivity monitored out of awareness.

Without going into the extensive detail of his arguments, where he renames several Freudian concepts according to more recent neurological and energetic research, I stress his conclusions that brain does not produce conscious subjectivity in a direct causal manner. Although his argument that consciousness begins in the ERTAS may seem to contradict this (i.e. direct causation of arousal), he avoids this contradiction through his analysis of a complex self-organising system that is neither brain nor mind. It is this system involving an "extended form of homeostasis", he argues, that gives rise to subjectivity. This functional organisation is neither purely physiological nor psychological. His is a dualist position that states that while both may seem to be separate and causally linked through efficient causation (normally understood as cause and effect), they are more linked through systemic organisation. Both mind and physiological functions have a common base function. This function is located within the deep brainstem responsible for arousal and the feeling of experience itself.

I'm not fully convinced that Solms has wholly evaded the popular notion that consciousness is "caused by" brain functioning – the ERTAS is part of the brain, albeit not the cortex, and it does seem to lie at an originating point. That is, there is no room for a spiritual cause beyond body. However, the self-organising function that creates both physiological and psychological functions that together form consciousness and subjectivity can be understood, I believe, as a formal cause in the Aristotelian sense. It is a functional form that enables consciousness. This formulation of consciousness challenges the Cartesian dichotomy of mind/body, as does its formulation of the unconscious in contra-distinction to consciousness. Moreover, Solms places free will as a fundamental principle of self-organising systems. The "something" function of a self-organising system is yet to be more fully understood, however interesting it is as a working hypothesis.

Solms' project (Solms and Turnbull 2011; Solms 2018) is to reinvigorate or recast psychoanalysis through an intensive revision of Freud's own neurological papers, especially "Project for a Scientific Psychology" (1895). He quotes Freud's anticipation that one day neuroscience would be able to provide an underpinning for his ideas, but that given the lack of methodological research tools and evidence from the neuroscience of the late nineteenth century, this was not then possible. Surveying developments since then, Solms and his associates believe it is time now to revisit the relations between neuroscience and psychoanalysis, especially since new technologies allow studying the brain's dynamic processes.

Part of his argument regards the predictive nature of living systems. Neurological predictions, he argues, when successful and a matter of fact, are not consciously experienced. It is when unpredictability occurs that conscious activity is required (echoes of Jaynes).[5] When something occurs that is not explained by unconscious predictions, the thinking cortex comes into action. Consciousness is aroused, effects occur (effects being a response to a need) and corrections are made to "prediction errors" through "precision modulation".

How then does this relate to the repressed unconscious or something similar? For Solms, the unconscious is largely a vast automatised system of memory and associations. This is in the service of meeting needs for survival and problem solving. Solms brings in a cognitive view of the unconscious linked to such evolutionary behaviour. Memory moves from episodic memory (short-term and connected to life solutions and predictions about how to act) to semantic memory (involving rules, and what I think linguists would describe as signification) to procedural memory (which is not representational but associative and habitual – one thinks here of the associative unconscious). The move to long-term memory is done quickly and unconsciously in the cortex. This allows for the freeing of representational space in episodic memory. Such automatization supports most of behaviour through action programmes – things we don't have to think about consciously. All this involves predictions unconsciously made, by-passing conscious deliberation and based on experience (Solms 2022).

But things can go awry and Solms is a therapist interested in the entrenched symptoms of his patients. Many poor predictions become autonomized, leading to repetitive behaviours that don't work to solve problems but lead into maladaptive thinking and behaviour, and often, distressing emotions that recur. These are prediction errors. Many of these are autonomized during infancy and childhood before mature problem solving is possible. He names the Oedipus conflict as demonstrating such errors. The child seeks solutions to his or her wishes in relation to the parents – solutions that cannot be realised. But these prediction errors become "repressed" and autonomized, leading to repetitions that forever evade solutions. Solms names this as the subject aspiring beyond the means of achieving them (such as in the case of the Oedipal child in Freudian psychoanalysis) – the whole experience being one of distressed affective structures that are consciously experienced in associated situations.

> The cognitive unconscious consists in predictions that are *legitimately* automatized. That is, they are deeply automatized because they work so well; they reliably meet the underlying needs that they are aimed at.
>
> The repressed, by contrast, is *illegitimately* (or prematurely) automatized. Illegitimate automatization occurs *when the ego is overwhelmed by its problems*; that is, when it *cannot* work out how to satisfy id demands in the world. This happens a lot in childhood, when the ego is feeble.
>
> (Solms 2018)

Solms acknowledges that the complexities of psychoanalysis as theory and method are still beyond what he has translated into neurological terms, and he has some disagreements with the Freudian view. Nonetheless, he argues that the core concerns of psychoanalysis are being substantiated by neuroscience, citing numerous studies.

The work is new and evolving. For instance, whereas in 2011 he says:

> What we observed were dynamic phenomena, in which the primary interacting forces clearly revolved around emotional states. More-over, these emotionally determined dynamics caused important aspects of the cognitive processes involved to become unconscious. By intervening psychoanalytically in these dynamics, moreover, it was possible to reverse the dynamic process in question and return the repressed cognitions to consciousness.
>
> (Solms and Turnbull 2011, pp. 7–8)

By 2018, Solms claims that there is no return of the repressed – a conception central to Freudian psychoanalysis. There is a return of affect but not of memory.

Where I differ from Freud in this regard is that *I do not believe the repressed ever returns*, it is only the *affect* (which it fails to regulate) that returns. How many patients actually remember their Oedipal strivings, even in psychoanalysis, for example? This is because *non-declarative memories are just that: non-declarative*. Non-declarative memories are purely associative (and permanently unconscious) action tendencies of the kind described by LeDoux, as with Pavlov's dogs. No thinking occurs, not even implicitly.

(Solms 2018)

For Freud, the return of the repressed is in the form of a symptom, slip of the tongue, joke or dream. For Solms, the return is an emotion only. This has strong implications for the psychoanalytic treatment. If the emotion returns without cognitive representation, then the psychoanalytic meaning of symptom becomes questioned. In the treatment, transference becomes a reworking of old problems through an experience in the here and now of a repetitive pattern of behaviour and affect. For psychoanalysts generally, symptoms are signifiers and patients do have conscious experience of their symptoms, not simply the emotional effects of the symptoms. For instance, in obsessional neuroses, where the symptom is an obsessive thought or act that is repeated, the origins of the thought or act can be remembered – see, for example, the memories in the Wolf Man case (Freud 1918) where the patient remembered specific instances that led to obsessive acts. One such act was the necessity to breathe out strongly when encountering certain circumstances linked to the devil, including seeing cripples. This was traced back to a memory of visiting his father in a sanatorium and seeing him crippled, such a memory becoming what Freud describes as a prototype for his patient's reactions to any crippled person. The analysis surfaced the ambivalent emotions the patient held toward his father – strong love and hate – and that were transferred to his religious life and reactions to God and the Devil. And, yes, such emotion was central to the development of this breathing obsession. But the memories linked to its aetiology were also discovered and remembered. Transference, in such cases as this, is a re-living of meaning, not simply of affect.

There will continue to be developments and criticisms of this neuropsychoanalytic approach, and the question of brain/mind parallels will continue to be explored. The more difficult issue is of causation – an issue confronted by Solms through his dual aspect monistic approach and his reference to self-organising systems. While the unconscious is seen primarily in cognitive terms as automatised behaviour patterns – a position, aspects of which are well supported by research – any other aspect of the unconscious is still left as mysterious. And although it is through the ERTAS that arousal occurs, as Jaynes (1976) has discussed, arousal is not identical to subjectivity, which itself may have different layers and forms; alongside different levels and forms of consciousness (see, for example, the Barrett Seven Levels of Consciousness model (2023) that works with different levels of what might be called self-consciousness, and ideas of altered states of consciousness, all affecting subjective experience).

As stressed earlier, definitions are crucial. Henriques (2023), for example, differentiates three different kinds of consciousness which he designates as Mind 1, Mind 2 and Mind 3. Mind 1 he names as functional awareness and reactivity; not necessarily needing a brain as demonstrated by drones, for example, that can be programmed to be responsive to aspects of the environment. Mind 2 is named as the subjective experience of being, which includes perception and qualitative experience, which he argues is found in many animals as well as humans. Mind 3 is "explicit, recursive, self-consciousness" (Henriques 2023, p. 1) that has evolved with language and civilisation. Differentiating mind from subjectivity through these three definitions perhaps allows for a better understanding of the complexities of what we mean by consciousness and unconsciousness, although the hard question of how it is that subjectivity arises is still a curiosity.

As I have pointed out, basic awareness and reactivity in humans and animals, Solms argues is primarily emotional. There is no evidence that the reactivity that Henriques notes is programmed into machines involves emotion. The machine does not have an equivalent of the parts of the old brain responsible for arousal. Henriques' theory is based on the idea that "life, mind and culture emerge as novel dimensions as a function of new information processing and communication systems" (Henriques 2021) harking back to some ideas in Jaynes, although now with an even stronger behavioural perspective involved in their study.

Intensively comparing such approaches, as the dual aspect neuropsychoanalytic theory of Mark Solms and neuro-psychological/behavioural unitary theories such as that propounded by Henriques, is not my purpose. Nonetheless, although vastly different, Jaynes, Solms and Henriques, are theories of emergence depending on evolution and survival in dynamic environments.

It will be in the next chapter that the ideas of consciousness and unconsciousness in nature are explored more fully. The idea of emergence and its link to free will continues to be of importance.

Notes

1 There are many other approaches to the unconscious from the perspective of the neurosciences. See, for example, Weinberger and Stoycheva (2020), who look at the unconscious primarily in terms of normal cognitive functions and who discuss Computational Neuroscience, examining how the brain computes experience.

2 It should be clear though that the Jaynesian inner space "I" is not directly equivalent to the psychoanalytic subject, despite similarities, because of the very different theoretical positions of Jaynes and Psychoanalysis.

3 As with Freud's 1915 contention, Solms insists that emotions are not unconscious. It is the very nature of feelings that we feel them. They are consciously experienced.

4 Whereas Jaynes regards the left and right hemispheres as providing functional differences about bicameral and modern consciousness, Solms locates functional

differences between the old brain (consciousness) and the cortex (mainly unconscious) in accordance with current neurological research.
5 I can't find any reference in Solms to Jaynes' work although both seem to be "playing in a similar space" where the interiority of mind emerges.

References

Barrett, R. (2023). 'Seven Levels of Consciousness Model', https://www.barrettacademy.com/7-levels-of-consciousness [accessed 5 October 2023].

Berlin, H. (2011). 'The Neural Basis of the Dynamic Unconscious', *Neuropsychoanalysis*, vol. 13, no. 1, pp. 5–31.

Boxer, P. (2022). 'How Are We to Distinguish a "Repressed Unconscious" from a "Radically Unconscious"?' *Lacanticles*. https://lacanticles.com/how-are-we-to-distinguish-a-repressed-unconscious-from-a-radically-unconscious/ [accessed November 2022].

Carhart-Harris, R.L. and Friston, K.J. (2010). 'The Default-mode, Ego-functions and Free-energy: A Neurobiological Account of Freudian Ideas', *Brain*, vol. 133, no. 4, pp. 1265–1283. https://doi.org/10.1093/brain/awq010

Chalmers, D.J. (1996). *The Conscious Mind: In Search of a Fundamental Theory*. Oxford: Oxford University Press.

Derrida, J. (1978). *Writing and Difference*. Alan Bass (trans.). Chicago: University of Chicago.

Detel, W. (2021). 'On the Conception of the Unconscious', *Academia Letters*, Article 1684. https://doi.org/10.20935/AL1684

Eisold, K. (2010). *What You Don't Know You Know*. New York: Other Press.

Fertuck, E.A. (2011). 'The Scientific Study of Unconscious Processes: The Time is Ripe for (Re)Convergence of Neuroscientific and Psychoanalytic Conceptions: Commentary', *Neuropsychoanalysis 2011*, vol. 13, no. 1, pp. 45–48.

Freud, S. (1895). 'Project for a Scientific Psychology'. *Standard Edition of the Complete Psychological Works of Sigmund Freud*, vol. 1, pp. 295–397.

Freud, S. (1918). 'From the History of an Infantile Neurosis', J. Strachey (ed.). *Standard Edition of the Complete Psychological Works of Sigmund Freud*, vol. XVII, pp. 7–122.

Hassin, R.R., Uleman, J.S. and Bargh, J.A. (eds.) (2012). *The New Unconscious, Social Cognition and Social Neuroscience*. 2006; online ed. Oxford Academic, 22 March. https://doi.org/10.1093/acprof:oso/9780195307696.001.0001 [accessed 4 February 2024].

Henriques, G.R. (2021). 'How to Solve the Mind-Body Problem with the Unified Theory of Knowledge', https://medium.com/unified-theory-of-knowledge/how-to-solve-the-mind-body-problem-with-the-unified-theory-of-knowledge-ffc1fc83f543 [accessed 9 October 2023].

Henriques, G.R. (2023). 'We Need a Better Vocabulary for Mind and Consciousness: Differentiating Consciousness from the Concept of Mind2', https://www.psychologytoday.com/au/blog/theory-of-knowledge/202310/we-need-a-better-vocabulary-for-mind-and-consciousness [accessed 9 October 2023].

Ikiseh, B.N. (2021). 'Unconscious Bias: The Unconscious Conscious Effect', *Academia Letters*. https://doi.org/10.20935/AL2291

Jaynes, J. (1976). *The Origin of Consciousness in the Break-Down of the Bicameral Mind*. Boston: Houghton Mifflin Co.

Kahneman, D. (2011). *Thinking Fast and Slow*. Harmondsworth: Penguin.

Kuijsten, M. (ed.) (2022). *Conversation on Consciousness and the Bicameral Mind: Interview's with Leading Thinkers on Julian Jaynes's Theory*. A Julian Jaynes Society Publication. www.julianjaynes.org

Kunstadt, L. (2013). 'The "Conscious Id": A Game Changer with Lots of Challenges: Commentary', *Neuropsychoanalysis*, vol. 15, no. 1, pp. 55–58.

Long, S.D. (ed.) (2016). *Transforming Experience in Organisations: A Framework for Organisational Research and Consultancy*. London: Routledge.

McVeigh, B.J. (2024). 'Consciousness Is the Holy Grail of Neuroscience: Why We Still Misunderstand a Crucial Concept in Psychology', https://www.academia.edu /114147694/Consciousness_Is_the_Holy_Grail_of_Neuroscience_Why_We_Still _Misunderstand_a_Crucial_Concept_in_Psychology?uc-sb-sw=5545557

Neuropsychoanalysis. (2023). https://www.tandfonline.com/action/ journalInformation [accessed September 2023]. Taylor & Francis online.

Solms, M. (2013). 'The Conscious Id' *Neuropsychoanalysis*, vol. 15, no. 1, pp. 5–19. https://doi.org/10.1080/15294145.2013.10773711

Solms, M. (2018). The Neurobiological Underpinnings of Psychoanalytic Theory and Therapy, *Frontiers in Behavioral Neuroscience*, Pathological Conditions, vol. 12. https://doi.org/10.3389/fnbeh.2018.00294 [accessed 15 March 2024].

Solms, M. (2022). *The Source of Consciousness*. YouTube Video [accessed 5 October 2023].

Solms, M. and Turnbull, O. (2011). 'What Is Neuropsychoanalysis', *Neuropsychoanalysis*, vol. 13, no. 2, pp. 133–145.

Standford Encyclopedia of Philosophy. (2014). https://plato.stanford.edu/entries/ consciousness/#CauStaCon [accessed 5 October 2023].

Weinberger. J. and Stoycheva, V. (2020). *The Unconscious: Theory Research and Clinical Implications*. New York: The Guilford Press.

10 The Unconscious in Nature

We are the cosmos made conscious and life is the means by which the universe understands itself.

(Brian Cox, particle physicist 2021)

Previous chapters have explored the idea of the unconscious as a phenomenon integrally tied to human beings, understanding "mind" with conscious and unconscious elements to be something specific to humanity. This chapter challenges the assumption within that idea and examines the possibility of forms of mind in non-human life. Although the cognitive psychology of the twentieth century eschewed the Freudian unconscious as unscientific and unobservable,[1] authors such as Bargh and Morsella (2008) point to the work done in biological sciences about unconscious behavioural dispositions that are evolutionarily adaptive; what they term the natural unconscious of evolutionary behaviour. For example, the operation of mirror neurones in unconscious learning processes; unconscious and almost immediate solutions to different conflicting behavioural tendencies and unconscious automatic links between perception and behaviour are all indications of unconscious mental processes that precede action and consciousness. This is consistent with the neurological theories of Solms presented in the last chapter where it is seen that many unconscious predictive behavioural patterns are built into the nervous system.

But is the unconscious, as formulated in this manner, a conceptual development beyond the Freudian unconscious, or is it a move away, eschewing the repressed and dynamic unconscious and losing the creative aspect of unconsciousness as an active form of thinking in human beings?

The idea of the unconscious in nature raises many questions about the definitions of life, mind and consciousness more broadly. I am committed to seeing how ideas of consciousness and the unconscious help to understand the deep connections throughout nature. Notwithstanding the important contributions from psychoanalysis, we may need to extend our ideas about the nature of "mind" and how its various forms emanate in all living things and in the planet as a whole. This at least requires exploration, not simply for the future of the human race through the interconnectedness that sustains us, not only for our place as the means by which the universe can understand itself,

DOI: 10.4324/9781003559818-10

but also for the deep meaning of our choice for life and our ethical responsibilities in pursuing this choice.

Mind

The question of whether non-human animals or other forms of life have consciousness, and given this, something akin to unconsciousness – that is, a mind as we think of it, has overwhelming complexity because we still don't have a firm grip on what consciousness and a mind are anyway. Many years ago Bion said, "If we consider that there is a thing called a mind or a character, is there any way in which we can verbalize it which is not a complete distortion?" (Bion 1976, pp. 317–318, quoted in Civitarese 2013). And, as Bion goes on to say, how might such a mind be regarded when seen from different perspectives or what he named as different vertices?

An opinion held by many since the Cartesian[2] cogito "I think, therefore I am" and its implication "I am conscious" is that human consciousness is so different from any kind of animal "mind" that a vast discontinuity is the case, especially evidenced by the human capacity for language and other symbolic activities, along with the idea of human culture. This view posits that animal "mind" if it even exists, cannot be in any way equivalent to the human mind. Yet, there also exist beliefs that have occured throughout history that animals have human-like minds. For example, in medieval times and even later in Europe, animals were thought by many, even the educated classes, to have minds including intentionality, a belief displayed in animal criminal trials, where animals such as cows, pigs and horses were brought before courts for crimes, and punished with the belief that the animal would understand the reasoning behind its punishment (Dinzelbacher 2002). Moreover, in a complementary argument, there is a common belief that humans retain much of animality within them. Kan (2016) for example examines this belief through a study of its expression in the literature of the nineteenth century, with some reference to modern literature. There she finds beliefs about specific characteristics believed to be unique to humans overcome and concludes that the authors she studied base their work on the premise of many animal-like characteristics in the human character and mind. How much of this is due to human projections onto animals or a valid recognition of nature is an object for research.

There have been and still are contrasting arguments that consider whether the human mind, including consciousness, is continuous or discontinuous with animality and the rest of the natural world. From the examination of earlier theories, it might be said that for many, humanity retains animality within the mind. Schelling, for example, as noted earlier, had the idea of the "Barbarian Principle" (Wirth and Burke 2013) that can be understood as nature without regulation by human cognition and language, with humanity considered as part of that nature. Such a principle perhaps continues to be present in the Freudian "id", at least in the idea of the instincts prior to their transformation into the drives. The idea of an unconscious outside of cultural influence remains (Boxer 2022). Evolution would suggest a continuity of the development of mind, evidence being of consciousness as recently defined by neuroscience within animals with neural systems for over half a billion years (Irwin 2024) and evolutionary evidence of conscious learning through selective attention and prediction errors in animals and insects (Van Swinderen 2024). The question of the unconscious still remains.

Many theorists both philosophical and scientific have questioned the Cartesian and other divisions of nature implying humanity as the only thinking animal. To understand if the concept of the unconscious is at all viable in relation to nature beyond humanity, the idea of consciousness in nature requires a deeper understanding, although I can here only briefly touch on this vast area of study. In this field of study, distinctions are needed between the differing definitions of the increasing sophistication of consciousness, from consciousness as basic awareness, through consciousness as a basis for cognition, to phenomenal consciousness – a sense of being – and higher forms such as self-reflective consciousness, available to humans but still under study if any form is available to other living organisms. Although, the evidence is growing that many creatures other than humans have self-consciousness (Irwin 2024; Feinberg and Mallatt 2020). This is demonstrated especially in vertebrates but also in other forms of life. Even Freud expressed the idea that mind with its unconscious is unexplored in relation to animals other than humans.

> We are describing the state of affairs as it appears in the adult human being, in whom the system Ucs. operates, strictly speaking, only as a preliminary stage of the higher organization. The question of what the content and connections of that system are during the development of the individual, and of what significance it possesses in animals – these are points on which no conclusion can be deduced from our description: they must be investigated independently.
>
> (Freud 1915, p. 188)

So, what of consciousness? Biology has expanded the idea of consciousness and cognition to areas well outside what has been considered "mind" in humans and has noted the complexity of these ideas in so doing. The scientific study of animal consciousness is relatively new and contrasting arguments are in the mix (Allen and Trestman 2016; Irwin 2024). Nonetheless, enough evidence has been gathered to make viable claims for many aspects of a complex consciousness being present in non-human animals, for instance, the capacity for some animals to have a sense of past, present and future. Non-human animals are demonstratively capable of deliberative decision-making and other high-level cognitive functions (Smith et al. 2003; Smith 2009; Budaev et al. 2019). Most telling is the evidence that some non-human species have high-level language skills beyond simple communication, including recursive syntax (Ferrigno and Cheyette 2020; Liao et al. 2022). Recursion occurs when a problem is solved through smaller sections of the problem being solved first. Structures are embedded in other structures. Liao et al. (2022) amazingly demonstrate, for example, how crows are capable of using recursive syntax.

> Recursion, the process of embedding structures within similar structures, is often considered a foundation of symbolic competence and a uniquely human capability...We reveal that crows have recursive capacities; they perform on par with children and even outperform macaques. The crows continued to produce recursive sequences after extending to longer and thus deeper embeddings. These results demonstrate that recursive capabilities are not limited to the primate genealogy and may have occurred separately from or before human symbolic competence in different animal taxa.
>
> (Liao et al. 2020, article abstract)

Next time a crow arrives in your town, look at it differently. Old ideas that animals have no consciousness, even high levels of problem solving and self-consciousness are no longer viable. "Life and consciousness are system features of embodied organisms" (Feinberg and Mallatt 2020).

From the perspective of evolutionary science, it is noted that self-organisation and the capacity to adapt to changing environmental conditions are properties of all living systems, together with systemic coupling to the environment such that environmental niches co-evolve with specific organisms (Maturana and Varela 1980a, 1980b), even to the extent that the genetic makeup of organisms can influence the genetic makeup of others (Dawkins 2016). This includes the evolution of consciousness and cognitive and social behaviours (Galef, 1995; Varela 2019). All of which are commensurate with definitions of consciousness such as "consciousness is 'the process by which an animal has perceptual and affective experience or feelings, arising from the material substrate of a nervous system'" (Irwin 2024) and includes all forms of phenomenal consciousness.

But beyond such arguments and evidence is the recognition of the tendency of Homo sapiens to think of animal consciousness from their own human perspective, as if all consciousness needs to be similar to ours. Animal consciousness researchers are attempting to understand consciousness from an evolutionary perspective that regards it as relative to the animal's context and as such quite different for different species (Van Swinderen 2024).

So, with demonstrated consciousness, what can be said of the unconscious in non-human animals? Alen and Trestman (2016) report studies that examine "blindsightedness" in monkeys – a phenomenon studied in humans who demonstratively perceive a stimulus without knowing it, a kind of unconscious – at least in the sense of out of awareness perception. But let it be clear – here I am not talking of the Freudian repressed unconscious but establishing initially that mind in some form with unconscious function can be hypothesised in non-human species. Clearly instinctual behaviours and emotions occur unconsciously, as in out of awareness. But what of indications of subjectivity? Although difficult to study, there is evidence for metacognitive "feelings of knowing" or subjectivity in some mammals and birds and studies are attempted to discern the subjective experiences of animals, despite complex methodological problems – just as there are complex methodological problems in studying subjectivity in humans (Irwin 2024; Feinberg and Mallatt 2020). Who can really experience the consciousness of another?

Animals and humans share non-verbal aspects of memory such as implicit memory that occurs outside of awareness. It is gained through learning without conscious effort, not requiring language. While studies of human implicit memory are linked to subjective experience, we can only conjecture this link in non-human animals. Semenza (2017) discusses the distinction between explicit (declarative) and implicit memory. Implicit memory works mostly unconsciously, with aspects of its processes being called "emotional memory".

> It contributes to formation of the self. The internal sense of who one is results not only from what one can explicitly recall, but also from implicit recollections. Such recollections create one's inner mental models and internal subjective experience of psychic contents (like images, sensations, emotions) and influence behavioural responses and moral behaviour.
>
> (Semenza 2017, p. 105)

Might we hypothesise that the implicit emotional memory function of non-human animal species also contributes to subjectivity, even to a form of morality, an idea widely debated in animal studies (Fitzpatrick 2024)?

Although *human* natural languages do not appear in other species, complex communication patterns do and as noted previously, basic aspects of language such as recursive syntax have been found to operate in some non-human species, including mammals and birds. Moreover, there is an argument to be made that expecting human-like language in other species is misguided and that animal subjectivity will have its own "language" of bodily, here-and-now experience (Lijmbach 1998). This requires that we understand semiotics in nature more fully.

Semiotic theory examines the way that signs occur in nature, from the very simple tropes of plants to the complex social communicative behaviours of mammals and insects. Temple Grandin (2015), renowned animal scientist, writes and talks of her own development with autism. She claims to have developed her extraordinary understanding of and communication with animals through her own way of thinking with images rather than words. She says "I have no language-based thoughts at all. My thoughts are in pictures, like videotapes in my mind" (2015). Her work illustrates the similarities between animal and human emotions (Grandin and Johnson 2008) but most interesting is that she talks of animal thinking as primarily associative. This is borne out by scientists Feinberg and Mallatt (2017) who examine the rise of consciousness in primitive species and note the early behavioural signs of associative cognition, necessary for the negotiation of complex environments. Such associative thinking bears much similarity to human thinking despite the (seeming) absence of symbolic/linguistic type signifiers. Indeed, dreams, those royal roads to the unconscious noted by Freud, predominantly appear as images decipherable as a rebus, a pictogram or hieroglyphic: an early form of human writing and language (Freud 1900). And it appears that many animals dream (Marshall 2023) although, it is not suggested here that rebus-type dreams occur in species other than humans – a phenomenon perhaps unable to be studied. Eco-semiotics considers how signs occur in ecosystems including their geographical contexts. It is often thought that humans are the only creatures to create meaning through emotional and cognitive capacity, yet eco-semiotics regards meaning-making and intentionality as integral to life in its context (Harney 1984, 2019). This is perhaps a very different view of what constitutes meaning-making. It is a kind of embodied meaning rather than a Cartesian logos; it is closer to somatic intelligence.

> Living systems are meaning-making systems. In other words, they are sign-using systems, or communicative systems. By definition, communication is an interaction based on sign relations. Many traditional scientific approaches take this obvious feature into account only implicitly. However, since the meaning-making may have a direct impact on the organization and dynamics of the systems under study, including the geographical systems, it makes sense to explore the descriptions in which the role of sign processes is made explicit.
>
> (Maran and Kull 2014, p. 41)

Many communicative meaning-making systems in nature occur without conscious deliberation – a kind of inbuilt unthought known, understood as instinctive and inherited, not learned, with what might be thought of as unconscious deliberation. The system of nature speaks through us (Green 2016). And when such instinctual patterns are disrupted, conscious deliberation enters the scene. Anticipating the future is an important aspect of mind in this regard. In recent biology and in psychology, life in general is regarded as anticipatory. This is not a teleological but a systemic process. That is, models for anticipations of the future reside in living systems and these steer current behaviours; an idea put forward, amongst others, by theoretical biologist Robert Rosen (Rosen 1985, 1991). Louie (2010) cites Rosen:

> An anticipatory system is a natural system that contains an internal predictive model of itself and of its environment, which allows it to change state at an instant in accord with the model's predictions pertaining to a later instant.
>
> (Louie 2010, p. 19)

Living systems from an eco-semiotic perspective then, have unconscious patterns built into their instinctive behaviour: an inherited natural system that

operates unconsciously without conscious deliberation, until what is anticipated fails to occur. Conscious deliberation then takes over. This is consistent with the descriptions provided by Solms in the last chapter. However,
Louie, following the work of Rosen, describes a critical distinction between
feedback and feedforward processes that distinguish anticipation. Feedback
control processes are governed by discrepancies between current system states
and the state the system should be in in its environment. This is a mechanistic
model able to be incorporated into machines. Feedforward, however, acts on a
(unconsciously learned) preset internalised model of prediction – drawn upon
in conscious and unconscious decision-making.

> We know from introspection that many, if not most, of our own con-
> scious activities are generated in a feedforward fashion. We typically
> decide what to do now in terms of what we perceive will be the con-
> sequences of our action at some later time. The vehicle by which we
> anticipate is in fact a model, which enables us to pull the future into the
> present.
>
> (Louie 2010, p. 21)

To take this further, maladaptive and self-destructive learned processes,
including internal anticipatory models, can be discerned in nature, in response
to changed and human-influenced environmental conditions, seen often in
the behaviour of pets or animals in captivity. Is this perhaps analogous to
a repressed unconscious with observable behavioural symptoms (Robertson
et al. 2013)? I remember many years ago when a man who had married an
Indonesian woman told me that Asians did not have an unconscious. I was
astounded at how he arrived at this and how wrong he was in his closed and
bigoted mind. Are we caught in the same trap when thinking about the animal
mind?

Emergence

As has been described in earlier chapters, much of psychoanalysis argues that
the repressed unconscious is formed not simply as an ongoing continuous
expression of nature but occurs in tandem with human consciousness in an
emergent, one might say, discontinuous manner. The two: i) human consciousness, meaning self-consciousness and subjectivity, and ii) unconsciousness, are understood to co-emerge (Bion 1962).[3] But given the recent animal
research, why should an animal consciousness/unconsciousness not also
emerge in a similar fashion? Especially since many animal scientists argue for
forms of culture amongst species other than humans (Laland and Galef 2009).

In Lacanian psychoanalytic terms, this brings forward the question of how
the Symbolic arose from the Real of nature,[4] or more precisely, how Symbolic
and Real – which are part of the emergent human mind – co-emerged. It
appears that the Lacanian and other psychoanalytic formulations require

recognition of the distinctiveness of the human social condition with its laws and symbolic function as basic to the development of the human mind (including the Freudian super-ego). But can such emergence also be within animal cultures? This question requires a discussion about emergence.

Emergence is a dynamic not explicable by the step-by-step effects of efficient causation. In many ways it is a mystery unsolvable by logos. One form becomes another. Given temperature changes, water becomes steam or ice. Yes, this is explained due to molecular movement, but still, it is somewhat mysterious. How is it that one form becomes another when the foundational components remain much the same? We might say that speech, language and the symbolic emerged from a nature that pre-existed and was ground to its emergence. The idea of "ground to" is different from the idea of efficient step-by-step causation manifest across time. It is somehow about a ground that inherently already contains that which is to come. David Bohm explains this more intricately than I when he describes the explicate order as that which can be investigated and is the unfolding of an implicate order that cannot be directly observed. "In terms of the implicate order one may say that everything is enfolded into everything" (Bohm 1980, p. 225). Although dealing primarily with particle physics, Bohm makes philosophical investigations into the nature of knowledge and consciousness that roam across a study of the physical world into mental phenomena. He describes through examining many processes how this enfolding and unfolding occur.

> I would say that in my scientific and philosophical work, my main concern has been with understanding the nature of reality in general and of consciousness in particular as a coherent whole, which is never static or complete, but which is in an unending process of movement and unfoldment.
>
> (Bohm 1980, p. x)

I am grateful to Gordon Lawrence who introduced me to Bohm's work because it is this idea of (i) wholeness and the links between every form of life, including all in the physical and mental worlds, an understanding of potentiality held and expressed, plus (ii) an understanding of the very practical needs within life that require this wholeness to be fragmented so that thinking can occur. This grounds my approach to "mind".

So, I'll return to that specific fragmentation of the whole that distinguishes the mind of humanity from the mind in other forms of life. For many psychoanalysts, it is the unconscious that makes humanity distinct. Following the teachings of Deleuze who, taking a different path to the Freudian and emphasising the creativity of the unconscious and its genesis in the nature of memory, Kerslake says, "It is the unconscious that gives rise to the real split between human beings and the rest of nature, not consciousness" (Kerslake 2007, p. 5); the unconscious here being understood in terms of associations held in memory.[5] And for Lacan, subjectivity only occurs for humanity and emerges from the gap created by entry into language and the symbolic.

This conceptualisation, however valid or not, still leaves open the question of its emergence. And although this is a question that Carew (2015) says cannot be answered and should not even be formulated; (he claims it just *did* emerge), the ground for such a human consciousness/unconsciousness, with its inbuilt implicate anticipatory form is worth investigation. So, we might say that speech, language and the symbolic emerged from nature, which was ground to its emergence. Its emergence was slow and accompanied by cultural and behavioural change and most likely is still evolving. Taking a Lacanian reading of Schelling, Zizek[6] names this emergence from the Real of nature to the Symbolic as an emergence into subjectivity: an eruption from nature into culture (Carew 2014, 2015). From a psychoanalytic and philosophical perspective, just as we cannot consciously trace the emergence of our own subjectivity and identity from a prior state; just as we cannot be at the birth of our own emergence because the present of our subjectivity was not there to witness the past; so, the emergence of culture and consciousness from nature is inexplicable to us. If logos and meaning are part of an exclusively human Symbolic order and prior to that there was none, attempts to find meaning there (in nature outside of culture) may be fruitless.

But much of this assumes that culture, subjectivity, symbolic thought, or their equivalence is nowhere but in humanity. As argued earlier, this is challenged by animal researchers. Feinberg and Mallatt (2020) argue for three stages within which the qualities of consciousness and subjectivity have emerged: 1. Life 2. Nervous systems and 3. Special neurobiological features that include capacities for self-reflection. Following general ideas in systems thinking they say, "emergence occurs in *complex systems* in which novel properties emerge through the *aggregate functions* of the parts of that system" (quote from the web version). Hierarchical emergence allows then for reciprocal relations between different hierarchical levels in complex patterns. The hierarchical emergence of the special neurobiological features basic to the emergence of subjectivity, they argue, occurs across many species.

Nonetheless, can we still say that the issue of human culture is special? If culture is defined in terms of the transmission of learning, then the evidence for animal culture is plentifully available. If culture, however, is defined in terms of human symbolic function, the evidence is scantily available and as Galef (1992) suggests "It may be misleading to treat animal traditions and human culture as homologous (rather than analogous) and to refer to animal traditions as cultural". We are left in that difficult space of finding parallels between "others" (humans and other species) that are different yet share superordinate qualities.

Taking the nature of emergence, the idea I can arrive at is of the human mind as a continuity of human origins in, and with, animality. Is this a complex ground to the emergence of quite a new kind of thinking, a kind of complex continuity perhaps needing new definitions of subjectivity, not based primarily on cognitive and emotional capacity, variously defined and observable across a variety of species? Because all species have emergent qualities – cognitive and emotive – that adapt to specific niches in their ecosystems, and none can be said to be more "evolved" than others in this regard.

The nature of human evolutionary emergence is still to be understood along with its ethical implications (Rogers 2020). As creatures of a complex evolutionary process leading to unique emergent capacities, perhaps another argument is that these capacities lie in an ethical domain rather than in the emotional and cognitive domains of consciousness and the unconscious. It may be that it is the capacity for ethics and morality that delineates the primary human distinction. It may be the distinctive nature of our human cultures to include this domain, notwithstanding those humans who too often, individually and collectively choose unethical and destructive paths.

But even this as uniquely human might be questioned. For instance, it is argued that it is the human ability to concisely communicate between individuals that makes us aware of moral and ethical behaviour, yet some animals – particularly those in packs – demonstrate similar behaviours that humans would name as ethical or moral (Monso et al. 2018), some animals even help others when there is no gain for them and sometimes a disadvantage. Jenny Gray, C.E.O. of Zoos Victoria, states that in all animals exhibiting play, adults demonstrate self-regulation with younger individuals – what she describes as pre-moral behaviour (2024), and those that don't show self-regulation are not played with. Each knows the rules and can distinguish when to play by them. And again, animal morality and ethical capacity may well be of quite a different nature to human morality. Perhaps in the end, human dominance comes simply from our basic aggressivity and the important evolutionary advantage of opposable thumbs.

Nonetheless, we are burdened or blessed with the unconscious choice between good and evil as Schelling first described or at least have this as a symbolic possibility. As such, our morality and our evolved consciousness/unconsciousness are inextricably linked.

Riker (1997) develops a new moral psychology in which the reality of unconscious functioning is included within a theory of responsibility, and the agent's primary ethical concern becomes knowing what her unconscious motivations are and integrating them into a morally and psychologically mature self.

And an ethical evolution of the human mind would indicate our responsibility for broad systemic issues and to eschew an instrumental approach to nature and take up an ethical approach as caretakers (McGrath 2018; Hoggett 2023). Such an approach would stretch beyond caring for the natural world simply to extend our own health and survival benefits. It would mean an active care for that of which we are essentially part. For such an active care to occur, our thinking needs to change. Instead of seeing ourselves at the apex of all abilities with the rights to exploit all else, there is a need to see ourselves as just one part of a complex living system, each part of which is adapted to a particular niche in a wider ecosystem.

Beyond Living Individuals

Can we recognise systems beyond individual organisms as being alive, let alone having a mind? The Gaia hypothesis was developed by Lovelock and Margulis (1973). It argues for the earth as a living system where biological, atmospheric and geological systems co-evolve according to principles of natural selection. While the hypothesis has been modified since its initial formulation, its fundamental claim now stands at the basis of the earth sciences discipline. For instance:

> The Gaia hypothesis postulates that the Earth's surface is maintained in a habitable state by self-regulating feedback mechanisms involving organisms tightly coupled to their environment...The dominant atmospheric gases, nitrogen and oxygen, are biological products: atmospheric oxygen is the result of past photosynthesis, and denitrifying organisms maintain atmospheric nitrogen (the thermodynamically stable form of nitrogen in the presence of oxygen should be as nitrate dissolved in the ocean). The proportions of these gases are particularly suited to the dominant organisms. Nitrogen serves to dilute oxygen, which at 21% of the atmosphere is just below the level at which fires would disrupt land life. Yet oxygen is sufficiently abundant to support the metabolism of large respiring animals such as humans.
>
> (Lenton 2003, p. 815)

Margo Lockhart and I have recently taken this up as fundamental.

> Consistent with the Gaia hypothesis of Lovelock and Margulis (1973; Lovelock 1979), the basis of our ontology is that the earth is a living planet and that we, as a living species on this planet, are connected to, and indeed interwoven with, the fabric of earth systems.
>
> (Long and Lockhart 2021)

Over the past fifty or so years, scientists have increasingly become concerned about the sustainability of life on our planet. Climate-caused changes resulting in species loss, climate disasters, ocean level rises and other ecological and even geological changes are noted. Recognition of this, together with studies of human activity since prehistoric times, has led to our age being named the Anthropocene: a geological epoch where human activity has deeply affected the various earth systems of climate, geology and ecology (Zalasiewicz et al. 2011; Lewis and Maslin 2015). "The Anthropocene, on current evidence, seems to show global change consistent with the suggestion that an epoch-scale boundary has been crossed within the last two centuries" (Zalasiewicz et al. 2011, p. 835), although it is recognised that human influence far precedes this. This influence is not simply biological or industrial but includes the way humans think. Maran and Kull (2014), for example, argue that the human tendency to categorise and compartmentalise the components of broad eco-systems (as in separate sciences) is part of the problem of environmental degradation. As Bill McKibben states in the introduction to the latest edition of *The End of Nature*, his 1989 groundbreaking book: "We are no longer able to think of ourselves as a species 'tossed about by larger forces', now we <u>are</u> those larger forces" (McKibben 2006, p. xviii).

Capra (2019) summarising the views of more recent biology and his own work, claims the earth is a living, self-regulating system. Human bodily systems, down to each individual cell, are seen as cognitive entities, and evolution is regarded as a "collaborative dance" rather than a competitive struggle for existence. He argues for a science of qualities to meet the complexity of life, of systemic approaches and the drive for innovation in life. Providing a framework for such studies that he calls "The Systems View of Life", he names the biological, cognitive, social and ecological dimensions that require a new form of thinking about patterns, systems and context. His main theme is that biology has moved from seeing living organisms as machines, to seeing them as networks at every level. This includes the work of other scientists who extend the ideas of intelligence and cognition not only to other species of animals, but also to plants (Wohlleben 2016; Mancuso 2021; Kimmerer 2022; Plant Consciousness). As an example of such research and thinking about all living systems, theoretical biologist Robert Rosen (1991), while arguing that complex systems cannot be reduced to their components, names a distinct quality called "organization". This he attributes to all life as the basis of that life, including the living universe, from biological cells to planetary systems. All this echoes back to the beginning of this book, to the work of Schelling and his *Naturphilosophie*.

> Nature must be seen as capable of organizing itself, generating life and the human consciousness capable of knowing nature.
>
> (Gare 2011 p. 28)

The systems views of Capra parallel the view of human organisations as complex systems provided by the Grubb Institute's "The Transforming Experience Framework" (Long 2016) and the work of Ralph Stacey (2010) who argues for the unpredictability of emergent systemic processes and hence the understandability of why senior managers fail to predict the future in their work organisations. It applies to all living systems including the planet; perhaps inferring the idea of groups, organisations and even societies as living systems.[7]

The idea of the earth as a self-regulating system raises the questions of earth consciousness and unconsciousness, however much these fly in the face of our normal understanding. In the last chapter, it was noted that some definitions place awareness and reactivity as a basic form of consciousness. For example, Henriques (2023), using this as a basic definition of what he calls "Mind 1" goes further to say that some machines can be shown to have awareness of and reactivity to their specific environments. Do we think of them as conscious? At this stage, I think not, but where the boundary between machines as mechanical and machines as conscious is, may be challenged. Developments in artificial intelligence (AI) already broach this as a possibility (Mc Dermott 2007), although most scientists agree that no machines or other current AI products are conscious by any definition, despite recent extreme hypotheses suggesting the possibility that we are all living in a virtual world developed by some super artificial intelligence, and our consciousness is part of that (Virk 2019). (For my part, I put those hypotheses in the improbable basket – impossible even to investigate.)

Although there are criticisms that the earth itself cannot be considered as subject to natural selection (Dawkins 2016) and that rather than being creatively self-correcting, nature is essentially self-destructive (Ward 2009), increasingly the views of the earth as a living system are being accepted by scientists, even some who first opposed the idea (Doolittle 2023).

The Gaia hypothesis has been transformed in the earth sciences to the study of the co-evolution of living and non-living earth elements, observable scientifically. The notion of the earth as a living and perhaps conscious entity is still controversial. The nature of such a consciousness, however, is difficult to ascertain or study and remains an unconfirmed hypothesis. Nonetheless, within such a hypothesis, many of the processes involved could be understood as unconscious, occurring with little self-conscious deliberation – given it is argued that plant intelligence, driven by evolution, can plan the plant's own growth processes and modify such planning according to environmental conditions. Can we see such anticipation as an unconscious directive?

Four Views of the Unconscious in Nature

Four distinct views of the unconscious in nature start to emerge:

(i)   the unconscious as implicate in all of life, including the earth as a system;
(ii) the unconscious of instincts and internal models evident in habitual behaviours and communicated through basic signs;
(iii) the repressed unconscious of psychoanalysis, evidenced in symbolic functions, described as a human process and unknown as to its existence in other life forms; and
(iv) the unconscious in ethical evolution evidenced through the development of conscience and accountability (again, with some basics observed in species other than human).

The question of whether we have stretched the idea of unconscious process beyond its utility arises. One quest in this book has been to consider in what ways we as humans have free choice or are doomed to the "slings and arrows of outrageous determinism", to borrow from Shakespeare. Psychoanalysis would have it that the more we explore and accept through bringing to consciousness our unconscious desires and memories, the more we can have some choice in our lives. Cognition and intelligence are increasingly shown to be understood as relative to the capacity to modify the environment and hence to have capacity to learn and adapt. Ideas about the nature of mind, intelligence, learning capacity, consciousness and the unconscious press us to extend knowledge in each of these areas and to open our own minds to possibilities. Humanity may be erroneously anthropocentric in believing in its cognitive, and emotional supremacy on earth.

Considering all this, what can be said about choice except that defining and understanding choice is exceedingly complex? It does seem that human choices in the ethical field are now needed for our ecosystems to survive. Our own freedom in the long term depends on this.

Notes

1 Psychoanalysis has never claimed that the unconscious is observable, only its effects from which the unconscious is inferred. Moreover, the philosopher Charles Peirce cogently argues that the first step of even the most conservative definitions within science is formed through abductive logic – the logic used in psychoanalytic and socioanalytic methods (see Long and Harney 2013).
2 Descartes believed that animals had no consciousness but were sophisticated machines.
3 See, for example, Bion

> I have proposed the theory that alpha-function, by proliferating alpha-elements is producing the contact-barrier, an entity that separates elements so that those on one side, are and form, the conscious and on the other side are, and form, the unconscious.
>
> (Bion 1962, p. 54)

4 This is a question that appears to have preoccupied the philosopher Zizek amongst others (Zizek 2006; Carew 2015).
5 This is not directly contradictory to the Freudian idea insofar as Freud does access the unconscious through associations and regards its structure as basically associative. The main difference is that Freudian repression is understood as active due to conflicts associated with the sexual drives, whilst the Jungian, Bergsonian and Deleuzian approaches do not agree with this as a primary basis for the unconscious.
6 It is noted here that Zizek's reading is controversial and believed by Boxer (2024) to be misguided because his reading of Lacan is incorrect.
7 It should also be noted that psychoanalytic and socioanalytic methodologies have always used the analysis of patterns, networks and complex systems in their approaches (Newton et al. 2011; Long and Sievers 2012; Long 2013). Psychodynamics uses a qualitative examination of patterns, systems and networks especially examining unconscious engagements.

References

Alen, C. and Trestman, M. (2016). 'Notes to Animal Consciousness', in *Stanford Encyclopedia of Philosophy*. Philosophy Department Stanford University. https://

plato.stanford.edu/entries/consciousness-animal/notes.html [accessed 20 August 2024].

Bargh, J.A. and Morsella, E. (2008). The Unconscious Mind, *Perspectives on Psychological Science*, vol. 3, no. 1, pp. 73–79. https://doi.org/10.1111/j.1745 -6916.2008.00064.x

Bion, W.R. (1962). *Learning from Experience*, 3rd ed. London: Maresfield library, Karnac.

Bion, W.R. (1976 [2008]). 'Evidence', in Francesca Bion (ed.). *Clinical Seminars and Other Works*, pp. 312–320. London: Karnac.

Bohm, D. (1980). *Wholeness and the Implicate Order*. London: Routledge.

Boxer, P. (2022). 'How Are We to Distinguish a "Repressed Unconscious" from a "Radically Unconscious"?' *Lacanticles*. https://lacanticles.com/how-are-we-to -distinguish-a-repressed-unconscious-from-a-radically-unconscious/ [accessed November 2022].

Boxer, P. (2024). 'Why Should Zizek's Misreading of Lacan Matter?' https://asy mmetricleadership.com/2024/02/24/why-should-zizeks-misreading-of-lacan -matter/ [accessed February 2024].

Budaev, S., Jorgenson, C., Mangel, M., Eailssen, S. and Giske, J. (2019). 'Decision-Making from the Animal Perspective: Bridging Ecology and Subjective Cognition', *Frontiers in Ecology and Evolution*, vol. 7. https://doi.org/10.3389/fevo.2019 .00164

Capra, F. (2019). 'Mind, Matter and Life Video Talk', https://www.findcenter.com/ video/41515/mind-matter-and-life-fritjof-capra [accessed 23 October 2023].

Carew, J. (2014). *Ontological Catastrophe: Zizek and the Paradoxical Metaphysics of German Idealism*. University of Michigan: Open Humanities Press. https://www .academia.edu/8370624/Reading_Schelling_Psychoanalytically_%C5%BDi%C5 %BEek_on_the_Fantasy_of_the_Ground_of_Consciousness_and_Language

Carew, J. (2015). 'Reading Schelling Psychoanalytically: Zizek on the Fantasy of the Ground of Consciousness and Language', *Symposium: Canadian Journal of Continental Philosophy*, vol. 19, no. 1 (Spring). [accessed 10 February 2024].

Civitarese, G. (2013). 'Bion's "Evidence" and His Theoretical Style', *The Psychoanalytic Quarterly*, vol. LXXXII, no. 3, pp. 615–633.

Cox, B. (2021). *Universe*. BBC Documentary.

Dawkins, R. (2016). *The Extended Phenotype*. Oxford: Oxford University Press.

Dinzelbacher, P. (2002). *Journal of Interdisciplinary History*, vol. xxxii, no. 3, pp. 405–421.

Doolittle, W.F. (2023). 'Is the Earth an Organism?' *Aeon Newsletter*. https://aeon .co/essays/the-gaia-hypothesis-reimagined-by-one-of-its-key-sceptics [accessed 24 October 2023].

Feinberg, T. and Mallatt, J. (2017). *The Ancient Origins of Consciousness: How the Brain Created Experience*. Cambridge, MA: MIT Press.

Feinberg, T. and Mallatt, J. (2020). 'Phenomenal Consciousness and Emergence: Eliminating the Explanatory Gap', *Frontiers in Psychology*, vol. 11, p. 1041. Published online 12 June 2020. https://doi.org/10.3389/fpsyg.2020.01041

Ferrigno, S. and Cheyette, S. (2020). 'Piantadosi, S. and Cantlon, J. Recursive Sequence Generation in Monkeys, Children, U.S. Adults and Native Amazonians', *Science Advances*, vol. 6, no. 26. https://www.science.org/doi/full/10.1126/ sciadv.aaz1002

Fitzpatrick, S. (2024). 'Animal Morality: What Is the Debate About?' https:// philarchive.org/archive/FITAMW [accessed March 2024].

Freud, S. (1900). *The Interpretation of Dreams*. James Strachey (trans.). Revised by Angela Richards 1976. Pelican Freud Library, vol 4. Harmondsworth: Penguin Books.

Freud, S. (1915). *The Unconscious*. J. Strachey (trans. and ed.)., S.E. vol. XIV, pp. 159–215. London: Hogarth Press.

Galef, B.G. (1992). 'The Question of Animal Culture', *Human Nature*, vol. 3, pp. 157–178. https://doi.org/10.1007/BF02692251

Galef (jnr.), B.G. (1995). 'Why Behaviour Patterns That Animals Learn Socially Are Locally Adaptive', *Animal Behaviour*, vol. 49, no. 5, pp. 1325–1334.

Gare, A. (2011). 'From Kant to Schelling to Process metaphysics: On the way to ecological civilization', *Cosmos & History: The Journal of Natural and Social Philosophy*, pp. 26–69.

Grandin, T. (2015). 'Thinking the Way Animals Do: Unique Insights from a Person with a Singular Understanding', *Western Horseman*, November 1997, pp. 140–145. https://www.grandin.com/references/thinking.animals.html

Grandin, T. and Johnson, C. (2008). *Animals Make Us Human*. New York: Houghton-Mifflin Harcourt.

Gray, J. (2024). 'Free Will, Liberty and Aristotle in the Animal Kingdom', *ABC Podcast*, 12 June 2024. https://www.abc.net.au/listen/programs/conversations/zoos-ethics-jenny-gray-history-animals-wilderness-science/103844130

Green, R. (2016) 'The Semiotics of The Unconscious', in G. Deleuze and R. Barthes (eds.) *Religious Theory E-Supplement to the Journal for Cultural and Religious Theory*. crt.org/religioustheory/2016/12/19/the-semiotics-of-the-unconscious-in-gilles-deleuze-and-roland-barthes-roger-green/

Irwin, L. (2024). 'Growing Confidence and Remaining Uncertainty about Animal Consciousness', *Qeios Open Access*. https://doi.org/10.32388/KOVD1Z.2 [accessed 7 July 2023].

Harney, M.J. (1984). *Intentionality, Sense and the Mind* (Series Phaenomenologica 94). Dordrecht: Martinus-Nijhoff.

Harney, M.J. (2019). 'Intentionality: Evolution of a Concept', in P. Wong, S. Bloor, P. Hutchings and P. Bilimoria (eds.) *Considering Religions, Rights and Bioethics: For Max Charlesworth*, pp. 139–153. Springer. https://link.springer.com/book/10.1007%2F978-3-030-18148-2

Henriques, G.R. (2023) 'We Need a Better Vocabulary for Mind and Consciousness: Differentiating consciousness from the Concept of Mind2', https://www.psychologytoday.com/au/blog/theory-of-knowledge/202310/we-need-a-better-vocabulary-for-mind-and-consciousness [accessed 9 October 2023].

Hoggett, P. (2023). 'Imagining our Way in the Anthropocene', *Organisation and Social Dynamics Special Issue: Organisational Systems and the Earth's Mega-systems*, vol. 23, no. 1 (Summer), pp. 1–14.

Kan, T. (2016). 'Renderings of the Abyss: Some Changing Nineteenth-century Literary Perceptions of the Animal/Human Divide', A thesis submitted for the degree of PhD Literature. University of Essex. https://repository.essex.ac.uk/19458/1/Post%20VIVA%20PhD%20Final%20123.pdf

Kerslake, C. (2007). *Deleuze and the Unconscious*. London: Continuum.

Kimmerer, R.W. (2022). 'The Intelligence of Plants Radio Talk', https://onbeing.org/programs/robin-wall-kimmerer-the-intelligence-of-plants-2022/ [accessed 17 May 2024].

Laland, K. and Galef, B. (eds.) (2009). *The Question of Animal Culture*. New York: Harvard University Press.

Lenton, T. (2003). 'The Gaia Hypothesis', in *Encyclopedia of Atmospheric Sciences*, pp. 815–820. Academic Press.

Lewis, S. and Maslin, M. (2015). 'Defining the Anthropocene', *Nature*, vol. 519, pp. 171–180. https://doi.org/10.1038/nature14258

Liao, D., Brecht, K., Johnson, M. and Nieder, A. 'Recursive Sequence Generation in Crows', *Science Advances*, vol. 8, p. 44. https://www.science.org/doi/10.1126/sciadv.abq3356

Lijmbach, S. (1998). 'Animal Subjectivity: A Study into Philosophy and Theory of Animal Experience', A thesis printed in the Netherlands by Grafisch bedrijf Ponsen & Looijen b.v.

Long, S.D. (ed.) (2013). *Socioanalytic Methods*. London: Karnac.

Long, S.D. (ed.) (2016). *Transforming Experience in Organisations: A Framework for Orgnisational Research and Consultancy*. London: Routledge.

Long, S.D. and Harney, M. (2013). 'The Associative Unconscious', in S. Long (ed.). *Socioanalytic Methods*, pp. 3–22. London: Karnac.

Long, S.D. and Lockhart, M. (2021). In Nature: Human Interaction with Living Non-human Co-inhabitants of Our World. Paper delivered to the OPUS Conference London 2021.

Long, S.D. and Sievers, B. (eds.) (2012). *Towards a Socioanalysis of Money, Finance and Capitalism*. London: Routledge.

Louie, A.H. (2010). 'Robert Rosen's Anticipatory Systems', *Foresight*, vol. 12, no. 3, pp. 18–29. https://www.researchgate.net/publication/228091658_Robert _Rosen's_anticipatory_systems [accessed 21 May 2024].

Lovelock, J.E. (1979). *Gaia: A New Look at Life on Earth*. Oxford: Oxford University Press.

Lovelock, J.E. and Margulis, L. (1973). 'Atmospheric Homeostasis by and for the Biosphere: The Gaia Hypothesis', *Telus*, vol. 26, no. 1 & 2, pp. 2–10.

Mancuso, S. (2021). *Nation of Plants*. Gregory Conti (trans.). London: Profile Books.

Maran, T. and Kull, K. (2014). 'Eco-Semiotics: Main Principles and Current Developments', *Geografiska Annaler: Series B, Human Geography*, vol. 96, no. 1, pp. 41–50.

Marshall, M. (2023). 'Do Animals Dream, and If So What About', *New Scientist*. https://www.newscientist.com/article/mg26034691-100-do-animals-dream-and -if-so-what-about/ [accessed 15 May 2024].

Maturana, H.R. and Varela, J. (1980a). 'Biology of Cognition', in *Autopoesis and the Living*. Holland: Springer Dordretch. https://doi.org/10.1007/978-94-009 -8947-4

Maturana, H.R. and Varela, J. (1980b). *Autopoesis and Cognition: The Realization of the Living*. Holland: Springer Dordrecht. Translated from Spanish.

Mc Dermott, D. (2007). 'Artificial Intelligence and Consciousness', in P.D. Zelazo, M. Moscovitch, and E. Thompson (eds.) *The Cambridge Handbook of Consciousness*, pp. 117–150. Cambridge: Cambridge University Press.

McGrath, S. (2018). 'In Defense of the Human Difference', *Environmental Philosophy*, vol. 15, no. 1, pp. 101–115.

McKibben, B. (2006). *The End of Nature: Humanity, Climate Change and the Natural World*. New York: Viking.

McKibben, B. (2019). *Falter: Has the Human Game Begun to Play Itself Out?* Carlton: Black Inc.

Monso, S., Benz Schwarzberg, J. and Bremhorst, A. (2018). 'Animal Morality: What It Means and Why It Matters', *The Journal of Ethics*, vol. 22, no. 3, pp. 283–310. doi: 10.1007/s10892-018-9275-3

Newton, J. Long, S.D. and Sievers, B. (eds.) (2011). *Coaching in Depth: The Organisational Role Analysis Method.* London: Routledge.

Plant Consciousness. http://www.esalq.usp.br/lepse/imgs/conteudo_thumb/Plant-Consciousness [accessed 24 October 2023]. The-Fascinating-Evidence-Showing-Plants-Have-Human-Level-Intelligence--Feelings--Pain-and-More.pdf

Riker, J.H. (1997). *Ethics and the Discovery of the Unconscious.* New York: Suny Press. https://sunypress.edu/Books/E/Ethics-and-the-Discovery-of-the-Unconscious

Robertson, B.H., Rehage, J.S. and Sih, A. (2013). 'Ecological Novelty and the Emergence of Evolutionary Traps' *Trends in Ecology and Evolution* published on *Research Gate* [accessed 24 October 2023].

Rogers, C.D. (2020). 'Psychoanalysing Nature, Dark Ground of Spirit', *Journal of the Pacific Association for the Continental Tradition*, vol. 3, pp. 19–37.

Rosen, R. (1991). *Life Itself: A Comprehensive Inquiry into the Nature, Origin, and Fabrication of Life.* New York: Columbia University Press.

Rosen, R. (1985). *Anticipatory Systems: Philosophical, Mathematical and Methodological Foundations.* Oxford: Pergamon Press.

Semenza, C. (2017). 'The Unconscious in Cognitive Science: A Few Suggestions for Psychoanalysis', in M. Leuzinger-Bohleber, S. Arnold, and M. Solms (eds.) *The Unconscious: A Bridge between Psychoanalysis and Cognitive Neuroscience*, pp. 93–112. London: Routledge.

Smith, J.D. (2009). 'The Study of Animal Metacognition', *Trends in Cognitive Sciences*, vol. 13, no. 9, pp. 389–396.

Smith J.D., Shields, W.E. and Washburn, D.S. (2003). 'The Comparative Psychology of Uncertainty Monitoring and Metacognition', *Behavioral and Brain Sciences*, vol. 26, pp. 317–373.

Stacey, R. (2010). *Complexity and Organizational Reality: Uncertainty and the Need to Rethink Management after the Collapse of Investment Capitalism.* London: Routledge.

Van Swinderen, B. (2024). *Discussion on the ABC Program All in the Mind – Episode Animal Consciousness*, Broadcast 31 March 2024.

Varela, J. (2019). 'The Correlated Evolution of Social Competence and Social Cognition', *Sensory Ecology and Cognition in Social Decisions.* https://doi.org/10.1111/1365-2435.13416

Virk, R. (2019). *Simulation Hypothesis.* Kindle Books.

Ward, P. (2009). *The Medea Hypothesis: Is Life on Earth Ultimately Self-Destructive?* Princeton: Princeton University Press.

Wirth, J.M., and Burke, P. (2013). *The Barbarian Principle: Merleau-Ponty, Schelling and the Question of Nature.* Albany: State University of New York Press.

Wohlleben, P. (2016). *The Hidden Life of Trees: What They Feel; How They Communicate.* Melbourne: Black Inc.

Zalasiewicz, J., Williams, M., Haywood, A. and Ellis, M. (2011). 'The Anthropocene: A New Epoch of Geological Time', *Philosophical Transactions of the Royal Society A*, vol. 369, pp. 835–841.

Zizek, S. (2006, originally published 1996). *The Indivisible Remainder: On Schelling and Related Matters.* London: Verso.

11 The Spirit in Things

The words used for spirit – pneuma (Greek), ruah (Hebrew), wind (English) – express a reality that is invisible but with discernible effects, as the unconscious is invisible with discernible effects.

(Morgan-Jones et al. 2010, p. 1)

My grandfather told me that a Sangoma must be able to draw knowledge from what he called "the hidden lake". There is, he said, a huge unseen lake somewhere in the spirit world where al the knowledge of the universe – past, present, and future – is to be found. You must never again say that you do not know something. You must just ask the lake, the unseen lake. To provide you with the knowledge that you seek.

(Credo Mutwa 2003)[1]

This book has wandered through one person's perspective on the history of the idea of the unconscious, beginning with the philosophy of Friedrich Schelling and the notion of the unconscious as pure will, willing only to become. In the twentieth century and the early twenty-first, the psychoanalytic venture captured the idea of the unconscious and continues to utilise it in amazingly fruitful ways. Especially it has shown how ideas inhabit our minds and affect our feelings and behaviours outside our conscious knowledge of this, and how much is rationalised in an attempt to make sense for ourselves both as individual persons and in groups. Social scientists took up the idea of the unconscious and linked the dynamic of repression to ideas of societal and political repression. Later, neuropsychoanalysis has taken the idea and looked for physical bases of behaviours conducted outside of awareness, while biologists and cosmologists explore the possibilities of all life and even the universe itself having something akin to a mind that displays an unconscious component.

I am a supporter of science with its close observation and empirical methods. It has brought much that is good to the world through its understanding of nature. Yet still we are left with the existence of spirit – something strongly within experience, yet seemingly outside scientific observation. It is something deep inside the idea of the unconscious born in the philosophy of Schelling and his philosophical ancestors: spirit as pure will/spirit before any mind. And

DOI: 10.4324/9781003559818-11

indeed, Lev (2017, 2023) explores the ways in which psychoanalysis can be considered a spiritual practice, citing many contemporary psychoanalysts who explore such an idea. This chapter will take me back with connections to a range of theories that have been approached in earlier chapters because spirit provides a different vertex from which to explore them. I am not a religious person, although Quakerism, with its ideas of the inner teacher, is appealing, and I have had the privilege of supervising the theses of two spiritual advisors who use approaches analogous to psychodynamic explorations. Others have told me I am spiritual, in the nature of humanity. Something that I am not quite sure about was seen, and, on this basis, the late Bruce Irvine invited me to work on his conferences developed through the Grubb Institute, and Leslie Brissett, formerly of the Tavistock Institute, has said something similar. At these conferences in London and Bangkok, I became more closely acquainted with the Transforming Experience Framework (TEF) (Long 2016) and allowed my interest in spirit to grow. The TEF names purpose and spiritual realms of experience as "Source" which I interpret as "that which gives meaning, is a bedrock, gives energy and purpose, and is beyond ego"…"whether one regards this as God, the Big Bang of physics, Bion's 'O' or infinity" (Long 2016, p. 87). Source is linked to the spiritual experience.

Just to be clear about the focus here though, in this chapter, I don't wish to discuss in detail, for example, the differences or indeed the similarities between psychoanalysis and religion or even psychoanalytic analyses of religious experience. This has been done extensively by others (see, for example, Meissner 1984; Palmer 1997; Jones 2001; Parsons 2021) each with attempts to integrate or bridge the different perspectives rather than have them diametrically opposed. Meissner, a psychoanalyst and Jesuit, for instance, sees the psychoanalyst Donald Winnicott's idea of transitional phenomena as providing insight into the importance of religious illusion, illusion being an essential aspect of psychological development: not delusion, but an essential meeting of the inner subjective with the external world, religious illusion being one example of a spiritual experience. I think the wonder of illusion and its creativity have always drawn me to the work of this aspect of psychoanalysis. But nor will this chapter move into the kind of "new age" spirituality that deals with totally scientifically uninvestigable and philosophically dubious phenomena.

Before I begin, I should state some of the underlying assumptions that permeate my work:

1. Mind is different to its substrate – the brain. The reticular activating system (RAS) is responsible in the brain for arousal of consciousness, but the experience of consciousness and its processes is in the mind – an emergent property.
2. Emotion is at the basis of consciousness and is experienced even without the cortex (evidence from animals and children born without a cerebral cortex, Solms (2018)).
3. Bion argues that thinking is the transformation of emotion and the mind is developed as a thinking organ and container for thoughts.

4. Mind is social; within and between people.
5. Spirit dwells in the collective system of life and is incorporated into personal experience.

A difficult concept to discuss, spirit, as I see it, is not the same as an individual soul that is somewhat linked to a living personality and regarded as progressing either to a heaven or through to another life as some religions would have it. For me, spirit is infinite and unknowable, is yearned for and basic to life, is linked to life-force, a pure will without object. This is neither a life-force in the sense of the early biological theory of vitalism, now generally discounted – arguing the presence of a kind of substance, energy or unknown something thought to distinguish inanimate matter from living matter (Coulter et al. 2019). Nor am I regarding it as the same as the life-force posited by Yoga with the theory of Chakras. Such theories and practices I do not feel competent to examine or question, although they do have something to do with human experience. Moreover, there is a discipline of psycho-spiritual studies (Niemiec, Russo-Netzer and Pargament 2020) that considers spiritual experience as linked to mental health at individual and cultural levels: an interesting rabbit hole not to be explored here. There are numerous ways in which spirit might be conceived or given meaning. Mine comes through my understanding of the unconscious.

Following the previous chapter, I will come at the idea of spirit from its embeddedness in the natural world. Such a perspective ran through Schelling's work, and he never gave up completely on his nature philosophy despite developing additional ideas (Grant 2006; McGrath 2010; Schelling 1861). It permeated his later work. For instance, the early Schelling attempts to find intuitive forms of thought in nature and links nature to spirit through this unconscious ground (McGrath 2012). "Schelling proposed nature as unconscious spirit, and spirit as nature become conscious of itself" (Matthews 2012). This was an idea of God, Spirit, the infinite as revealed through nature: "The universe or totality is the self-revelation of the absolute" (Schelling et al. 1942, p. 17). Important in this argument is Schelling's view that the initial state of Spirit is unconsciousness, and that consciousness and subjectivity could only arise once "other" was actualised and that in that process, difference, otherness, narcissism and free will are revealed. All were there in potential, but the initial negation or drawing inward of spirit was the actualising force. Hence, the unconscious is ground to and prior to consciousness. The idea of potentiality, that is, all of nature and consciousness, comes from the unconscious defined this broadly.

This perspective also links to the work of Wilfred Bion (see Chapter 4 of this book). For instance, take the idea of "O". As indicated earlier, "O" echoes Schelling's ideas of the unconscious as infinite and ground to an aesthetic completeness (Grotstein 1997; Glover 2009). As noted in the chapter on Schelling, both Bion and Schelling acknowledge the influence of the Kabbalah. Spirit, although seen as part of nature – meaning the whole of nature, its biological, geological and physical whole – is expressed in the human mind, as part of our essence as social creatures, deeply hidden in culture.

Such a view of spirit is imbued in the idea of the sacred. The sacred is not to be confused with organised religion or religiosity. Although a dichotomy is often made of religious/secular, I want more to emphasise sacred/profane – this distinction being one seen as critical to religious thinking by sociologist Durkheim. It is one of attached value rather than an institutionalised form. Religious institutions contain much that is profane, and secular society can and does contain the sacred. A culture of the sacred has always underpinned human history and culture in different forms. It remains a nascent presence despite the secularisation of societies (Zondervan 2016). One might say that it stays in the cultural associative unconscious.

There is much written about the sacred by both religious scholars and anthropologists. I don't claim to have read extensively in this literature, nor do I wish to provide summaries. But one book that caught my interest is by a mid-twentieth-century anthropologist, Eliade (1987) who writes about the nature of religious experience as the experience of living in a sacred cosmos: an experience held unconsciously. This experience is essentially different from what he terms the profane experience of everyday living and the world of most modern humans living in a desacralised world. Eliade argues that the sacred is deeply lodged in human history and culture. Despite its eschewal in contemporary living and the desacralization of much of culture – what Sociologist Philip Rieff (2006, 2007, 2008) describes in the trilogy *Sacred Order/Social Order* as a destruction of the sacred order – Eliade argues that the sacred is still present in nascent form, deeply embedded in the unconscious. This perhaps seems a closer affinity to Jung than to Freud.

Through an anthropological study of many cultures across time, Eliade argues for the concrete and immediate experience of the sacred as it shows itself in objects, places, times and activities: the quality of the sacred being its "otherness"; its superordinate reality. "Man (*sic*) becomes aware of the sacred because it manifests itself, shows itself, as something wholly different from the profane" (Eliade 1987, p.1). Sacred places are revealed in different ways or are founded by different activities, but they form a space of centrality where chaos is held at bay. "Every sacred space implies a 'heirophany', an eruption of the sacred that results in detaching a territory from the surrounding cosmic milieu and making it qualitatively different" (Eliade 1987, p. 5). As with place, there are sacred times distinguished from profane time, experienced as a sanctification of time, the meaning of which is in renewal – a renewal of the sacred.

In contrast to the Freudian view of religious experience as mostly a defence against reality, Eliade states:

> We have no warrant for interpreting periodic return to the sacred time of origin as a rejection of the real world and an escape into dream and imagination...for the wish to reintegrate the *time of origin* is also to wish to return to the presence of the gods, to recover the strong fresh pure world...it is at once thirst for the sacred and nostalgia for being.
>
> (Eliade 1987, p. 8)

Myth, he argues, echoing the late Schelling and then Jung, is a history of the sacred that is imbued into sacred activities and life. Although religious experience is described as of the sacred, formal religions throughout their histories have both stayed true to and turned aside from the authentically sacred. Eliade argues that although much of the experience within modern society has been desacralised, vestiges remain in certain societal traditions. More importantly, humanity has a long history of religious experience. Life is a sacred cosmos, and this history remains unconsciously a part of us.

> The modern man of non-religious societies is still nourished and aided by the activity of his unconscious, yet without thereby obtaining to a properly religious experience and vision of the world…from one point of view it could almost be said that in the case of those moderns who proclaim that they are non-religious, religion and mythology are "eclipsed" in the darkness of their unconscious…in his deepest being he still retains a memory of it (the religious experience).
>
> (Eliade 1987, p. 10)

Most definitions of sacred see it as holy and deserving of respect. Certainly, the everyday meaning holds something sacred as being precious and not to be defiled. So, what then is the dynamic source of the sacred?

I cannot leave a discussion about the sacred without turning to the work of René Girard (1977, 1986). Girardian analysis locates the sacred alongside its companion word "sacrifice"; the sacrificial dynamic being a means to appease the gods, to prevent or stop violence and aggression, and to engender prosperity and peace. Girard's theories account for a manner of dealing with violence and escalating counter-violence, such as evidenced in long-standing feuds between warring groups, through the process of creating scapegoats onto which both sides can project their anger. The scapegoat is expelled or often sacrificed to appease the revenge of all parties. His extensive research of so-called primitive cultures, especially those with cannibalistic practices, is given in support of this thesis. A practice he notes is that often the people who will become the victims of sacrifice are given a type of sacred position in the tribe for months or even years before the sacrifice. This analysis sees the dynamics of the cessation of violence at the basis of what is sacred, taking this further into the Christian tradition by regarding Christ as the ultimate scapegoat for all sinners (Girard 1986).[2] Replacing the scapegoat dynamic in modern cultures is the instigation of the Law, at least in name, although it is evident the scapegoat dynamic still operates in small and large groups, families and corporations.

Stein's (2019) idea of the lost good self argues that whistleblowers are not stigmatised and hated, perhaps made into scapegoats, wholly because they represent a hated other but because they represent a lost part of the self that would think and feel as the whistleblower does but is no longer available. We might at first think that this analysis runs counter to Girard's position about the scapegoat carrying a sacred position in order to end violence. However, Stein's is more an interpersonal examination of unconscious projective mechanisms that place into the scapegoat a lost good self. Girard looks to a group process whereby the group sacralises a person. This may be regarded as a process of projecting the good into the scapegoat, so may fit with Stein's object relations perspective.

Spirit in Organisations

At a conference in Tasmania conducted by the then Australian Institute of Socioanalysis (AISA), on entering one of the groups that formed as part of an experiential exercise, I began thinking of groups as having a primary spirit. I had walked into one of the groups and became aware of something that seemed to be driving the group other than the task at hand. We discussed this and further developed our thinking about it at the conference. Alastair and Joshua Bain (2002) take the idea further forward saying, "we are defining primary spirit as that which breathes life into an organisation. The animating principle" (p. 100). They go on to say that an organisational primary task requires primary spirit: "a group needs to 'carry in' the primary spirit so as to 'carry out' the task for which it exists" (Bain and Bain 2002, p. 103). This is much akin to the idea of "source" in the TEF: that is, the purpose, held as a spirit, grounding thought and action.

The Grubb Institute's "Transforming Experience through Authentic Action in Role Framework" works with experiences gained through person, role, system, context and Source. The framework acknowledges that experience is gained through the lens of each of these (if not more perspectives, as yet unarticulated). Important here is the idea of connectedness with Source. This is because Source is seen in relation to the other dimensions of experience as it "permanently and continuously permeates and influences all the others whether we know it or not" (Bazalgette and Reed 2016, p. 197). Source is centrally about connectedness: between people and between all things. When that is recognised and lived, albeit perhaps only in small moments and fleetingly, spirit is reached as a resource. In that moment "self" and "other" are neither split apart nor condensed into one; but both are together: "the both and also of complexity" (Brissett 2024). I think this is exemplified in Shapiro's idea of finding how the other is right (Shapiro 2020): distinct but connected through a higher purpose, if only this superordinate value or belief might be found. Good negotiators help antagonistic groups to find such a superordinate space (see, for example, the work of Bar-On et al. 1996, 1998; Volkan, Scholtz and Fromm 2023). Freud (1921), despite his disdain for religion, pointed to this Source, without naming it as such in the leading idea or leader with whom group members could identify and hence with each other. Source here is the glue for the group – the esprit de corps; the common ideal. Source is the spirit in the bond of recognition between fellow sufferers. Released as a resource, it gives courage, direction and meaning. Source is engaged when group members recognise that something beyond themselves connects them.

Spirituality and connectedness to source are often regarded as highly personal. They are manifest in different states of consciousness; in an experience of being in a state beyond self; in a connectedness with the infinite or with nature or in art (De Cortinas 2009). When body and spirit come together, the experience may be ecstatic; a passion that touches the sacred and connects to the aesthetic (Aurelio 2012). Take, for example, Bernini's sculpture *The Ecstasy of St. Teresa* or Baglione's painting *The Ecstasy of St. Francis* as depicting such states.

How then can we think of spirituality as an unconscious collective, part of our social nature?

Here I can give an example from my own consulting work at an adolescent psychiatric unit in a large hospital. The purpose was to work in an inpatient setting to contain and treat adolescents with severe mental illness problems. The spirit was one of camaraderie amongst staff and extended to the young people especially during situations such as violence on the ward or the display of extreme anxieties. Staff had to "read" each other in the sense of anticipating how to work in concert around these issues. The spirit was held within an atmosphere of vigilance, care and contained assertion. There were times when staff discussed and argued with each other in meetings about care plans, treatments and other issues related to the young people, and of course times when the young people were able to "suss out" staff differences and use these to manipulate situations. There were times when experiences were fraught. But the essential spirit of the place, with good leadership, held the team together to work effectively.

What might be said of Source here? My work in a reflective space with staff for over 20 years was that I did not have to induce a spirit of work; they brought it with them to the task, as Bain indicates, but I had to help them hold it through easy and hard times. Is this the same as group cohesion? I wonder if cohesion is an outcome of spirit in a group. What lies behind cohesion is more ineffable. It involves the psychodynamics of groups such as involved in leadership, followership, collaboration, trust, knowledge of differing roles and their tasks, boundary management and so on. But just as mind is an emergent process from brain in context, and group mind is emergent from conscious and unconscious associative connections, so spirit is infused in group mind and – the best I can articulate at the moment – is a ground to, engine to, purpose to group mind: the connectedness that makes the many one and the one many.

Rieff (1966) argues that the destruction of the authority of the sacred is exemplified by the rise of psychological man – Freud's "triumph of the therapeutic", at least as carried out by his followers. Secular Western culture, he argues, is dominated by the ideas of self-authorisation, self-improvement and ego development. All seeming positive attributes, but such a culture can become swamped with narcissism and selfishness – to follow Christopher Lasch (1979) – even of perversity should purely egoistic concerns become dominant (Long 2008). Freud (1930) saw a deep division between the desires of humans and civilisation with sublimation of desires being the only "healthy" way forward. Such a view held little place for the sacred. Yet if we are to take the work of Wilfred Bion, Matte-Blanco and Gordon Lawrence, we might see that the unconscious as infinite touches the experience of the sacred, transcendent of individual or even collective ego. The unconscious as social – as an associative field of experience both between and within people – transcends the ego and gives entry to an experience of belongingness together with respect for, and experience of otherness. Despite being a secular psychiatric organisation, with the social/medical purpose of aiding the psychological health of the young people, I came to experience the work of the adolescent facility at its best as touching the essence of its young patients – reaching towards their authenticity. Yes, this was in the form of the therapeutic move towards developing self-confidence and personal authority and accountability for action by the young people; but done through very personal contacts that rested on a more transcendent authority, the authority of human worth and connectedness with others. Such was the sacredness of this work and the spirit of the organisation.

Unconscious Sacred Order

How then might this sacred order be present unconsciously, not only in human cultures but in the wholeness of life? Important here is the strong desire to achieve meaning: the will to meaning and identity. While all is connected in a totality, Bohm indicates the cognitive and scientific need to fragment the wholeness of the universe to gain meaning. One large fragment of the whole is the propensity of living things to group. There are herds of animals, flocks of birds, schools of fish, forests of trees, colonies of insects, vast grasslands and bales of seaweeds, societies of Homo sapiens. Bion (1961) stresses that humans are basically social animals.

In previous chapters I have examined some of the ideas around consciousness and unconsciousness in groups, organisations, society and nature more broadly. Here I want to suggest spirit as embedded in these groupings, and experienced throughout them as part of mind, conscious and unconscious, remembering that individual minds are but part of a greater connected social mind (Harre 1984; 1979; Long and Harney 2016). This is recognised in such ideas as "esprit de corps", "community spirit", "team spirit" and "spirit of the tribe".

It's an interesting phrase "esprit de corps" – literally spirit of the body but initially and largely applied to a military body. There is a colloquial recognition that a group, a battalion, a nation has an essential spirit; something at the core that drives, gives purpose and coherence. Much of modern organisational language includes its heritage in military forms. We talk of delegation, authority, hierarchy, deployment, "pulling in the same direction", strategy and tactics. Deeply entrenched in the history of modern enterprise are metaphors and images of military might and battles, as well as of collaborative effort and teamwork. Armies, at least in theory, rely on connectedness, both on the positive connectedness between their personnel, but also on the negative connectedness in the creation of "other" as enemy.

Spirit, it seems, may be divisive as well as connecting. Something beyond us may not connect us with the whole but connect us with only a split-off part of the whole. This is so often the case with international and intergroup enmities where the connection is with the part that we identify as good, split from the part we identify as bad. It is so easy to despoil the sacred in other cultures, for other people. Often because of a lack of understanding, sometimes out of anger, fear or envy. This is currently evident in the war of Russia on Ukraine and the war in the Middle East, where the Palestinians are suffering in Gaza and Israeli society is split between anger and despair. For true reparation to occur between different cultures, there needs to be an acknowledgement and deep recognition of damage done (Long 2021). Perverse and narcissistic practice so easily can occur. The truly sacred across all groupings recognises not just an acquisitive stance where personal, societal or organisational gain is concerned, but a true recognition of what can bring us together. Schelling's ideas of the sacred in nature, the recognition of otherness, the shared human history in myth and the unconscious substrata of being provide a foundation.

In working with Margo Lockhart, I have attempted to explore a worldview that underpins the connectedness of all things, such as in the Gaia hypothesis and in the philosophy of Schelling. We (Long and Lockhart 2021) have built on a relational ontology in accord with, but not limited to, the ontology of many indigenous peoples. To give a flavour of this, the Australian indigenous academic Mishel McMahon describes Relational Ontology as:

> the view of reality that all entities: plants, animals, elements, seasons, skies, waterways, the land, the spirit world and humans are in relationship, like a web.
>
> (McMahon 2021)

This is akin to the Gaia hypothesis (Lovelock and Margulis 1973; Lovelock 1979), the Systems view of Capra (2019), and the philosophy of Bohm described in the previous chapter but with the addition of spirit. There I suggested that as creatures of an evolved self-consciousness with unique emergent mind capabilities, our differences from other forms of life lie not so much in sentience, or even in cognitive capacity when this is defined in terms of co-evolution with environmental habitat. A shark, for example, has a greater intelligence and cognition of the ocean as habitat for survival than we do, despite scientific understanding. The realm of difference, I believe, lies with the ethical responsibility that our evolution brings. I note that spirit connects in part with the realms of ethics, responsibility and eco-consciousness.

McGrath (2018, p. 101), with reference to the problems of the Anthropocene, viz. human contributions to climate change, extinction of species and even to the degradation of the earth's geology, says:

only a re-awakening of this responsibility can restore health to anthropocenic nature. The non-human cannot effect this restoration, for that is not its vocation. A difference in vocation is not necessarily a difference in moral worth, and so the human difference does not justify denying the "intrinsic value" of the non-human. Humanity is uniquely responsible both for the mess we are in and for cleaning it up.

Sometimes, I despair that the spirit in collective humanity has turned to an unending divisive "them" and "us" position, a stance perhaps necessary for survival in the tribes of pre-history; a stance that Freud recognised and despaired of himself when looking at discontents. And, I become caught in the possibility or impossibility of my own agency or free will, a question unanswerable although struggled with by many including Schelling (Welchman 2006). But then I am also reminded of the everyday honesty and kindness of friends and neighbours and those who gather together in the face of tragedies. There will always be acquisitiveness, greed, envy, anger, instrumentalism and hatred born of a defensive and misguided self-protection in the face of life's harshness. This is our human heritage. But a truly civilised culture, if I can use that word without its negativity, can face such a nature with compassion, care and justice and help unconscious will to find its place in life and joy. This may sound simple, but it takes facing much pain with courage. It takes also a deep understanding of the complexity of all living things, in whatever ways such an understanding can reach us: scientific, intuitive, spiritual or plain honest everyday living. Today calls for a new stance if only we can reach it. This is a new ethic where unconscious will might recognise its position in a whole-of-earth spirit.

Notes

1 Thanks to Michelle May for sending me this quote and introducing me to Zulu Credo Mutwa's wisdom.
2 An ongoing annual colloquium is held on the theories of Girard conducted through the International Association of Scholars of Mimetic Theory – mimesis being a central concept in Girard's work – and an annual colloquium held on Violence and Religion, introduced to me by the late Rev. Tom Michaels. See also https://violenceandthesacred.podbean.com/

References

Aurelio, M.S.G. (2012). 'Schelling's Aesthetic Turn in the System of Transcendental Idealism', www.kritike.org/journal/issue_11/aurelio_june2012pdf.

Bain, A. and Bain, J. (2002). A Note on Primary Spirit Socioanalysis, vol 4. pp. 98–111.

Bar-On, D., Brendler, K. and Hare, A.P. (1996). *Something Went Wrong with the Roots…Israeli and German Youth Relates to the Holocaust.* Frankfurt: Campus.

Bar-On, D, Ostrovsky, T. and Fromer, D. (1998). 'Who Am I in Relation to the Other: German and Israeli Students Confront the Holocaust and Each Other', in

Y. Danieli (ed.). *International Handbook of Multigenerational Legacies of Trauma.* New York: Plenum.

Bazalgette, J. and Reed, B. (2016). Reframing Reality in Human Experience: The Relevance of the Grubb Institute's Contributions as a Christian Foundation to Group Relations in the Post-9/11 World, in S. Long (ed.). *Transforming Experience in Organisations: A Framework for Organisational Research and Consultancy*, pp.107–134.

Bion, W.R. (1961). *Experiences in Groups.* London: Tavistock Publications.

Brissett, L. (2024). Personal email [accessed 9 June 2024].

Capra, F. (2019). "Mind, Matter and Life Video Talk", https://www.findcenter.com/video/41515/mind-matter-and-life-fritjof-capra [accessed 23 October 2023].

Coulter, I., Snider, P. and Neil, A. (2019). 'Vitalism – A Worldview Revisited: A Critique of Vitalism and Its Implications for Integrative Medicine', *Integra Med (Encinitas)*, vol. 18, no. 3, pp. 16–73.

Credo Mutwa, V. (2003). *Zulu Shaman: Dreams, Prophesies and Mysteries.* Stephen Larsen (ed.). Rochester, VT: Destiny Books.

De Cortinas, P. (2009). *The Aesthetic Dimension of the Mind; Variations on a Theme by Bion.* London: Karnac.

Eliade, M. (1987). *The Sacred and the Profane: The Nature of Religion.* San Diego: A Harvest Book, Harcourt, Brace.

Freud, S. (1915 [1957]). *Instincts and Their Vicissitudes.* S.E. vol. XIV, pp. 117–140. London: Hogarth Press.

Freud, S. (1921). *Group Psychology and the Analysis of the Ego.* S.E. vol. 69, pp. 69–143. London: Hogarth Press.

Freud, S. (1930). *Civilization and Its Discontents.* S.E. vol. XXI (1927–1931), pp. 57–146. London: Hogarth Press.

Girard, R. (1977). *Violence and the Sacred.* Patrick Gregory (trans.). Baltimore: John Hopkins University Press.

Girard, R. (1986). *The Scapegoat.* Yvonne Freccero (trans.). Baltimore: John Hopkins University Press.

Glover, N. (2009). *Psychoanalytic Aesthetics: An introduction to the British School.* London: Karnac.

Grant, I.H. (2006). *Philosophies of Nature after Schelling*, London and New York: Continuum.

Grotstein, J.S. (1997). 'Bion the Pariah of "O"', *Bharatiya Janata Party*, vol. 14, no. 1, pp. 77–90.

Harre, R. (1979). *Social Being: A Theory for Social Psychology.* Totowa, NJ: Rowman and Littlefield.

Harre, R. (1984). "Social Elements as Mind", *British Journal of Medical Psychology*, vol. 57, pp. 127–135.

Jones, J.W. (2001). "Chapter 5. Towards a Psychoanalysis of the Sacred", in *Contemporary Psychoanalysis and Religion*, pp. 111–136. New Haven: Yale University Press. https://doi.org/10.12987/9780300161922-007

Lasch, C. (1979). *The Culture of Narcissism: American Life in an Age of Diminishing Expectations.* New York: Norton.

Lev, G. (2017). 'Getting to the Heart of Life: Psychoanalysis as a Spiritual Practice', *Contemporary Psychoanalysis*, vol. 53, no. 2, pp. 222–246. https://doi.org/10.1080/00107530.2017.1295773

Lev, G. (2023). *Spiritually Sensitive Psychoanalysis: A Contemporary Introduction.* London: Routledge.

Long, S.D. (2008). *The Perverse Organisation and its Deadly Sins.* London: Karnac.

Long, S.D. (ed.) (2016). *Socioanalytic Methods: Discovering the Hidden in Organisations and Social Systems.* London: Karnac.

Long, S.D. and Harney, M. (2016). "The Associative Unconscious", in S. Long (ed.). *Socioanalytic Methods: Discovering the Hidden in Organisations and Social Systems.* London: Karnac.

Long, S.D. (2021). Repairing the damage: wishful, defensive, or restorative? *Organisational & Social Dynamics*, vol. 21, no. 1, pp. 28–39.

Long, S.D. and Lockhart, M. (2021). *Unpublished Plenary Talk at the OPUS Conference.* London.

Lovelock J.E. (1979). *Gaia: A New Look at Life on Earth.* Oxford: Oxford University Press.

Lovelock, J.E. and Margulis, L. (1973). 'Atmospheric Homeostasis by and for the Biosphere: The Gaia Hypothesis', *Telus*, vol. 26, no. 2, pp. 2–10.

Matthews, B. (2012). *Schelling: Heretic of Modernity. An Intellectual Biography of Freidrich Wilhelm Joseph von Schelling (1770–1854).* http://philosophy project.org/schelling/ [accessed 11 September 2014].

McGrath, S.J. (2010). 'Schelling on the Unconscious', *Research in Phenomenology*, vol. 40, pp. 72–91.

McGrath, S.J. (2012). *The Dark Ground of Spirit: Schelling and the Unconscious.* E version London and New York: Routledge. (Originally published 2011).

McGrath, S.J. (2018). 'In Defense of the Human Difference', *Environmental Philosophy*, vol. 15, no. 1, pp. 101–115.

McMahon, M. (2021). 'Yarning about First Nations Worldviews with Mishel McMahon', *Edgy Ideas Podcast Episode*, vol. 34. https://audioboom.com/posts/7962268-yarning-about-first-nation-worldviews-with-mishel-mcmahon

Meissner, W.W. (1984). *Psychoanalysis and Religious Experience*, New Haven and London: Yale University Press.

Morgan-Jones, R., Long, S., Sher, M., Armstrong, D., Bell, J., Sirota, J., Rogovsky, I., Guerin, M., Jones, K., Dempsey, K., Nossal, B., Eden, A. and van den Hooff, H. (2010). *Small Group Discussion Notes.* Elsinore, Denmark: ISPSO Members Day, 17 June.

Nimiec, R.N., Russo-Netzer, P. and Pargament, K. (2020). 'The Decoding of the Human Spirit: A Synergy of Spirituality and Character Strengths towards Wholeness', *Frontiers of Psychol*, vol. 11. https://www.frontiersin.org/journals/psychology/articles/10.3389/fpsyg.2020.02040/full

Palmer, M. (1997). *Freud and Jung on Religion.* London: Routledge.

Parsons, W.B. (2021). *Freud and Religion: Advancing the Dialogue.* Cambridge: Cambridge University Press.

Rieff, P. (1966). *The Triumph of the Therapeutic: Uses of faith after Freud.* Harmondsworth: Penguin.

Rieff, P. (2006–8). *Sacred Order/ Social Order.* Trilogy of books Charlottesville: University of Virginia Press.

Schelling, F.W.J. (1942). *The Ages of the World* (written 1814–15). Fredrick de Wolfe Bowman Jnr. (trans.). Columbia University Press.

Schelling, F.W.J. (1861 [2006]). *Philosophical Investigations into the Essence of Human Freedom*. Sämmtliche Werke, VII Edited by Karl Friedrich August Schelling. Stuttgart: Cotta. With an introduction by Jeff Love and Johannes Schmidt (trans.).

Shapiro, E. (2020). *Finding a Place to Stand: Developing Self-Reflective Institutions, Leaders and Citizens*. Chicago: Phoenix.

Solms, M. (2018). The Neurobiological Underpinnings of Psychoanalytic Theory and Therapy, *Frontiers in Behavioral Neuroscience*, Pathological Conditions vol. 12. https://doi.org/10.3389/fnbeh.2018.00294 [accessed 15 March 2024].

Stein, M. (2019). The Lost Good Self: Why the Whistleblower is hated and stigmatised. Organization Studies, vol. 42, no. 7 pp. 1–20.

Volkan, V., Scholtz, R. and Fromm, G. (2023) (eds.) *We Don't Speak of Fear: Large Group Identity, Societal Conflict and Collective Trauma*. Bicester: Phoenix Publishing House.

Welchman, A. (2006). 'Schelling's Moral Argument for a Metaphysics of Contingency', in E. Correiro and A. Dezi (eds.) *Nature and Realism in Schelling's Philosophy*. Torino: Academia Press.

Zondervan, A.W. (2016). *Sociology and the Sacred: An introduction to Philip Rieff's Theory of Culture*, Reprint edition. Toronto: University of Toronto Press.

12 Revisiting Theories of the Unconscious with the Idea of the Spirit Within

Following the last chapter and the position at which my exploration of the concept of the unconscious has arrived, how can we think of ethical responsibility and the unconscious? Surely ethics, responsibility and morality are all based on conscious deliberation. Let me briefly revisit the theorists encountered in this book and interrogate them. I address two questions. The first is about the nature of freedom and the emergence of ethical choice. The second is our collective as well as individual responsibilities, given I am arguing for the unconscious in collectives.

For Schelling ethical responsibility lies with our free choice. This however appears contradictory because it is not a free conscious choice but an unconscious one. It appears as if there is no choice, only an unconscious determinism. But for Schelling the unconscious will *is* within choice. I return to Schelling's formulation of freedom as "the capacity for good and evil" (Schelling 2006, p. 23), notwithstanding that this may not be a simple choice, with good and evil being defined in many ways and in relation to many contexts. From here, individual action comes from the somewhat paradoxical position that freedom is both choice and unconscious necessity:

> individual action results from the inner necessity of a free being...But precisely this inner necessity is itself freedom; the essence of man is fundamentally his own act; necessity and freedom are in one another as one being.
>
> (Schelling 2006, p. 50)

Schelling argues for the existence of evil and the possibility of its choice because of an unconscious choice, an unconscious character freely but unconsciously chosen that wills our moral and ethical choices. This may seem to us counterintuitive, but it is fundamental to the further development of the concept of the unconscious. Welchman, regarding Schelling, argues that the choice is necessarily unconscious.

> At the level of the transcendental decision, this opacity of ourselves to our own rational scrutiny manifests itself in the fact that the "free act

DOI: 10.4324/9781003559818-12

which becomes necessity cannot occur in consciousness, insofar as it is mere self-awareness and only ideal consciousness, since the act precedes it as it precedes all *Wesen* and indeed produces it".

(quote from Kosch 2006, p. 386 in
Welchman para 54)

This perspective of Schelling privileges the unconscious in the place of pure willing, "In the final and highest analysis, there is no other being than willing. Willing is primordial being". (Schelling 2006, p. 21). It is through willing that God and creation, for Schelling, can become, can materialise out of infinite chaos. Just as evil is included in the ground of God before immanence, and just as God "become" is displayed in nature, humans have the propensity for evil. The freedom of choice is instigated in the first willing. For Schelling, this is then played out in the history of the world, through collective humanity.

In a review of Kosch's 2006 book, *Freedom and Reason in Kant, Schelling and Kierkegaard*, Welchman (2007) says,

> Kosch's explanation makes everything clear: the aesthetic life is (at its most sophisticated) the view of Schelling's *System of Transcendental Idealism*, the conception of freedom in history as a drama in which each of us is an individual actor and at the same time co-author.

So, the idea of the unconscious as first systematically articulated in Western thought in Schelling's philosophy, is integrally tied to our choices; at least the choice of good or evil lies in our unconscious being, there to be lived and discovered. Moreover, this choice lies not in us simply as individual personalities, but in the history and further development of humanity. This is the philosophy behind the birth of the idea about the unconscious and is echoed throughout much of psychoanalytic theory.

The Freudian view is that unconscious will, in the form of instinct, cannot be directly conscious. Instincts, deeply unconscious, he argues, "lie on the frontier between the mental and the somatic" (Freud 1915, p. 122). As such, can we have responsibility for them? Perhaps only insofar as their mental representations become linked to conscious deliberations, thoughts and actions. But there they are subject to societal/parental condemnation or praise incorporated into the superego and to the anxieties of the ego and may return in the form of parapraxes, dreams or neurotic symptoms. The implications from Freudian theory are that we must take responsibility through consciously accepting and working with and realistically ameliorating the dangers within the perpetual push of the unconscious drives and their expression in us. This ethic of responsibility and choice impregnates psychoanalytic theory even through its changes. And it is not a simple ethic of pursuing the pleasure principle. Freud's optimism was muted, and he called simple human unhappiness the best that might be achieved and endured (Freud and Breuer 1895) whether individually or as whole cultures (Freud 1930). Yet the psychoanalytic method that he discovered does offer the hope of knowing ourselves, both the good and the evil.

For Bion, it is "O" – the infinite truth – that guides and draws us; an infinity that comes into being, is emergent, through the emotional experience of living. We gradually come to this truth, not ruthlessly but through communion with others (Bion 1958). This implies the presence of "O" as both in and of community, and also transcendent to it, a seeming paradox but integral to the nature of transcendence. Here, will is expressed through communion. In general, the psychoanalytic ethic looks to finding truth through a deep realisation of one's fundamental wishes and desires, albeit constrained by the demands of an external reality and the responsibilities inherent in that. For Bion, truth is found through the pain inherent in life and found deeply in the in-between. The proto-mental space, the development of a mind to think communal thought (the communal thought being what I have called the associative unconscious, the thoughts without thinkers or thoughts yet to find thinkers), and the struggle between mystic and establishment are all found in the struggle of human living.

Lacan spent a seminar series on ethics, and in this he stresses the place of desire in forming human subjectivity. To know one's desire and to live it is the aim of psychoanalysis and a basis of its ethic. This involves the recognition of the basis of one's subjectivity.

> Desire for Lacan has a significance much wider than that of a pleasure principle involving sexual or other drives; rather, it is a constitutive and problematic ingredient in becoming a human subject. For him, the non-satisfaction of desire is a foundational human problem, installed with the emergence of the subject in early life…The basic condition of lack and the longing for restoration of a lost wholeness it inspires, Lacan proposed, stimulate fantasies connected with what is conceived of as lost. These fantasies and their derivatives invest life with idiosyncratic passion and meaning, even as they may at times disregard or overthrow practical realities. The ethics of psychoanalysis, for Lacan, are based on this new way of conceiving and addressing desire.
>
> (Kirshner 2012, para 13)

Hence the reference in Chapter 4 of this book to "not give ground to one's desire". It is not self-satisfaction that is involved, but self-knowledge. As I intimated at the end of Chapter 4, the Lacanian perspective is somewhat bleak. It is a choice between being in a madness outside of "normal" social being or living within a society of illusion estranged from our basic nature – a compromise life, perhaps Freud's life of simple human unhappiness. Self-knowledge is a difficult passage in this choice. And I am left wondering about the ethic of the desire of others; about empathy and love.

The idea of the unconscious in social theory, as discussed in Chapter 5, is often linked to egalitarian and democratic political positions, taking the psychoanalytic ethic into a broader systemic arena. Human choice appears strongly constrained by the sometimes unseen and often surreptitiously engineered inequalities and power differentials in social conditions, such conditions being unconsciously built into the very fabric of social institutions as propounded by Marx and followers such as Louis Althusser (1970), who argues that the infiltration of ideologies is at the basis of concrete or actual subjectivities, and says "ideology is eternal, exactly like the unconscious" (Althusser 1970). Again, a somewhat bleak picture.

Theorists from the Frankfurt School emphasise a need to raise awareness and challenge such conditions. For instance, Erich Fromm and those who study what he named as a social unconscious, look to human unconscious connectedness in a group mental fabric. Implicit is a recognition of what is shared and hence of group and communal responsibilities. For Fromm, real freedom can be terrifying and the "escape from freedom" with its anxieties, possible alienation and responsibilities, leads to a turning from freedom towards authoritarianism. Again, the ethic is to face responsibilities with courage.

It seems that the psychoanalytic ethic is extended to social systems where choice and responsibility rest on the capacities to bring unconscious forces to awareness and to tolerate the anxieties consequent upon this, and hence to bravely reflect on action, individually and especially collectively. Much of systems psychodynamic or socioanalytic organisational consulting is premised on finding the expression of repressed or defended dynamics in the structures and cultures of workplaces (Menzies-Lyth 1988; Hirschhorn 1977; Stapley 1996; Long 2016; Lawler and Sher 2022, 2024) and in transforming these through conscious reflection, toleration of anxieties, working through and systemic change.

Psychoanalytic neuroscience, while throwing a new light on the unconscious through modern brain research, continues a similar ethic insofar as it looks to the development of learned unconscious behavioural patterns with a therapeutic aim to repattern. Here the route to change modifies the traditional talking therapy. But always there is the aim to modify the effects of the unconscious learning of dysfunctional habits and ways of living.

Reaching into the unconscious in nature – perhaps an altogether new paradigm within the idea of the unconscious – brings us squarely to our ethical responsibility as creatures of the planet. No longer can we claim to be the only living forms with conscious awareness and alongside all living creatures, this is constrained through the exigencies of our specific contexts, both internal and external, physical and social and our learning and experience. This book is not putting forward a deep and complex philosophical examination of choice and ethics. Without much further study, I am not competent to do that. But I have suggested that our human development has placed us in a position within the world as an ecosystem, where we have the capacity to think ethically about our actions. This is not a purely cognitive or even emotional capacity, but an emergent collective spiritual one. What we can think of as unconscious in nature is that which binds the fractured whole. We had best listen to it.

How then might we proceed in listening to the unconscious in its different guises from individual through to institutional and whole-of-nature?

Moving beyond our human ego-centric perspective may allow us a healthier space for living on our planet. Biosemiotics takes the stance that communication at any level of organism is intentional and does not require a Cartesian mind (Harney 1984, 2019). Signs within nature hold knowledge, much of which is unconscious. Such signs range from the complex languages of human cultures through the simple tropisms of plants.[1] Nature holds many messages through her signs. In terms of evolution, "an organism is a message to future generations that specifies how to survive and reproduce" (Sharov 2015).

Understanding more of the biosemiotics within the earth-as-an-organism may give us a deeper understanding of what is unconsciously available to us as earth inhabitants and integrally part of that system. While the intentionality in biosemiotics appears initially as teleological – a stance rejected by psychoanalysis in its acquiescence to the science of the day – such a teleological view is from a mechanistic perspective. By contrast, intentionality is not a property simply of conscious will, but a systemic property of living, evolving organisms (Harney 2019). Human thinking must include an understanding of our own meaning and intention within the world as we enact it. "Without the premise of intentionality, it makes no sense to speak of the moral dimension of human experience" (Harney 2019, p. 139). Anticipatory and intentional aspects of all living systems, many of which are unconscious, must be at the basis of a living ethic.

If we understand the associative unconscious as that social network of thoughts (including ideologies – both useful and misguided) and signs together with their associated emotions that give rise to our consciousness, then access to its riches is essential for our health as individuals and as societies. Without that access, we become isolated and subject to a limited, shallow and ego-filled consciousness. For many reasons we may fail to access this unconscious network – the reasons given to us by Freud, Jung, Fromm, Foulkes and many others. And it is these reasons that bring about destructive processes for the person and for groups, organisations and society. But throughout human history many have found access through, for instance, dreams, art, science, poetry, therapy, communion with others and spiritual contemplation. It may be that the use of such reflective practices as are used in the arts and the sciences via abductive logic will allow more creative solutions to our social and organisational maladies.

Closing but not Ending

The unconscious as an idea has a long history in Western thought, and it continues to evolve. While in the twentieth century it was predominantly an idea within psychoanalysis, where it still thrives and is given new directions as a phenomenon in human psychology and cultures, the twenty-first century brings it forward as an idea to inform us of much that is deeply hidden in nature and the universe. As an idea expands as this has, it is in danger of dissolving into meaninglessness, where in trying to describe everything, it can describe nothing. Each of the theories presented in this book avoids this in their own specificities and definitions. "The Unconscious", while evoking many definitions and perhaps is too broad a term, has a general common cultural meaning. It is the hidden that influences and prompts us outside our awareness. It is that which is mysterious and yearned for, yet seems dangerous and is feared because it presages dread and anxiety because it too often challenges established certainties. It seems to be a master of destiny, blindly followed. Stories and myths from antiquity would have it as the will of the gods. But in exploring how it has been described and studied over the past few centuries, I have come to respect its influence and to understand some of its signs, messages, symptoms, entreaties and anticipations to help me in my decisions in life. In their recognition, I may not meet that which is unconscious directly, but can attempt as best I am able, to choose my actions by discovering what compels. And I can listen to the messages from the unconscious (my own, that of my groups and from the deep unconscious of nature) to create some of the good in life.

The Edge

Do you dare stand at the edge?
And look into the vastness.
He had thought everything was fine.
He could control his fate.
He outranked nature.
But then, caught with his pants down,
No matter others could not see,
He was naked to himself.
Exposed!
In his vulnerability he saw for the first time
How excavators and mechanical bob-Cats tore down the perfect picture
of the forest.
He saw, through the gloom, eyes Blue, brown, black and white
At war.
How had he missed such violence?
Machines that killed and healers not reached.
Starkly,
In pain and sadness, he saw,
How he wished he had not!
Coloured bruises on the skin
Of a child.
Where was the path that he had lost?
Did the shores he could not reach hold reminders from an unearthed
past?
Presentiments of the future

This strange excursion shook his heart
And yellowed his brain.
I can't go back, I can't go back, He wept.
Again, I ask Do you dare to stand at the edge?
For if you fall
It is into a space
That after many years
Will land you back into the future
At the edge of the infinite.

(Susan Long, poem inspired by an International
Dream matrix June 2020)

Note

1 The meaning of a sign depends on the relationship between the sign vehicle, the object and the interpretant (the processes elicited by the sign vehicle). For instance, the information within the sign for fire may be as follows: sign vehicle = smoke; the object = fire; the interpretant = the thought of fire (whether in a human or animal or even the unconscious reaction of other flora, such as in the biological makeup of plants in bushfire or wildfire prone areas whose seeds can only germinate under conditions of fire).

References

Althusser, L. (1970 [1971]). 'Ideology and Ideological State Apparatuses: Notes towards an investigation', in B. Brewster (trans.) *Lenin and Philosophy and Other Philosophical Essays*. Monthly Review Press. https://www.marxists.org/reference/archive/althusser/1970/ideology.htm
Bion, W.R. (1958). 'On Arrogance', *International Journal of Psychoanalysis*, no. 39, pp. 144–146.
Freud, S. (1915 [1957]). *Instincts and their Vicissitudes*. S.E. vol. XIV, pp. 117–140. London: Hogarth Press.
Freud, S. (1930). *Civilization and its Discontents*. S.E. vol. XXI (1927–1931), pp. 57–146. London: The Hogarth Press.
Freud, S. and Breuer, J. (1895). *Studies on Hysteria*. S.E. vol. 2, pp. 1–306.
Harney, M.J. (1984). *Intentionality, Sense and the Mind*. Boston: Martinus Nijhoff.
Harney, M.J. (2019). "Intentionality: Evolution of a Concept", in P. Wong, S. Bloor, P. Hutchings and P. Bilimoria (eds.). *Considering Religions, Rights and Bioethics: For Max Charlesworth*, pp. 139–153. New York: Springer. https://link.springer.com/book/10.1007%2F978-3-030-18148-2
Hirschhorn, L. (1977). *The Workplace Within: Psychodynamics of Organizational Life*. Boston: MIT Press.
Kirshner (2012). 'Towards and Ethics of Psychoanalysis: A Critical Reading of Lacan's Ethics', *Journal of the American Psychoanalytic Association*, vol. 60, p. 6. https://doi.org/10.1177/0003065112457876
Kosch, M. (2006). *Freedom and Reason in Kant, Schelling and Kierkegaard*. Oxford: Oxford University Press.

Lawler, D. and Sher, M. (2022). *An Introduction to Systems Psychodynamics: Consultancy, Research and Training.* London: Routledge.

Lawler, D. and Sher, M. (2024). *Systems Psychodynamics: Theorist and Practitioner Voices from the Field.* London: Routledge.

Long, S.D. (ed.) (2016). *Socioanalytic Methods: Discovering the Hidden in Organisations and Social Systems.* London: Karnac.

Menzies-Lyth, I.E.P. (1988). *Containing Anxiety in Institutions. Selected Essays.* London: Free Association Books.

Schelling, F.W.J. (1861 [2006]). *Philosophical Investigations into the Essence of Human Freedom.* Sämmtliche Werke, VII. Edited by Karl Friedrich August Schelling. Stuttgart: Cotta. With an introduction by Jeff Love and Johannes Schmidt (trans.).

Sharov, A. (2015). *Biosemiotics.* https://home.comcast.net/~sharov/biosem/welcome.html [accessed 12 March 2015].

Stapley, L. (1996). *The Personality of the Organization: A Psychodynamic Explanation of Culture and Change.* London: Karnac.

Welchman, A. (2007 [2006]). *Review of Michelle Kosch, Freedom and Reason in Kant, Schelling and Kierkegaard.* Oxford: Oxford University Press, 236pp. *Notre Dame Philosophical Reviews* https://ndpr.nd.edu/reviews

Index